Marxist Left Review

Number 21 – Summer 2021

Editor
Omar Hassan

Editorial Committee
Mick Armstrong
Sandra Bloodworth
Omar Hassan
Louise O'Shea

Reviews Editor
Alexis Vassiley

© Social Research Institute

Published by Socialist Alternative
Melbourne, February 2021

PO Box 4354
Melbourne University, VIC 3052

www.marxistleftreview.org
marxistleftreview@gmail.com

Contributions to *Marxist Left Review* are peer-reviewed

ISSN 1838-2932
rrp. $17

Subediting and proofreading
Tess Lee Ack
Diane Fieldes
Tom Bramble

Layout and production
Oscar Sterner

Cover
James Plested

Printed by IngramSpark

Marxist Left Review is a theoretical journal published twice-yearly by Socialist Alternative, a revolutionary organisation based in Australia.

We aim to engage with theoretical and political debates on the Australian and international left, making a rigorous yet accessible case for Marxist politics. We also seek to provide analysis of the social, political and economic dynamics shaping Australian capitalism.

Unless indicated otherwise all articles published reflect the views of the individual author(s).

We rely on our readers' support to continue publication.

Subscribe at *marxistleftreview.org*

Marxist Left Review Number 21 – Summer 2021

FEATURES

1 OMAR HASSAN
   Pandemic politics: 2020 in hindsight,
   and a perspective for 2021

25 SANDRA BLOODWORTH
    Celebrating the Paris Commune of 1871:
    "Glorious harbinger of a new society"

75 JORDAN HUMPHREYS
    Capitalism, colonialism and class: A Marxist
    explanation of Indigenous oppression today

149 MICK ARMSTRONG
     Between syndicalism and reformism: Founding
     the Communist Party of Australia

185 TESS LEE ACK
     Reds at the blackboard: Militancy in the teacher unions

213 RICK KUHN
     Economic crises are unavoidable under capitalism

243 TERRY IRVING
     From the rising tide to Govett's Leap: The
     socialist life of Gordon Childe

continued on next page →

REVIEWS

263   LIZ ROSS
Gordon Childe and the fatal lure of politics

267   RYAN STANTON
The real history of World War I

277   DIANE FIELDES
Radical Australian trade unionism

281   EMMA NORTON
The making of Australia's security state

287   IAN BIRCHALL
Victor Serge's final words

OMAR HASSAN

Pandemic politics: 2020 in hindsight, and a perspective for 2021

Omar Hassan is an editor of *Marxist Left Review*. He has been active in anti-fascist and Palestine solidarity work, and has written extensively on the Middle East.

THE YEAR 2020 is gone, but it will not be forgotten. Like 1914, 1929, 1974 and 2001, historians will record it as a moment when the social and economic status quo was radically disrupted and a new era of politics was born. As with each of these evocative dates, the events of last year have both concrete and general aspects; triggered by particular and unpredicted incidents, yet fundamentally conditioned by longer-term contradictions that have been exposed and intensified by the crisis.

The catalyst in this case, of course, was the disease dubbed COVID-19. Marxists such as Rob Wallace, author of *Big Farms make Big Flu*, have written extensively about the connection between intensive capitalist agricultural practices and the emergence of this and other viruses, so there is no need to repeat their arguments here. Their essential point is that COVID-19 should not be seen as an exogenous shock (that is, something coming from the outside) to our otherwise healthy social system. Rather, the pandemic is a side effect of capitalism's extractive relationship with the natural world, mediated through and multiplied by globalised chains of production, distribution and travel. This growing likelihood of global pandemics is just one example of how this dynamic will have deadly consequences far beyond planetary warming. If policies remain unchanged, we will see the unravelling of many more of the ecological processes that have kept us safe until now.

The health crisis that spread from China across the world in turn triggered an unprecedented global economic meltdown. The second quarter of 2020 saw the largest fall in GDP ever recorded in the US, a stunning 9.5 percent contraction. This was no outlier; records were smashed in country after country, dwarfing the economic contractions of the Great Depression. Yet the world recession was triggered voluntarily, as governments locked down their economies to try to stop the spread of the virus. As such, there was a substantial bounce in the third quarter: record-setting growth followed record-setting contractions in a range of wealthy economies.

States responded to the initial crisis with unprecedented levels of monetary and fiscal support for the economy. According to a survey conducted by Statista in early October, Japan had expended the equivalent of 21 percent of annual GDP to hold off an economic meltdown, while the numbers for Australia and the US were around 14 percent each.[1] Compare this with the 2009 peak of the global financial crisis, when Australia and the US deployed stimulus worth the equivalent of just 2 percent of GDP.[2] While welfare spending has been a bigger feature of measures this time around, big capital remains by far the biggest beneficiary. It is hard to predict the political and ideological impact that this spending will produce, but it seems likely, in the short term, that core neoliberal principles of budgetary discipline and aversion to debt will be set aside. Having said that, the ruling class offensive against workers goes on, as shown by the new anti-union legislation proposed by Scott Morrison's government.

In addition to direct fiscal spending, the loose monetary policy of the last decade has continued, with interest rates bottoming out and, in a number of cases, heading into negative territory. The unimaginably large amounts of credit flowing through the system have produced a range of odd and potentially destabilising side effects. First, contra the voodoo economics of modern monetary theory, the debts accumulated by states will have to be paid back at

1. Statista Research Department 2020.
2. International Monetary Fund 2009.

some point. While some advanced economies – most notably the US – can borrow enormous sums on the basis of strong credit ratings and economic fundamentals, most are not so lucky. Despite some leniency from the IMF and other international lending agencies early in the pandemic, a number of so-called emerging economies are facing sovereign debt crises. As a result, they've been forced to cut social spending and devalue their currencies, making life harder for workers and the poor, further undermining economic growth and increasing the burden of repayment where state debts are denominated in foreign currencies such as the US dollar.

A second side effect of cheap credit is a boom in share markets, which have continued to rise despite little evidence of profit growth. The historic average of the share price to real earnings (PE) ratio for the S&P 500 (an index measuring the performance of 500 of the largest listed companies in the US) is about 15. It currently sits at an inflated 37 – the third highest ever recorded.[3] Tech companies are in a distorted league of their own, leading one *Financial Times* writer to speculate that US stocks may be on track to become the largest bubble in history.[4] Zoom's PE ratio reached an astronomical 800 last year before settling at more than 250. At the time of writing, newly launched Airbnb shares are trading at more than $140, while DoorDash is selling for $170. Neither company has ever made a profit. In an interview with *Red Flag* last year, Marxist economist Joel Geier pointed out that even established companies have been affected by this bubble:

> Apple had profits of US$58 billion last year, compared to $59 billion two years ago. Its stock market valuation two years ago was $720 billion, but in [October] it was valued at $2 trillion![5]

Further adding uncertainty is the fragile state of the world economy prior to the crisis, evidenced by the manufacturing recession and slowing growth visible in late 2019. This followed a decade of anaemic growth in the aftermath of the global financial crisis, a period described by British Marxist economist Michael Roberts as the

---

3. S&P 500 PE Ratio 2020.
4. Parlin 2020.
5. Hassan 2020.

weakest economic recovery ever recorded.[6] In the US, there is evidence that government stimulus and the Federal Reserve's bond-buying programs have disproportionately assisted large companies, which have survived the crisis better than smaller rivals. It is yet to be seen whether this leads to the kind of economic rationalisation and restructuring required to boost profits, or merely the unnatural survival of unprofitable zombie companies. The main short-term impact is a rapid expansion of the wealth of big capital. The world's 2,200 billionaires added an eye-watering $1.9 trillion to their portfolios in 2020.[7] In Australia, billionaires increased their wealth by more than 50 percent.[8]

For now, the biggest factor weighing on the global economy is the terrible mishandling of the virus. The recovery in the third quarter of 2020 will not be sustained; the resurgence of the virus in most of Europe and the US has sent many economies into recession again. The hospitality and tourism sectors are some of the hardest hit, but are by no means alone. Commercial real estate markets have been plunged into crisis as businesses abandon expensive office space and encourage their employees to work from home. Airlines have been losing money at an extraordinary rate, though many have been kept afloat by government handouts worth $160 billion.[9] In October, almost 200 European airports were said to be close to bankruptcy, even before the second wave snuffed out hopes of a quick revival in travel.[10] While many businesses hung on during the first lockdowns, the new wave of infections and lockdowns could be the knockout blow for many small and medium enterprises that have less access to credit.[11]

Demystifying the lockdown debate

With a few notable exceptions, ruling classes have responded to the pandemic with negligence and incompetence. Their policies have

---

6. Smith 2020.
7. Petersen-Withorn 2020.
8. Hurst 2020.
9. IATA 2020.
10. Eccles 2020.
11. Wigglesworth et al 2020.

resulted in the death of nearly 2 million people, and the immiseration of many more. Their first instinct was to do nothing and hope for the best. A *Financial Times* investigation found that New York Governor Andrew Cuomo stalled for weeks before closing schools and non-essential industries, resulting in the worst recorded urban outbreak with the highest death rate in the world.[12] The same article assessed New York to have been a crucial node in the spread of coronavirus across the US, while the *New York Times* reported that the delays cost the lives of at least 36,000 people.[13] This experience was by no means isolated to New York or the US. Governments everywhere were slow to react, more worried about economic growth than the lives of their citizens. Borders were left open, large gatherings went ahead, and the deadly virus was allowed to make its way across the globe. Here in Australia, the federal government delayed imposing serious border controls until after the Ferrari Formula One team – fresh from virus-ravaged Italy – arrived in Melbourne for the Grand Prix. For its part, the Victorian Labor government refused to call off the most bourgeois of all sporting events until thousands had begun queueing outside the racetrack. The farcical incident clarified the lines of the debate that would define the year: a conflict between corporate profiteering and public health.

In comparison to what followed, however, the policies implemented in the first phase of the crisis seem positively enlightened. After a few months of dithering, most governments implemented social distancing measures and stay-at-home orders while cases were still at relatively manageable levels. But as the economic implications of the lockdowns became apparent, governments eased public health measures, despite the obvious risks. In Italy and Spain, for instance, restrictions were lifted when daily case numbers, adjusted for population, were higher than at the peak in Australia. A number of US states ended their first lockdowns with daily case numbers higher than when they started. And as the second wave of the virus broke in the second half of 2020, governments were much slower to act: it took daily death tolls in the hundreds before rigorous public health measures were reintroduced.

---

12. Kuchler and Edgecliffe-Johnson 2020.
13. Glanz and Robertson 2020.

Though much attention has focused on hard-right opposition to public health measures – most notably, Trump – the ruling class response to the pandemic has cut across traditional left-right divisions: the Socialist/Podemos alliance in the Spanish state has acted more or less identically to liberal Emmanuel Macron in France and conservative Angela Merkel in Germany. New Democracy in Greece has been more decisive than most on the European continent, with schools and the hospitality industry largely closed since November. The general pattern has been leaders delaying necessary action until the last possible moment and then opening the economy before the virus is under control, all the while trying to shield corporations from as much of the economic fallout as possible. Even socially liberal Sweden, which refused to lock down for most of 2020, has now fallen into line, though an entire year had to pass before the government mandated the simple act of mask wearing. One exception is several governments in Asia, which, having experienced SARS and other pandemics more recently, were prepared to rapidly implement strong health measures to good effect.

Another exception has been a minority on the hard right, such as Donald Trump and Jair Bolsonaro, who have downplayed the virus and refused to take any significant action. These figures have caused damage to their countries through their reactionary populism, yet their political success has been mixed. In Hungary, Viktor Orbán faces a united parliamentary opposition and declining popular support, and Trump was decisively defeated in the US. The story in Brazil is mixed: a program of cash handouts to the poor has kept Bolsonaro's support from crashing, but he remains vulnerable. This highlights the fact that though much of the hard-right base is imbued with COVID denialism as part of a broader anti-scientific conspiracist outlook, it remains a relatively small part of the population. There is so far little evidence of the right expanding its political support through this approach, with strict public health measures enjoying mass support almost everywhere.

In Australia, there has been arguably the most serious political fight around public health in the advanced capitalist world. Politicians started the crisis by singing from the same songbook, as Morrison's national cabinet, consisting of the PM and the state premiers, implemented a range of measures. The impact was to substantially boost the credibility of governments at every level. Western Australian Premier Mark McGowan, for example, enjoys a record 92 percent popularity rating for his strong handling of the issue. But after the virus escaped from Melbourne's poorly supervised quarantine hotels, politics reasserted itself in a brutal way. Labor Premier Daniel Andrews came under sustained assault from the Liberal state opposition, the Liberal federal government, big business groups and members of his own party. While some of the criticisms focused on the botched hotel quarantining procedures, their real target was his reintroduction of one of the world's most severe lockdowns, and his insistence that it be maintained until daily cases dropped below five. The media – led ably by the ABC – did its best to create a sense of social and governmental crisis. Interviews with small-minded business owners obsessed about making a profit filled the news day after day, supplemented by a contrived concern for our collective mental health. They hoped to generate a mood of absolute hostility to the Andrews government that would force it to relent and open the economy ahead of schedule. It failed miserably. A serious political polarisation ensued, but polls repeatedly showed that Andrews enjoyed overwhelming public support for his strong public health measures. It is significant that working-class solidarity allowed so many to hold the line – against a tidal wave of capitalist propaganda – that people's lives are more important than the needs of business and "the economy". The results speak for themselves: while the UK and Victoria had a similar number of daily cases in the middle of June, as of writing this piece Victoria had one, while Britain had more than 60,000. While it is yet to be seen if other countries follow the lead set by the Andrews government, his preparedness to preserve the lockdown to the point of elimination has set a new benchmark and will undoubtedly make it harder for other Australian leaders to get away with letting the virus rip.

The question of lockdowns has vexed the radical left for much of the year. Many have allowed concerns over authoritarianism and racism to overshadow the need to protect workers from the pandemic. This error was somewhat understandable at first, given the novelty of the pandemic, and that the left everywhere has spent years campaigning against border restrictions and the anti-democratic expansion of police powers. Some on the left have also been hostile to lockdowns because of the effect it can have on workers and their livelihoods, especially in countries with more minimal welfare.

Yet it has been clear for many months now that the ruling class has been more interested in maintaining business as usual than in using the crisis to opportunistically quash democratic rights. This has been true even of hard-right governments like those of Trump, Bolsonaro and Modi, who might have been expected to grant themselves new powers under the cover of this major catastrophe. The general needs of capital accumulation – and lack of a clear threat on their left – means that these leaders have emphasised instead the value of freedom to live and work unburdened by concern for others. Some countries have seen major attacks on workers' rights in this period, including Greece and France, but this is no reason for the left to abandon the argument for public health. In any case, it is incontrovertible that the scale of the health crisis requires enormous and intrusive action by the state. Most left (and right) critics of lockdown acknowledge this implicitly, by arguing for tracking and tracing as a supposedly less authoritarian alternative. Yet in many ways, tracking and tracing systems – especially when integrated into mobile and CCTV networks – entail more granular surveillance and control over the population, and are also more likely to be maintained after the pandemic.

Understanding the pandemic in class terms is essential. In responding to this new and dynamic situation, our guiding principle should be to defend the lives and interests of workers against the profits and power of the bourgeoisie. The experience in China, Australia, New Zealand and elsewhere decisively shows that elimination of the virus – often mocked as a utopian dream by the ruling class – is achievable. Strict lockdowns are an essential tool, one that the ruling class has generally refused to deploy until too late for fear of the economic consequences. In this context, Panagiotis Sotiris' critique of the ruling class' alleged "lockdown strategy" is way off the mark both empirically and politically.[14] Far from representing a new phase of neoliberal authoritarianism, public support for lockdowns indicates widespread feelings of social solidarity and a preparedness to sacrifice for the common good. That such attitudes exist even when few political organisations have argued for them, such as in the US, is evidence that it is a product of working-class good sense, rather than neoliberal propaganda. While we should be prepared to fight against inevitable excesses that go with any mobilisation of state power, the first priority is to ensure that the basic measures needed to protect public health are taken.

The alternative is a kind of workerist libertarianism that has nothing to do with working-class politics: the arguments that lockdowns increase the powers of the state could easily be applied to welfare systems and road rules. As well, it's important to remember that it is workers, the poor and the racially oppressed who've been disproportionately impacted in terms of deaths and long-term illnesses, because they are concentrated in more dangerous jobs that cannot be completed from the safety of home. It is therefore ridiculous to argue that keeping society and the economy running more-or-less as normal is in any way anti-racist or pro-worker. Rather, to the extent that governments pursue these policies, it's to preserve profits for the capitalists. There are occasions when the left will need to oppose authoritarian overreach, a position made tricky due to our overall support for staunch public health measures. The successful Democracy is Essential campaign, initiated in Sydney by Socialist Alternative and NSW Greens leader David Shoebridge, demonstrated exactly how this can be done:

> The crackdown on protest cannot be justified on the basis of legitimate health concerns. We, along with the majority of Australians, support the various restrictions and lockdowns that have been in place in recent months to control the spread of the deadly Coronavirus. Indeed, many of us have argued that they should go further. But at the moment, protests are being singled out in an absurd and hypocritical way. In NSW, up to 10,000 are

---

14. Sotiris 2020.

now allowed to attend NRL matches, and 50 in a single corporate box. 300 can be in a casino, pub, or restaurant. Schools are not closed. Thousands are once again flocking to beaches. 500 can attend community sporting events. And yet 21 protesters, socially distanced and wearing masks, is deemed illegal... Some will say that protests should be put on hold for the moment, given the danger of COVID-19. The problem with this is twofold. Firstly, we don't know how long this ban on protests could last... Secondly, the injustices and urgent causes about which we are protesting have not been put on hold.[15]

On the same lines, raising the slogan of internationalism in opposition to border closures and lockdowns is fundamentally mistaken. While some have pointed to the impossibility of locking down countries such as India and Peru as proof that the tactic is flawed, these places could have avoided the virus altogether if China had locked down earlier. Even after it spread from Wuhan, millions of lives could have been saved if New York, northern Italy and other early hotspots had acted decisively. Bourgeois reluctance to lock down and close borders needs to be understood as a reflection of their commitment to minimising disruption to the world economy, rather than some concession to ethical principles. Germany, for instance, has insisted on allowing migrant workers from Eastern Europe to continue crossing borders that were otherwise closed. This policy risked the lives of hundreds of thousands of low-paid workers and their families to ensure agribusiness could make a profit.[16] In Australia, university bosses have been campaigning to allow the early entry of international students – who pay exorbitant fees and are often forced to live and work in squalid conditions – despite the risks to the broader population. Against this liberal defence of murder, we should insist that the best thing a country can do for the international working class is eliminate the virus in its own territory, freeing up resources to be allocated to more needy regions. Wealthy countries like Australia should be exporting doctors, medical equipment and other forms of aid to the worst hit

---

15. DemocracyNSW 2020.
16. Edwards 2020.

areas, and welcoming tens of thousands of refugees for treatment and resettlement. But all of this is only possible once the virus is under control.

Of course, lockdowns on their own are insufficient. A range of additional measures are required to make the process as humane and effective as possible. To avoid permanent lockdowns, and to facilitate internationalism, countries need dramatically improved testing, tracing and quarantining facilities run by the government, not by profit-seeking corporations.[17] The most obvious is that governments pay for workers' wages and massively improved welfare systems to ensure that nobody falls through the cracks. Serious programs of public education are also necessary to give people the tools to understand how social solidarity from below can assist the measures taken from above in keeping everyone safe. Public amenities should be drastically improved so that those who live in working-class neighbourhoods can enjoy green spaces and other essential elements of a good life. Finally, there needs to be quality tracking and tracing systems that ensure the preservation of privacy. This final point is often counterposed to lockdowns, but in reality is complementary to them. Given the exponential growth in contacts with each new case to trace, keeping overall numbers low is crucial for tracing to be a realistic option. If this all sounds utopian, the unprecedented spending splurge unleashed by governments proves yet again that there are sufficient resources to fund everything we've ever asked for; it's simply a matter of priorities and building the forces that can fight for what's needed.

It would be churlish to deny the challenges that the pandemic has posed to the kind of organising needed to win such demands. Social distancing and lockdowns make much of the organising that the left takes for granted more difficult. On the other hand, the social and economic devastation caused by the virus – and the necessity of continued work in a range of industries – has provided trade unions with opportunities. Unions could have reversed a long-term trend of declining membership and engagement by fighting to protect their members' lives and conditions. Short of mass industrial action,

---

17. Kaine and Josserand 2020.

it would be well within unions' capacities to organise campaigns of sick-outs and stayaways like those which spontaneously occurred in the early days of the pandemic. Essential workers continue to have enormous economic and political leverage due to their vital role during the pandemic. This could be used to demand better equipment, services and conditions for themselves and the class more broadly. As well, unions could have experimented with massive online events and creative actions for workers stuck at home, raising demands for more public housing, moratoria on evictions, permanently increased welfare payments, spending on counselling, tutoring and women's services, and so on. The experience of the National Education Union in the UK is illustrative. That union has spearheaded two separate rebellions in favour of shutting down schools, both of which achieved meaningful victories. On 3 January, it held an online meeting viewed by almost 400,000 participants, having recruited 6,000 new members in the 24 hours after taking a defiant stand against Boris Johnson's drive to reopen schools.[18] This action forced the government into an embarrassing U-turn and implementing a broader lockdown.

Far from driving similar campaigns, the union movement in Australia has been asleep at the wheel. It entered the crisis in its weakest state in well over a century, both organisationally and politically. The idea of class collaboration, that is, the policy of conflating the interests of workers and bosses, is totally unchallenged. Faced with Australia's first economic crisis in decades the union bureaucracy's instincts for class collaboration kicked in automatically, with leaders keen to prove their loyalty to capital and the "economy" over their own members. This policy was driven from the top, ACTU Secretary Sally McManus spending much of the year in meetings with the government and heads of big business. Little wonder that she received plaudits from a wide range of ruling-class figures (establishment journalist Michelle Grattan wrote glowingly of her constructive and pragmatic relationship with the Liberal government).[19] This mirrors the basic approach of federal Labor leader Anthony Albanese, who has made his title of opposition

---

18. Robinson 2021.
19. Grattan 2020.

leader redundant by signing off on every major policy of the Liberal government.

Though the ACTU and the ALP have long been an embarrassment to any decent unionist, individual unions have been no better. The teachers' unions have done their bit to keep the economy running as usual, refusing calls by rank-and-file teachers to shut down schools on multiple occasions. Their stubborn defence of the safety of in-class teaching was contradicted by the decision of some AEU branches to bar organisers from visiting schools on OHS grounds. The powerful CFMMEU has spent the year aggressively championing the "right" of the construction sector to work through the pandemic, putting out joint press releases and radio advertisements with the Master Builders' Association.[20] But the prize for the most disgraceful union betrayal of 2020 goes to the National Tertiary Education Union, which offered university bosses an historic 15 percent wage cut in exchange for a role in overseeing the restructuring of – read: swingeing cuts to – the sector. While Socialist Alternative members and supporters in NTEU Fightback were successful in beating back this scandalous assault on workers' living standards,[21] the attacks have come thick and fast at a local level with little resistance from the NTEU leadership. This despite there being some evidence that university budgetary catastrophes flagged earlier in the year may not be eventuating due to better than expected student enrolments.[22] Overall, Australian unions have been at best irrelevant to defending their members in this historic crisis, even when controlled by a "left" bureaucracy as in the CFMMEU, AEU and NTEU.

Vaccine apartheid

News that scientists had developed multiple viable vaccines has been celebrated across the world. The world owes a lot to the dedication and talent of the research teams that achieved this breakthrough in record time. Yet the discovery raises as many political issues as the pandemic itself. First, it suggests that the decades spent developing vaccines for diseases that plague poor countries are at least partly

---

20. Master Builders Victoria 2020.
21. Fieldes & Humphreys 2020.
22. NTEU Fightback 2020.

a function of under-investment rather than technical limitations. Roughly $20 billion[23] was invested in developing a vaccine for HIV between 2000 and 2018, while as of August 2020 $39.5 billion[24] had been invested into a vaccine COVID-19.

The vast sums of money that governments have directed to coronavirus research this year have been crucial to the breakthrough. Despite nearly two decades passing since SARS emerged in 2002, little funding was allocated for developing an understanding of the coronavirus. The rapid end of the SARS pandemic meant that there was no economic incentive to support scientists overcome early obstacles to vaccine development. To kickstart research into COVID-19, governments gave out enormous grants. Pfizer has received $1.9 billion from the US government, while Moderna benefitted from $4.1 billion as of December.[25] In the year to November, the US government alone had spent $10.5 billion on vaccine development, manufacturing and distribution. In May, the *New York Times* reported that an EU-organised teleconference raised $8 billion in one day.[26] Yet these extraordinary outlays do not give governments control over the vaccine, a share of the profits made, or any other mechanisms of public accountability and control. Instead, taxpayers have simply subsidised the cost of developing an urgently needed social good from which these massive corporations will now be able to profit. This is just the latest instance of the parasitic relationship between drug companies and publicly funded research labs.[27] A 2018 report by the Center for Integration of Science and Industry found:

> [National Institutes of Health] funding contributed to published research associated with every one of the 210 new drugs approved by the Food and Drug Administration from 2010-2016. Collectively, this research involved >200,000 years of grant funding totalling more than $100 billion.[28]

---

23. HIV Prevention Research & Development Investments 2018.
24. Cornish 2020.
25. Cornish 2020.
26. Stevis-Gridneff and Jakes 2020.
27. Zaitchik 2017.
28. Cleary et al 2017.

This explains why Trump's attempts to cut funding to the National Institutes of Health have been rejected by Congress and big pharma alike.[29] This pattern is replicated globally. A 2008 paper estimated that the taxpayers cover two-thirds of all upfront drug research and development costs globally, and that roughly a third of new medicines originate in public research institutions.[30] The centrality of public funding for basic health research is yet another refutation of the myth that the market will direct resources to their most rational use.

Then there is the issue of vaccine distribution. There are enormous logistical challenges involved in administering the vaccine in much of the underdeveloped world, where the necessary equipment and human resources are rare to non-existent. Thus we have the absurd scenario where a country like India is planning to export hundreds of millions of doses of a vaccine that it will struggle to distribute to its own population.[31] But India is relatively fortunate compared to many countries, which lack any means of accessing a vaccine because the wealthy countries early in the pandemic signed deals with drug companies to corner the market. A report by the People's Vaccine Alliance found that wealthy countries have purchased enough doses to immunise their populations three times over, while just 10 percent of the underdeveloped economies will get access this year. It also reported that all of Moderna's, and 96 percent of Pfizer's, predicted output for 2021 has already been purchased by rich countries, which means it could take until 2023 for poorer regions to be fully immunised.[32] Nothing highlights this divide more starkly than the situation in Israel, which is rolling out the vaccine for its own citizens while refusing access for Palestinians suffering under their endless occupation.

Even within national borders, there are important debates about who gets first access to the precious early doses. Alongside healthcare workers, US states such as New York and Illinois have included financiers and bankers on the list of essential workers, meaning

---

29. Ledford et al 2019.
30. Boldrin and Levine 2008.
31. Vaidyanathan 2020.
32. The People's Vaccine Alliance 2020.

they could get early access even as they work from the safety of their penthouses and gated communities.[33] This is just one quirk of the depraved US health system, which also lacks a coordinated method for distributing the vaccine rationally and efficiently. The result is a decentralised mess perfectly suited to being corrupted by corporate interests, and incapable of deploying the doses already received in a timely manner. There are already signs that a black market will emerge as the wealthy and politically connected do all they can to secure early doses.

Ongoing crises

While the vaccine may eventually end the pandemic, it will not be for many months now. Officials in the US, which is likely to have best access, have indicated it will take until at least the end of June for everyone that wants a vaccine to get it.[34] If the death rate stays at around 2,000 per day, another 300,000 Americans will have died by then. In Australia, the government has promised that everyone will be immunised by October, but that leaves plenty of time for new waves if health restrictions are lifted recklessly. We should expect the pandemic to continue ravaging the advanced capitalist nations for months to come, and for substantially longer for poorer regions. The health crisis and its devastating economic side effects are ongoing.

There are other, arguably more fundamental, factors shaping global politics beyond the coronavirus. As mentioned earlier, the pandemic is just one symptom of a broader ecological catastrophe that continues to develop. Unsurprisingly, both market mechanisms and UN summits have failed to deliver the radical shift away from fossil fuels required to prevent disastrous global warming. A shocking $269 billion of recovery funding has been earmarked for the fossil fuel industry, with just $177 billion for renewables.[35] And while certain pro-capitalist commentators celebrate statistics showing that investment in renewables will surpass fossil fuels for the first time this year, the fossil fuel industry remains overwhelmingly

---

33. Stacey and Kuchler 2020.
34. Collman 2020.
35. Energy Policy Tracker 2020.

dominant[36] as the source of global energy, with almost all of the major players planning to significantly expand oil[37] and gas[38] production by 2030. The climate movement has been subdued in the past year, but the sentiment that drove the climate strikes, and in Australia the enormous demonstrations against the bushfires, has not disappeared. The disjunct between the ecological views of the majority and the destructive policies of the ruling class will continue to be an important political factor, one that will interact dynamically with the increasingly volatile realities of climate change at a local and global level. This will manifest most obviously in mass mobilisations that are likely to continue in various forms, but will also have political ramifications, contributing to the ongoing crisis of legitimacy faced by mainstream political parties.

In another sign of the underlying fragilities of the world capitalist system, there was yet another wave of insurgent movements for democracy in 2020, rocking country after country despite the dangers posed by the pandemic. Places as diverse as Thailand, Belarus, Chile, India, Iran, Nigeria and Poland witnessed enormous mobilisations as activists stood up to repressive regimes with courage and persistence. Following the experience in Hong Kong and Lebanon in the previous year, most of these movements are motivated by a desire for genuine democratic control over society, rather than strictly economic grievances. While specifically working-class actions have been missing from many recent protest movements, in Belarus and especially Iran, the working class has been central, both symbolically important and the resistance's driving motor. Considering that organisers in Hong Kong tried (and failed) to launch a general strike in 2019, the mixed but generally positive experience of climate and women's strikes, and the massive strikes of both workers and farmers in India, we can tentatively say that the idea of the strike is being re-established in the popular imagination as an important tactic for popular resistance. Having said that, workers in most places have little to no capacity to shut down the means of production at a national level. There are no shortcuts to building that kind of power. The rank-and-file

---

36. Smil 2017 and BP Statistical Review of World Energy.
37. Brower et al 2020.
38. IEA 2020.

networks required to organise mass industrial action – as opposed to school walkouts, lunchtime stunts or management-supported workplace shutdowns – take serious organising underpinned by political commitment. Regardless, this process of reconstituting a specifically working-class culture of activism will be made easier in the conditions of general political rebellion that are likely to persist.

The most important of these movements in 2020 – in the advanced capitalist world at least – was the Black Lives Matter protests in the US. The scale of the demonstrations was unlike any anti-racist movement in US history, the *New York Times* reported on separate polls estimating that between 15 and 26 million Americans participated in protests[39] during May and June. The movement was far larger and more multiracial than in the first iteration of BLM in 2014, many overwhelmingly white towns hosting substantial mobilisations. Its impact was both national – winning majority support[40] – and global, generating sizeable mobilisations in Britain, France and Australia, among others. Democrats, many of them Black, control the cities where the police are most violent and where the movement was strongest. Unfortunately, this didn't stop many activists from framing the effort to elect Joe Biden[41] as central to ending police violence in US cities, an approach that saw the movement essentially wound up by August. Though some momentum has undoubtedly been squandered as a result, the killing of Blacks by racist cops will continue. Given that, and that Biden has less talent than Obama's toenails, it's safe to say that future explosions are inevitable.

Institutional racism is just one factor that could destroy Biden's attempt to stabilise US politics. There is a long and growing list of challenges for his administration to overcome, including the pandemic, the ongoing fragility of the real economy, political mobilisations on the left and the right, economic turmoil in the underdeveloped economies, the growing confidence of regional powers to act independently of US interests across the world, the shenanigans of

---

39. Buchanan et al 2020.
40. Cohn and Quealy 2020.
41. Blake 2020.

the hard right, and most of all, the rise of China. It may turn out that distributing a vaccine for COVID-19 will be the easiest part of Biden's presidency. For the radical left, we can only hope that's the case.

References

Blake, Justin 2020, "Joe Biden, Black Lives Matter activists helped you win Wisconsin. Don't forget us", *The Guardian*, 16 November. https://www.theguardian.com/commentisfree/2020/nov/16/joe-biden-black-lives-matter-wisconsin-jacob-blake

Boldrin, M and D Levine 2008, "The Pharmaceutical Industry", in *Against Intellectual Monopoly*, Cambridge University Press.

Brower, Derek, David Sheppard, Jude Webber and Myles McCormick 2020, "The oil sector's bumpy road ahead", *Financial Times*, 1 October. https://www.ft.com/content/50764b35-9b68-4894-8a7c-d610c8ee568f

Buchanan, Larry, Quoctrung Bui and Jugal K Patel 2020, "Black Lives Matter May Be the Largest Movement in U.S. History", *New York Times*, 6 June. https://www.nytimes.com/interactive/2020/07/03/us/george-floyd-protests-crowd-size.html

Cleary, Ekaterina Galkina, Jennifer M Beierlein, Navleen Surjit Khanuja, Laura M McNamee and Fred D Ledley 2017, "Contribution of NIH funding to new drug approvals 2010-2016", PNAS. https://www.pnas.org/content/115/10/2329

Cohn, Nate and Kevin Quealy 2020, "How Public Opinion Has Moved on Black Lives Matter", *New York Times*, 10 June. https://www.nytimes.com/interactive/2020/06/10/upshot/black-lives-matter-attitudes.html

Collman, Ashley 2020, "The White House coronavirus testing czar says all Americans will have access to the vaccine by the end of June", Business Insider Australia, 29 December. https://www.businessinsider.com.au/vaccine-available-to-all-americans-by-june-official-says-2020-12?r=US&IR=T

Cornish, Lisa 2020, "Funding COVID-19 vaccines: A timeline", Devex, 21 August. https://www.devex.com/news/funding-covid-19-vaccines-a-timeline-97950

DemocracyNSW 2020, "Democracy is Essential – Open Statement", 31 August. https://democracyisessential.wordpress.com/2020/08/31/statement/

Eccles, Mari 2020, "193 European airports at risk of closure due to crisis, says industry lobby", *Politico*, 27 October. https://www.politico.eu/article/coronavirus-travel-economy-193-european-airports-risk-closure-due-to-crisis-industry-lobby/

Edwards, Maxim 2020, "Fruit picking in a pandemic: Europe's precarious migrant workers", *Global Voices*, 14 July. https://globalvoices.org/2020/07/14/fruit-picking-in-a-pandemic-europes-precarious-migrant-workers/

Energy Policy Tracker 2020, "Track public money for energy in recovery packages", 30 December. https://www.energypolicytracker.org/

Fieldes, Diane and Jordan Humphreys 2020, "NTEU Fightback: Rank-and-file rebellion in a most unlikely union", *Marxist Left Review*, 20, https://marxistleftreview.org/articles/nteu-fightback-rank-and-file-rebellion-in-a-most-unlikely-union/

Glanz, James and Campbell Robertson 2020, "Lockdown delays cost at least 36,000 lives, data show", *New York Times*, 20 May (updated 22 May). https://www.nytimes.com/2020/05/20/us/coronavirus-distancing-deaths.html

Grattan, Michelle 2020, "When Christian met Sally – the match made by a pandemic", *The Conversation*, 28 May. https://theconversation.com/grattan-on-friday-when-christian-met-sally-the-match-made-by-a-pandemic-139562

Hassan, Omar 2020, "The crisis of the world economy", *Red Flag*, 26 October. https://redflag.org.au/node/7430

HIV Prevention Research & Development Investments 2018, "Investing to end the epidemic", July 2019. http://www.hivresourcetracking.org/wp-content/uploads/2019/07/rt_2018.pdf

Hurst, Daniel 2020, "Australia's billionaires became 50% richer during pandemic", *The Guardian*, 29 December. https://www.theguardian.com/australia-news/2020/dec/29/australias-billionaires-became-50-richer-during-pandemic?fbclid=IwAR29EgjpKUL_vOGQLNedhge6AfHzb075FXdNokfHYyNjRQMAFn6hHP3tdV8

IATA 2020, "Looming cash crisis threatens airlines", Press Release, 6 October. https://www.iata.org/en/pressroom/pr/2020-10-06-01/

IEA 2020, "Gas 2020. Analysing the impact of the Covid-19 pandemic on global natural gas markets", June. https://www.iea.org/reports/gas-2020/2021-2025-rebound-and-beyond

International Monetary Fund 2009, "Group of Twenty (Meeting of the Ministers and Central Bank Governors March 13-14, 2009 London, UK) Global Economic Policies and Prospects". https://www.imf.org/external/np/g20/pdf/031909a.pdf

Kaine, Sarah and Emmanuel Josserand 2020, "Melbourne's hotel quarantine bungle is disappointing but not surprising. It was overseen by a flawed security industry", *The Conversation*, 8 July. https://theconversation.com/melbournes-hotel-quarantine-bungle-is-disappointing-but-not-surprising-it-was-overseen-by-a-flawed-security-industry-142044

Kuchler, Hannah and Andrew Edgecliffe-Johnson 2020, "How New York's missteps let Covid-19 overwhelm the US", *Financial Times*, 22 October. https://www.ft.com/content/a52198f6-0d20-4607-b12a-05110bc48723

Ledford, Heidi, Sara Reardon, Emiliano Rodríguez Mega, Jeff Tollefson and Alexandra Witze 2019, "Trump seeks big cuts to science funding – again", Nature, 11 March. https://www.nature.com/articles/d41586-019-00719-4

Master Builders Victoria 2020, "Joint Statement from CFMEU and Master Builders Victoria", 6 September. https://www.mbav.com.au/news-information/news/ohs/media-release-joint-statement-cfmeu-and-master-builders-victoria?ohs

NTEU Fightback 2020, https://mailchi.mp/4b5a77f3d443/millionaire-vc-thinks-we-should-keep-calm-and-carry-on-4864812?e=f95f5d3142

Parlin, Andrew 2020, "This US stock bubble could rank among the biggest in history", *Financial Times*, 6 September. https://www.ft.com/content/9d12ae03-2f6b-4028-8464-e305269e7ee3

Petersen-Withorn, Chase 2020, "The world's billionaires have gotten $1.9 trillion richer in 2020", *Forbes*, 16 December. https://www.forbes.com/sites/chasewithorn/2020/12/16/the-worlds-billionaires-have-gotten-19-trillion-richer-in-2020/?sh=708708447386

Robinson, Sadie 2021, "Workers send message to Tories—keep all schools shut or we could walk out", *Socialist Worker*, 3 January, https://socialistworker.co.uk/art/51106/

S&P 500 PE Ratio 2020, 31 December. https://www.multpl.com/s-p-500-pe-ratio

Smil, Vaclav 2017, "Energy Transitions: Global and National Perspectives" and BP Statistical Review of World Energy, Our World in Data. https://ourworldindata.org/grapher/global-primary-energy?time=earliest..latest

Smith, Ashley 2020, "The Virus, capitalism, and the long depression. Interview with Michael Roberts", Spectre, 24 March. https://spectrejournal.com/the-virus-capitalism-and-the-long-depression/

Sotiris, Panagiotis 2020, "Thinking Beyond the Lockdown: On the Possibility of a Democratic Biopolitics", *Historical Materialism*, 28 (3), 29 September. https://brill.com/view/journals/hima/aop/article-10.1163-1569206X-12342803/article-10.1163-1569206X-12342803.xml

Stacey, Kiran and Hannah Kuchler 2020, "US states wrestle with what makes workers 'essential' in Covid jab rush", *Financial Times*, 12 December. https://www.ft.com/content/198e98cb-3e41-4323-b30c-89181a101d2b

Statista Research Department 2020, "Value of COVID-19 stimulus packages in the G20 as share of GDP 2020", November 26. https://www.statista.com/statistics/1107572/covid-19-value-g20-stimulus-packages-share-gdp/

Stevis-Gridneff, Matina and Lara Jakes 2020, "World leaders join to pledge $8 billion for vaccine as U.S. goes it alone", *New York Times*, 4 May. https://www.nytimes.com/2020/05/04/world/europe/eu-coronavirus-vaccine.html

The People's Vaccine Alliance 2020, "Campaigners warn that 9 out of 10 people in poor countries are set to miss out on COVID-19 vaccine next year", Amnesty International, 9 December. https://www.amnesty.org/en/latest/news/2020/12/campaigners-warn-that-9-out-of-10-people-in-poor-countries-are-set-to-miss-out-on-covid-19-vaccine-next-year/

Vaidyanathan, Gayathri 2020, "India will supply coronavirus vaccines to the world — will its people benefit?", Nature, 3 September. https://www.nature.com/articles/d41586-020-02507-x

Wigglesworth, Robin, Joe Rennison and Robert Armstrong 2020, "America's two-track economy: the small business credit crunch", *Financial Times*, 14 December. https://www.ft.com/content/1ae439b1-75e7-4b55-876c-66533ac37db8

Zaitchik, Alexander 2017, "Taxpayers – not Big Pharma – have funded the research behind every new drug since 2010", The Other 98%. https://other98.com/taxpayers-fund-pharma-research-development/

SANDRA BLOODWORTH

Celebrating the Paris Commune of 1871: "Glorious harbinger of a new society"[1]

Sandra Bloodworth has written extensively about Lenin and the 1917 Russian revolution, Marxist economics, women's and sexual oppression and pre-class societies.

ELEANOR MARX WROTE of the Paris Commune:

It is time people understood the true meaning of this Revolution; and this can be summed up in a few words... It was the first attempt of the proletariat to govern itself. The workers of Paris expressed this when in their first manifesto they declared they "understood it was their imperious duty and their absolute right to render themselves masters of their own destinies by seizing upon the governmental power".[2]

Karl, her father, had addressed the International Workingmen's Association (known as the First International) on 30 May 1871. He began with: "On the dawn of March 18, Paris arose to the thunderburst of 'Vive la Commune!' What is the Commune, that sphinx so tantalising to the bourgeois mind?"[3]

Marx went on to describe why he was so inspired. The Paris Commune

1. From Marx 1871. Thanks to the sharp eyes and insights of Omar Hassan and Mick Armstrong, the final result is vastly improved on the original draft.
2. Lissagaray 1976, introduction, p. 3.
3. This address would be published as part of the pamphlet, The Civil War in France.

was the first revolution in which the working class was openly acknowledged as the only class capable of social initiative, even by the great bulk of the Paris middle class – shopkeepers, tradesmen, merchants – the wealthy capitalist alone excepted.[4]

Many of the lessons Marx drew from this momentous event have in the last half century been largely lost to workers struggling to get control over their lives. But if we listen to the voices of the women and men of the Commune, if we examine the barbarous response of the National Government headed by the reactionary Adolph Thiers, we find that the lessons are just as relevant to our struggle many years later. As Walter Benjamin argued so poetically:

> The class struggle, which always remains in view for a historian schooled in Marx, is a struggle for the rough and material things, without which there is nothing fine and spiritual... They are present as confidence, as courage, as humour, as cunning, as steadfastness in this struggle, and they reach far back into the mists of time. They will, ever and anon, call every victory which has ever been won by the rulers into question. Just as flowers turn their heads towards the sun, so too does that which has been turned, by virtue of a secret kind of heliotropism, *towards* the sun which is dawning in the sky of history. To this most inconspicuous of all transformations the historical materialist must pay heed.[5]

In paying heed I will attempt to capture the incredible atmosphere of joy, experimentation and creativity which flourished. But we cannot flinch from the horror of that terrible last week, known as *la semaine sanglante*, where at least 30,000 people were slaughtered by a government determined to crush not just the physical presence of this social revolution, but also its spirit. The preparedness of the ruling class to inflict such violence should be burned into the consciousness of every anti-capitalist activist. Any movement with a vision of a new society must confront the vexed question of how to win in the face of such barbarism.

The Commune established a more thoroughly democratic

---

4. Marx 1871.
5. Benjamin 1968, pp. 254-55.

society than capitalism has ever seen before or since. The reforms introduced were far in advance of anything the capitalists had ever sanctioned, some of which still have not been won in many countries. The 150th anniversary of this marvellous event is a good time to revisit the inspiring first steps of the revolutionary workers' movement, and draw the lessons that can be learnt from its successes and ultimate defeat.

The uprising

It all began as the sun rose over the radical working-class arrondissements[6] of Montmartre and Belleville on 18 March 1871. Soldiers began seizing nearly 250 cannon deliberately placed in these working-class areas by the National Guard, a popular Parisian militia. The soldiers had been sent there by the head of the new republican government, Adolphe Thiers. Among other things, Thiers was widely despised for his role in the brutal suppression of workers' rebellions in 1848.

But contrary to Thiers' expectation of a swift exercise, the affair spun out of control. The incompetent army had forgotten to bring horses to drag the cannon, which gave the Guardsmen time to fraternise with soldiers. Expecting a treasonous crowd, the soldiers began turning their rifles up as the streets rang with declarations of *Vive la République!*

The London *Times* correspondent describes the scene as women came out to buy bread and prepare for the day: "Small savage groups of blouses [were] making cynical remarks upon everybody's cowardice… 'If they had only left them to us to guard they would not have been captured so easily'." This militancy and self-assurance of the working women of Paris, convinced that they could fight better than the men, will reverberate through the whole revolution. Our witness, moving along to the suburb of Belleville, recorded soldiers and Guardsmen finding they had much in common. Let's pause to witness a typical scene:

> There was something intensely exciting in the scene. The uncertainty for a moment whether the men were meeting as friends

---

6. An arrondissement is similar to a suburb in Australian cities.

or enemies, the wild enthusiasm of the shouts of fraternization, the waving of the upturned musket, the bold reckless women laughing and exciting the men against their officers, all combined to produce a sensation of perplexity not unmingled with alarm at the strange and unexpected turn things were taking.[7]

Fraternisation, courageous defiance by the masses of Paris and mutiny were the hallmark of the day. When troops blocked the entrance to the church of Saint-Pierre to stop anyone ringing the tocsin in order to alert the National Guard and citizens to the danger, workers got into other churches, climbing into the steeples. The tolling of the tocsins brought increasing numbers crowding into the streets.[8]

The correspondent described these areas as "rugged open spaces where the lawless crowds of these parts love to hold their meetings and park their cannon". Belleville, side by side with Montmartre on the right bank, is described as "[t]he most solidly working-class district in all of Paris, and the most revolutionary".[9] These cannon were regarded as *their* cannon, financed by workers' subscriptions to the National Guard since the revolution of 1848. And they were the only means of defence against the Prussian army shelling the city since Thiers had moved his troops to Versailles. When the *Times* correspondent queried a National Guardsman about possible fighting, he was rebuked: "*Sacrebleu*, do you suppose we are going to allow these *Canaille* to take our cannon without firing a shot?"[10] After all, the National Guard had deliberately positioned their cannon to defend these key suburbs.

Hostile crowds quickly gathered to block the soldiers trying to move the cannon. Eyewitness accounts all draw our attention to the large numbers of women and children. Louise Michel, one of the most flamboyant and radical figures of the Commune, later recalled the events at Montmartre:

Montmartre was waking up; the drum was beating. I went with

---

7. Edwards 1973, pp. 58-59.
8. Merriman 2016, p. 41.
9. Edwards 1973, p. 15.
10. Edwards 1973, pp. 59-60.

others to launch what amounted to an assault on the hilltop. The sun was rising and we heard the alarm bell. Our ascent was at the speed of a charge, and we knew that at the top was an army poised for battle. We expected to die for liberty.

It was as if we were risen from the dead. Yes, Paris was rising from the dead. Crowds like this are sometimes the vanguard of the ocean of humanity... But it was not death that awaited us... No, it was the surprise of a popular victory.

Between us and the army were women who threw themselves on the cannons and on the machine guns while the soldiers stood immobile.[11]

General Lecomte three times ordered the soldiers to fire on the crowd. "A woman challenged the soldiers: 'Are you going to fire on us? On our brothers? On our husbands? On our children?'" Lecomte threatened to shoot any soldier who refused to do just that. As they hesitated, he demanded to know if they "were going to surrender to that scum". Michel recalled:

[A] non-commissioned officer came out from the ranks and... called out in a voice louder than Lecomte's. "Turn your guns around and put your rifle butts up in the air!" The soldiers obeyed.
It was Verdaguerre who, for this action, was shot by Versailles some months later. But the revolution was made.[12]

Later, Lecomte and another General, Clément Thomas, were taken prisoner before being shot. This incident would become the centre of controversy for years to come, trotted out by enemies of the Communards to demonstrate their barbarism. Of course, the two men's role in perpetrating mass violence to crush the revolution of 1848 and Lecomte's repeated orders to kill women and children are rarely mentioned.

Hostile witnesses viewed events through the jaundiced eyes of those accustomed to wielding unchallenged authority, but the

---

11. Gluckstein 2006, p. 13.
12. Merriman 2016, p. 44. The government is often referred to as Versailles because it was ensconced there.

narrative is the same. A Versailles army officer recorded that where he was in charge they were

> stopped by a crowd of several hundred local inhabitants, principally children and women. The infantry detachment which was there to escort the cannon completely forgot their duty and dispersed into the crowd, succumbing to its perfidious seductions, and ending by turning up their rifle butts.[13]

A proclamation by Thiers was posted around the city: the taking of the cannon was "indispensable to the maintenance of order", the intention of the government was to rid the city of the "insurrectionary committee" propagating "communist" doctrines, threatening Paris with pillage. This slur that the rebels wanted to destroy Paris, issued by the reactionary who had abandoned Paris to be shelled and occupied by the Prussians, was the source of even more determined resistance.

Once the horses arrived, some soldiers succeeded in beginning to move some of the cannon in Belleville. Guardsmen and residents responded by building barricades to physically prevent their removal. The crowd swelled, transforming itself from a mass of spectators to increasingly angry and active participants. One observer wrote that they saw

> women and children swarming up the hillside in a compact mass; the artillery tried in vain to fight their way through the crowd, but the waves of people engulfed everything, surging over the cannon-mounts, over the ammunition wagons, under the wheels, under the horses' feet, paralysing the advance of the riders who spurred on their mounts in vain. The horses reared and lunged forward, their sudden movement clearing the crowd, but the space was filled at once by a back-wash created by the surging multitude.

In response to a call by a National Guardsman, women cut through the horses' harnesses. The soldiers began dismounting, accepting the offers of food and wine from the women. As they broke ranks they became "the object of frenetic ovations".[14]

---

13. Gluckstein 2006, p. 13.
14. Merriman 2016, p. 43.

Some time later the *Times* correspondent returned to Montmartre and visited the barricade, the first stone of which he had seen laid. It had now

> grown to considerable dimensions by reason of the rule which is enforced that every passer must place a stone, a pile of which is placed for the purpose on each side of the street... New barricades were springing up in every direction... It was now midday, and the whole affair wore a most strange and incomprehensible aspect to one not brought up to making barricades... Instead of a government blocking every street as was the case in the morning, a hostile cannon was now looking down every street.[15]

The barricades would develop their own centres of activity, drama and tragedy which would become a focus for historians. Eric Hazan, in his book *The Invention of Paris, a History in Footsteps*, includes a history of barricades and their "theatrical role" with reference to the Commune's use of them.[16]

Cordons of soldiers had been replaced by National Guards supervising barricade-building. The streets, so quiet first thing in the morning, were now "swarming with [Guardsmen], drums were beating, bugles blowing, and all the din of victory".[17]

By midday, General Vinoy, assigned to capture the cannon, was fleeing Paris. A Commune sympathiser wrote in his diary:

> Legally we had no more government; no police force or policemen; no magistrate or trials; no top officials or prefects; the landlords had run away in a panic abandoning their buildings to the tenants, no soldiers or generals; no letters or telegrams; no customs officials, tax collectors or teachers. No more Academy or Institute: the great professors, doctors and surgeons had left... Paris, immense Paris was abandoned to the "orgies of the vile multitude".[18]

How to explain this seemingly spontaneous mass mobilisation over a few hundred cannon? Paris had been under siege by the Prussians

---

15. Edwards 1973, pp. 60-61.
16. Hazan 2010, pp. 236-45.
17. Edwards 1973, pp. 61-62.
18. Gluckstein 2006, p. 14.

since 19 September 1870 and shelled relentlessly since 5 January. Anger with Thiers was intense. He had gone to war with Germany the previous July for the glory of the French empire. Confronted with defeat by Bismarck's army, he baulked at the idea of arming the population of Paris. And the bourgeoisie refused to support any defence of Paris while the National Guard, with its working-class membership, remained in control of armaments. It was clear that to win the war with Bismarck, all cities, especially Paris, needed to be mobilised under arms. But the history of France since the revolution of 1789 had been one of recurring social upheavals which terrified the bourgeoisie. An army general later summed up the problem: "the diplomacy of the government and almost all of the defence revolved around one thing: *the fear of revolt*".[19] So Thiers had conspired with Prussia's Bismarck to crush radical Paris as a condition of a treaty to end the war. Removing the cannon was part of that process.

"Paris armed is the revolution armed", remarks Marx. And so Thiers, "by surrendering to Prussia not only Paris, but all France... initiated the civil war they were now to wage, with the assistance of Prussia, against the republic and Paris".[20]

Attempting to seize the cannon was in reality simply the trigger which unleashed a well of bitterness fed by poverty and squalor in the overcrowded working-class districts. The restructuring of Paris by Georges-Eugène Haussmann,[21] appointed by Louis Napoléon Bonaparte, who ruled from his coup d'état in 1852 until September 1870, had been devastating. New, wide boulevards cut swathes through workers' districts, destroying 100,000 apartments in 20,000 buildings. This displaced thousands from central Paris, with the poor crowding into Montmartre and Belleville. In the midst of a booming economy, it is estimated that a majority of the working class required government assistance.[22] Alongside growing misery, the wealthy enjoyed glitzy arcades packed with elegant stores and cafés within walking distance of their magnificent private residences.

---

19. Edwards 1973, p. 22. Italics in Edwards.
20. Marx 1871.
21. Usually known as Baron Haussmann.
22. Gluckstein 2006, pp. 68-69.

As Merriman says, "the bourgeoisie's day had truly arrived".[23] The rebuilding of Paris, which was meant to stave off social unrest, had instead stoked it for decades.

The victorious movement of March 1871 had brought to life what became known as the Paris Commune. Its task was now to reorganise life in the city, based on principles of justice, equality and freedom from tyranny.

The Commune – a new power

As we follow events over the next 72 days we will witness truly awe-inspiring achievements. Innovative democratic institutions were established. And the experience of taking control over their society inspired mass involvement in debates about all aspects of their lives. They replaced the state with one under their control. They vigorously attempted radical reforms in the family, the conditions of women, in the workplace, and education, well ahead of the times, as they debated the role of science, religion and the arts in society.

Edmond de Goncourt – co-founder of the naturalist school of literature in France and whose will established the Goncourt Academy which annually awards the prestigious French literary prize – left this testimony to the Commune's proletarian character:

> The triumphant revolution seems to be taking possession of Paris…barricades are being put up everywhere, naughty children scramble on top of them… You are overcome with disgust to see their stupid and abject faces, which triumph and drunkenness have imbued with a kind of radiant swinishness…for the moment France and Paris are under the control of workmen… How long will it last?… The unbelievable rules…the cohorts of Belleville throng our conquered boulevard.

He is disgusted by their "mocking astonishment" at their achievement, noting that they wear their shoes without socks! He admits that the "government is leaving the hands of those who have, to go into the hands of those who have not".[24]

By midday on 18 March, the population had established a

---

23. Merriman 2016, pp. 7-8.
24. Merriman 2014, pp. 46-7.

situation of dual power: radical Paris in a standoff with the government in Versailles. On one side was Adolph Thiers, a reactionary through and through. His government, elected as recently as February, had already fled to the decadent safety of Versailles, accompanied by the army and a stream of bourgeois and respectable middle-class figures. Now it operated from the Grand Château of the Bourbon monarchy in Versailles, the reactionary centre of the centuries-old alliance between the Catholic church and the Bourbons. Thiers, determined to crush the Commune, would be backed by all of respectable opinion, both in France and across Europe.

On the other side of the barricades, workers created the most democratic institutions known to humanity at that time. Marx would write of their achievements: "[t]he great social measure of the Commune was its own working existence. Its special measures could but betoken the tendency of a government of the people by the people".[25] Such a state of affairs was a direct threat to the repressive rule of Thiers, the monarchy and the church.

Whenever the oppressed rise up and fight for their rights, a sense of revelry inevitably follows. This is what inspires sympathetic witnesses of revolutions to describe such moments as festivals of the oppressed. Paris in 1871 was no different. Even bitter enemies of the Commune could not but convey the joyous atmosphere in the wake of the victory of 18 March. One recorded the experience of standing in front of the Hôtel de Ville, the Paris town hall now occupied by the Communards, while the names of those elected to form a Commune Committee were read out:

> I write these lines still full of emotion... One hundred thousand perhaps, where did they come from? From every corner of the city. Armed men spilled out of every nearby street, and the sharp points of the bayonets, glittering in the sun, made the place seem like a field of lightning. The music playing was the *Marseillaise*, a song taken up in fifty thousand resolute voices: this thunder shook all the people, and the great song, out of fashion from defeats, recovered for a moment its former energy.

---

25. Marx 1871.

...An immense sea of banners, bayonets, and caps, surging forward, drifting back, undulating, breaking against the stage. The cannons still thundered, but they were heard only in intervals between the singing. Then all the sounds merged into a single cheer, the universal voice of the countless multitude, and **all these people had but one heart just as they had but one voice**.[26]

The elected Commune Committee was entrusted with the momentous responsibility of defending the city against Versailles, organising food supplies, care for the wounded; indeed, of reorganising the entire life of the city.

The state

The old state power had been demolished, a significant move Marx emphasised:

> [F]or the first time since the days of February 1848, the streets of Paris were safe, and that without any police of any kind. "We," said a member of the Commune, "hear no longer of assassination, theft, and personal assault; it seems indeed as if the police had dragged along with it to Versailles all its Conservative friends".

To emphasise the significance of this, Marx puts it in a broader context:

> The direct antithesis to the empire was the Commune. The cry of "social republic" [the popular slogan of the mass movement]...did but express a vague aspiration after a republic that was not only to supersede the monarchical *form* of class rule, but class rule itself. The Commune was the positive form of that republic.

> Paris, the central seat of the old governmental power, and, at the same time, the social stronghold of the French working class, had risen in arms against the attempt of Thiers...to restore and perpetuate that old governmental power bequeathed to them by the empire. Paris could resist only because, in consequence of the siege, it had got rid of the army, and replaced it by a National Guard, the bulk of which consisted of working men. This fact was

---

26. Gluckstein 2006, p. 53. Bold in Gluckstein.

now to be transformed into an institution. The first decree of the Commune, therefore, was the suppression of the standing army, and the substitution for it of the armed people.[27]

This revolutionary move was the basis on which the new democracy that Marx celebrates could be built.

> The majority of [the Commune Committee's] members were naturally working men, or acknowledged representatives of the working class. The Commune was to be a working, not a parliamentary body, executive and legislative at the same time. The Commune was formed of the municipal councillors, chosen by universal suffrage in the various wards of the town, responsible and revocable at short terms.

This was a key point Marx emphasised: how elected delegates and government officials can be made accountable. But not just elected delegates. "Like the rest of public servants, magistrates and judges were to be elective, responsible, and revocable."[28]

Work

Marx concluded that these innovative democratic structures were "the political form at last discovered under which to work out the economical emancipation of labour" and explained:

> The political rule of the producer cannot co-exist with the perpetuation of his social slavery. The Commune was therefore to serve as a lever for uprooting the economical foundation upon which rests the existence of classes, and therefore of class rule. With labour emancipated...productive labour ceases to be a class attribute.[29]

The Commune Committee was not just left to get on with decreeing reforms while everything went back to the old normal. Historians have documented the incredible flowering of organisation, debate and social experimentation that took place, adding a tapestry of rich

---

27. Marx 1871.
28. Marx 1871.
29. Marx 1871.

detail which illuminates Marx's theoretical generalisations. Many of the organisations and their proposals were based on demands which had been discussed by socialists and worker militants for decades. The difference now was that they were not just topics for debate and protest. Now they became the expression of the poor and oppressed as they began to take control of their lives.

The Committee set up a range of Commissions to deal with specific areas. The Jewish-Hungarian worker, Léo Frankel, a member of the International and collaborator of Marx, was appointed minister of labour to deal with workers' rights and working conditions. Night work by bakers was abolished; employers were banned from reducing wages by levying their employees with fines under any pretext, "a process in which the employer combines in his own person the parts of legislator, judge, and executor, and filches the money to boot".[30]

Some issues were complicated due to conflicting priorities. Military supplies were obviously of paramount importance. But the Commune's purchase of the cheapest equipment did not sit easily beside workers' demands for decent wages. The commissioner for finance, Proudhonist François Jourde, baulked at rewriting contracts with employers, hardly surprising given the Proudhonists supported private property. But as Frankel pointed out, "the revolution was made exclusively by the working class. I don't see what the point of the Commune is if we...do nothing for that class". In response to the workers themselves, new contracts specifying a satisfactory minimum wage were agreed. The employers were not consulted.

An additional clause decreed by the Labour Commission stated that where possible contracts be awarded "directly to the workers' own corporations". Workers' corporations can be understood here to refer to co-operatives, associations and trade unions. They were strongly backed by Frankel's Commission as a vehicle for socialism. The Commission also decreed that the enterprises of any employers who fled to Versailles were to be taken over by its workers.[31]

Another of Marx's collaborators in the International played

---

30. Marx 1871.
31. All the examples and quotes about the Labour Commission from Gluckstein 2006, pp. 28-31.

a key role in influencing the Labour Commission.[32] The Russian socialist Elisabeth Dmitrieff was central to establishing the *Union des Femmes*, or Women's Union. It was the women's section of the First International. A *mariage blanc*[33] had provided Dmitrieff with an escape route out of Russia. She had spent the last three months in London, where she met with Marx almost daily, discussing theories of revolution. Prior to that she had joined the International in Geneva, where she had met the future Communards Eugène Varlin and Benoît Malon. According to historian Kristin Ross, the *Union des Femmes* became the largest and most effective organisation in the Commune.[34] It met daily in almost every one of the twenty arrondissements. The membership was dominated by workers in the garment trades: seamstresses, laundresses, dressmakers and so on.[35]

The *Union des Femmes*' discussions included theoretical questions about ending private property and the issues of gender-based inequality, as well as solving the day to day struggle to provide fuel and food to families. At the same time they participated in the defence of the Commune, maintenance of barricades, tending to the sick and wounded. Ross sums up: "In some ways, the Women's Union can be seen as the practical response to many of the questions and problems regarding women's labour that had been the discussion topic [for years]".[36]

Another historian, Donny Gluckstein, argues: "[t]he Labour Commission's work was shaped by, and depended absolutely on, the Women's Union and the trade unions' workers' corporations, which in turn were empowered by the commission."[37] Spelling out their mission, the *Union des Femmes* declared: "We want work, but in order to keep the product. No more exploiters, no more masters. Work and well-being for all". At their urging, the Commune set up cooperatives

---

32. The International included this grouping, but also Proudhonists, who dominated the French section, Blanquists and others.
33. Many revolutionary women escaped the stifling pressure from their families by entering a "white marriage" in which the man expected no sexual relationship.
34. Ross 2016, pp. 27-29.
35. Thomas 1967, pp. 62-63.
36. Ross 2016, p. 27.
37. Gluckstein 2006, p. 50.

to make Guardsmen's uniforms, which provided well-paid work under the women workers' control.[38]

While women suffered special oppression, their working lives were also shaped by the broader conditions facing the working class. They made remarkable moves in the direction towards workers' control, in spite of limited time and conditions of war: "There were a dozen confiscated workshops, above all those linked to military defence... Five corporations had begun searching out the available workshops, ready for their confiscation". And state-owned establishments such as the mint and the national print shop were put under workers' management. Even the café workers, given these leads, began to set up a trade union.[39]

The radical clubs

The tradition of radical political clubs, inspired by the 1789-92 revolution and revived in 1848, had emerged from the underground in the year leading up to the Commune. They discussed a wide range of issues: political strategy, which reforms to prioritise, women's rights, attitudes to the church and science, how to better organise defence and strengthen the barricades and more. Previously these issues were confined to radical circles, but now the clubs attracted a wider audience and enthusiastic support for their proposals. Workers were the great majority of participants, but middle-class radicals also joined in. Between 36 and 50 clubs met daily, mostly in the working-class districts. Some were huge, involving thousands, with women playing a prominent role both in their own clubs and in mixed ones with men.[40] Many discussions resulted in sending resolutions to the Commune Committee, and there was an ongoing debate regarding its relationship to the clubs.

An anti-Communard gave a sense of the spirit which made the clubs such a vibrant part of the new democracy:

> From Rue Druout right up to the Montmartre district the boulevards had become a permanent public meeting or club

---
38. Ross 2016, pp. 26-28.
39. Gluckstein 2006, p. 31.
40. Gluckstein 2006, pp. 48-49.

where the crowd, divided into groups, had filled not only the pavements but also the road to the point of blocking...traffic. They formed a myriad of public assemblies where war and peace were hotly debated.[41]

Élie Reclus, an ethnographer given responsibility for the management and preservation of the Bibliothèque Nationale, called them "schools for the people", where constructive debate flourished and a heightened sense of community was created. Ross describes the clubs as "a quasi-Brechtian merging of pedagogy and entertainment".[42]

A week after the declaration of the elected Commune Committee, on the initiative of the club in the third arrondissement that was endorsed by the Commune Committee, churches across the city were commandeered as meeting places and organising centres. These venues, unlike street meetings, created a sense of seriousness and permanence in the clubs, even of high drama. Lissagaray, member of the International and author of one of the first books published about the Commune, penned a colourful description of one such meeting:

> The Revolution mounts the pulpits...almost hidden by the shadow of the vaults, hangs the figure of Christ draped in the popular oriflamme. The only luminous centre is the reading desk, facing the pulpit, hung with red. The organ and the people chant the Marseillaise. The orator, over-excited by these fantastic surroundings, launches forth into ecstatic declamations which the echo repeats like a menace. The people discuss the events of the day, the means of defence; the members of the Commune are severely censured, and vigorous resolutions are voted to be presented to the Hôtel de Ville the next day.[43]

It is wonderful to imagine such revolutionary proceedings taking place beneath soaring ceilings and beautiful stained glass windows. Occupying these odes to privilege and power was a constant reminder

---
41. Gluckstein 2006, pp. 45-46.
42. Ross 2016, p. 17.
43. Quoted in Gluckstein 2006, p. 49. Lissagaray uses oriflamme for scarlet banner which, in its literary meaning, denotes a principle or ideal that serves as a rallying point in a struggle.

of the momentous challenge the Commune had thrown down before the bourgeoisie, the monarchy and their ally, the church.

Separating church and state

Marx noted that once the state force was dismantled, the Commune

> was anxious to break the spiritual force of repression...by the disestablishment and disendowment of all churches as proprietary bodies... The whole of the educational institutions were opened to the people gratuitously, and at the same time cleared of all interference of church and state. Thus, not only was education made accessible to all, but science itself freed from the fetters which class prejudice and governmental force had imposed upon it.[44]

Anti-church sentiment was not just the preserve of small numbers of radicals. The Catholic church had thrown its wealth and power behind Bonaparte's dictatorship, never concealing its bitter hostility to republicanism. So the growing opposition to Bonaparte was organically anti-clerical, among both middle-class radicals and the urban poor. In the large cities, attendance at religious ceremonies had sharply declined before the revolution, especially among workers. It's not difficult to see why. The church taught that the poor would be rewarded for their suffering by passing from this vale of tears to the glories of heaven. But to enter that heaven you had to silently endure endless misery. As well, the church, in this time of the Enlightenment and a rapidly changing world, was seen as a bastion of ignorance, summed up by the *Syllabus of Errors* in 1864 which denounced modern society.[45] As Merriman writes: "[t]he church's close association with people of means had long drawn popular ire; the birth of the Commune merely unleashed it".[46]

State laws were strongly influenced by the church's teachings about the family, women's role and morality. So the programs for reforms raised in the clubs around such issues were more often than not entwined with anti-religious bitterness.

---

44. Marx 1871.
45. Merriman 2016, pp. 10-11.
46. Merriman 2016, p. 104.

There were no bounds to the irreverence displayed once the churches were commandeered. Mock masses, holy water replaced with a pile of tobacco, statues of the Virgin Mary dressed in the uniform of women supplying provisions to the National Guard, sometimes with a pipe in her mouth. At the same time the Communards in many cases allowed ceremonies for the devout to go ahead in the mornings before the clubs met. As such the meetings would often take place amidst flowers, crucifixes and other religious paraphernalia left behind from morning mass and other religious events.

Church properties provided much needed venues, a practical issue which just happened to intersect with the anti-church sentiment. Notre-Dame-de-Lorette became a barracks at one stage, then a jail for those arrested for refusing to fight. The Women's Union's cooperative was housed in Saint-Pierre in Montmartre, also used as a storage place for munitions and a school for girls. Another became a medical facility.[47] In a reversal of the old order, speakers in the clubs insisted that the clergy pay rent to the Commune for use of ecclesiastical spaces for "their comedies". Proceeds were to go to the widows and orphans of the fighting. The club of Faubourg Saint-Antoine suggested that church bells be melted to make cannon.[48]

The hostility to the church is a theme in many records of the time. For instance, when the archbishop, who had been arrested, called the head of police and court officials "my children", the sharp response was: "We are not children – we are the magistrates of the people!" Merriman cites a document in which the archbishop is described as "Prisoner A who says he is a servant of somebody called God".[49]

While one third of all students attended religious schools, the church exercised a virtual monopoly over the education of girls, a fact directly related to the lower rates of literacy among women.[50] In general, religious education was backward and stifling. A commission

---

47. Merriman 2016, pp. 107-9; Gluckstein 2006, p. 49.
48. Merriman 2016, p. 105.
49. Merriman 2016, p. 101.
50. Merriman 2016, p. 11.

headed by a range of artists, teachers and songwriters instigated closing down the church schools and removing religious symbols.[51] Where necessary, crowds took direct action to shut schools taught by religious figures, who had never been required to have the qualifications demanded of regular teachers. Many of them resigned, asking for lay teachers to replace them. By May religious teaching was banned in all schools.

Education

Members of the First International were prominent in debating and proposing innovations on a number of intersecting questions around education. The official journal of the Commune records that they were active in organising public educational meetings and reorganising education "on the largest of possible bases". Ross puts well how central was the issue:

> A lived experience of "equality in action", the Commune was primarily a set of dismantling acts directed at the state bureaucracy and performed by ordinary men and women. Many of these dismantling acts were focused, not surprisingly, on that central bureaucracy: the schools.[52]

Discussions about education went well beyond secularisation. A third of children had no access to education at all, and the Commune would try to implement compulsory and equal education for both boys and girls. Teachers' wages were raised, with women and men on equal pay. A school of industrial arts was established with a woman as director. Students would receive scientific and literary instruction, then use some of the day for the application of art and drawing to industry. One of the most enthusiastic supporters of the polytechnic schools was Eugène Pottier, member of the International and a supporter of the utopian socialist Charles Fourier's concept of "attractive work". A son of a box-maker, Pottier was a fabric designer and a poet. Unlike today, theoretical and practical debates about education were not carried out in the rarefied circles of academia, but in the clubs around the city. Declarations reflecting those debates

---
51. Ross 2016, pp. 39-40.
52. Ross 2016, p. 40.

were printed as posters and pasted on walls in the streets. One which bore Pottier's name read in part:

> That each child of either sex, having completed the cycle of primary studies, may leave school possessing the serious elements of one or two manual professions: this is our goal...the last word in human progress is entirely summed up by the simple phrase: *Work by everyone, for everyone.*[53]

"Secular nurseries" were also set up near workplaces employing women. They were guided by principles laid down by the utopian socialist Charles Fourier: caregivers were not to wear black or dark-coloured clothing, and were rotated to avoid boredom or tiredness setting in, "it being important that children should be looked after only by cheerful and young women, whenever possible". Religious representations were replaced with pictures and sculptures of real objects such as animals and trees, including aviaries full of birds. Boredom was thought to be "the greatest malady" of children.[54] We get a glimpse of some of what those children were taught in this anecdote from a gentleman who witnessed a "band" of 200 "toddlers" marching behind a drum and a small red flag. "They sing at the top of their lungs '*La Marseillaise*'. This grotesque parade celebrated the opening of a lay school organised by the Commune."[55]

Marx's collaborator, Benoît Malon, helped set up an asylum for orphans and runaways, where they could be offered basic instruction. Paule Mincke opened one of the first schools for girls. They requisitioned a Jesuit school, because it was endowed with the most advanced equipment and laboratories. Édouard Vaillant set up a professional school of industrial art for girls, occupying the École des Beaux Arts. This school introduced a new approach to teaching. Any skilled worker over the age of 40 could apply to become a professor.[56]

The emphasis on science as fundamental to the advance of society was a powerful theme. A young scientist from the US, Mary Putnam Jacobi, happened to be in Paris. Her experience in that

---

53. Ross 2016, p. 44.
54. Ross 2016, pp. 41-42.
55. Merriman 2016, p. 104.
56. Ross 2016, pp. 40-41.

spring "led to a political awakening" and inspired her to spend the next three decades campaigning against sexist assumptions about women's biology. She became a powerful advocate for the equal contribution of women to medicine and developed the philosophy that the advance of science and the advance of women were one and the same objective. She depathologised menstruation by disproving the then widely held notion that rest was necessary in order to prevent infertility, one of the reactionary ideas of the Proudhonists.

Women's rights and the family

Marx mocks "the absconding men of family, religion, and, above all, of property", and writes:

> In their stead, the real women of Paris showed again at the surface – heroic, noble, and devoted, like the women of antiquity. Working, thinking, fighting, bleeding Paris – almost forgetful, in its incubation of a new society, of the Cannibals at its gates – radiant in the enthusiasm of its historic initiative![57]

As already discussed, women were involved in pushing many of the Commune's most radical proposals. This is not surprising. Women – due to the specific nature of their oppression – can be the bearers of more conservative ideas in stable times, especially when trapped in the home. But when they challenge their chains of oppression, they often become the most dynamic element of mass movements, with less to lose and more to gain from a fundamental transformation of the status quo.

The Commune immediately made farsighted and fundamental improvements to women's lives. The remission of rents and the ban on sales of goods deposited at the pawn shops lifted a huge burden from workers' families. A decree on 10 April granted wives – legal or defacto – of Guardsmen who were killed defending the Commune a pension of 600 francs. Each of her children, legitimate or not, could collect 365 francs until they turned 18. And orphans would receive the education necessary "to make their own way in society".[58] As Edith Thomas, in her social history of women in the Commune, remarks:

---

57. Marx 1871.
58. Thomas 1967, p. 53.

"This was an implicit recognition of the structure of the working-class family, as it really existed, outside the context of religious and bourgeois laws". *Unions libres* were common among workers but not recognised by the church or the state, denying women their dignity, to say nothing of economic discrimination given that unmarried women were not eligible for any widow's allowance. And "[i]n a city where about a quarter of all couples were unmarried, the church, which normally charged 2 francs to register a birth, demanded 7.50 francs [about two days' wages for many] for an 'illegitimate' child".[59]

Thomas comments that the widows' pension was "one of the most revolutionary steps of its brief reign. That this measure outraged the bourgeoisie, and that it was received with jubilation by members of the Commune are indications of its significance". [60]

But women weren't passive recipients of reforms. It was mostly women who dragged the guillotine into Rue Voltaire and burned it on 10 April. Women were some of the most militant in both women's and mixed clubs. They were particularly strident in their denunciation of marriage. In a club in Les Halles, a militant woman warned that marriage "is the greatest error of ancient humanity. To be married is to be a slave. In the club of Saint-Ambroise a woman declared that she would not permit her sixteen-year-old daughter to marry, that she was perfectly happy living with a man "without the blessing of the Church".[61] At least one other club also voted in favour of divorce, a policy which was implemented by the Commune Committee. These kinds of discussions in the clubs were the catalyst for the kinds of reforms we have seen. They didn't just come from the Commune Committee on high. And marriage ceased to be a formal contract, it was simply a written agreement between couples, easily dissolved.[62]

Michel's *Club de la Révolution*, along with others, raised the right to abortion, which was endorsed by the Committee. At the Club of the Free Thinkers Nathalie Lemel – a book binder, and member of Marx's group in the International who worked with that other

---

59. Merriman 2016, p. 105.
60. Thomas 1967, p. 54.
61. Merriman 2016, pp. 105-6.
62. Gluckstein 2006, pp. 32-33.

comrade of Marx, Elisabeth Dmitrieff and her *Union des Femmes* – along with Lodoyska Kawecka, who dressed in trousers and wore two revolvers hanging from her sash, argued for divorce and the liberation of women.[63]

Many of the ideas about women's liberation, just as those about education, did not originate in the Commune. Marx's grouping in the International, along with feminists such as André Léo, had created a tradition of support for these attitudes among the most militant workers and socialists. But the revolutionary movement opened up a whole new opportunity for their ideas to win popular support.

The role of art

The anti-capitalist, anti-elitist orientation of the International naturally attracted artists, writers and other intelligentsia whose dependence on patronage and state subsidies curtailed their artistic and political expression.

Eugène Pottier has become famous for his authorship of *The Internationale*, a song imbued with all the internationalism and irreverence of the Commune. Before that he also wrote the founding manifesto of the Artists' Federation in which he penned the term "Communal luxury", adopted by Kristin Ross as the title of her book.[64] The founder and president of the Federation was Gustave Courbet, later persecuted because he was accused of ordering the demolition of the Vendôme column.[65] The Federation held debates about the role of art and the artist in society, the integration of art into everyday life and how to overcome the counterposition between beauty and utility. It attracted well-known artists such as Corot, Manet and Daumier, who scorned those who fled Paris for Versailles such as Cézanne, Pissarro and Degas. Émile Zola, who associated with the reactionaries in Versailles, disgraced himself with mocking attacks on Courbet for his participation in politics, a sphere considered foreign to artists.[66]

---

63. Cox 2021.
64. Ross 2016.
65. See below for an explanation of this demolition.
66. See Ross 2016, pp. 42-65 for an account of the debates in the Artists' Federation and the artists involved.

The Federation refused to deal with any artistic creations which were not signed by their creator. This was a response to the previous practice of artists having to sell their works unsigned so that a dealer could pocket the profits. The personal history of Napoléon Gaillard, another member of the International, demonstrates their theories. A shoemaker, Gaillard was appointed commissioner for barricades. But how to sign a creation as immense as a barricade? An enemy of the Commune explained how Gaillard solved this problem:

> [He] appeared so proud of his creation that on the morning of May 20, we saw him in full commandant's uniform, four gold braids on the sleeve and cap, red lapels on his tunic, great riding boots, long, flowing hair, a steady gaze…and with his hand on his hip, had himself photographed.[67]

In harmony with the theories developed in the Federation, Gaillard would write philosophical treatises on the foot and the boot, and invent rubber galoshes. There were people who would not wear any other shoe than those he designed, years after his death. From exile he wrote "[t]he Art of the Shoe is, no matter what one says, of all the arts the most difficult, the most useful, and above all the least understood". He insisted that he be known as both a worker and an "artist shoemaker". His stance and writings summed up the Artists' Federation's arguments for overcoming the counterposition of the useful to the beautiful, calling for the public to demand shoes made for the foot as it is, rather than as it is assumed it should be.[68]

The attempt to overcome the separation of art from industry and life in general became a subject of much debate and experimentation, strongly influencing the British socialist novelist and fabric designer William Morris.

The Commune's internationalism

Marx and Engels had argued in *The German Ideology* decades earlier that workers could only become fit to create a new society through struggle against the old. Paris in March 1871 illustrated their point dramatically. France had been at war with Prussia since July 1870, yet

---

67. Ross 2016, pp. 55-56.
68. Ross 2016, pp. 55-56.

the Commune was determinedly internationalist in spirit: "Within sight of that Prussian army, that had annexed to Germany two French provinces, the Commune annexed to France the working people all over the world". A Jewish-Hungarian worker was appointed to the key position of minister of labour. They "honoured the heroic sons of Poland [J Dabrowski and W Wróblewski] by placing them at the head of the defenders of Paris". And "to broadly mark the new era of history it was conscious of initiating, under the eyes of the conquering Prussians on one side, and the Bonapartist army...on the other, the Commune pulled down that colossal symbol of martial glory, the Vendôme Column".[69]

This was not just a militant, spur of the moment act. Great thought and planning went into the removal of the statue that was on top of the column. There is a photograph of a pile of rubble in the Place Vendôme, all that remains of Bonaparte's statue, surrounded by undamaged buildings: the Communards had employed their most skilled engineers and workers to bring it down. Indeed, their original goal was to move the monument to a museum, but it proved too fragile to survive the toppling. The Place Vendôme was renamed Place Internationale.[70]

Like many of the reforms being proposed, the ideas of internationalism had been developing among radical workers before March 1871. Lissagaray outlines the development of a combative working class, independent of the increasingly conservative liberal bourgeoisie. In 1870, as rumours circulated about the coming war with Prussia:

> [T]he revolutionary socialists crowd the boulevards crying, *Vive la paix!* And singing the pacific refrain – "The people are our brothers/And the tyrants are our enemies"... Unable to influence the bourgeoisie, they turn to the working men of Germany... "Brothers, we protest against the war, we who wish for peace, labour and liberty. Brothers, do not listen to the hirelings who seek to deceive you as to the real wishes of France".[71]

The Commune's embrace of foreign militants in their midst and the

---

69. Marx 1871.
70. Ross 2016, p. 23.
71. Lissagaray 1976, pp. 10-12.

demolition of the symbol of imperial might demonstrated that their internationalism was more than rhetorical.

Reorganising society democratically

Contemporary observers, both hostile and sympathetic, commented that the Commune's elected leaders were unknown. That was not as true as it might seem; many of them had already made their name in debates in the popular clubs. To respectable society, then as now, such mass leaders were invisible. The other comment which recurs throughout the observations then and through all the histories is their inexperience. And how could it be otherwise? As Marx stresses, this was the first time workers had been sufficiently formed as a class to lead a movement for change. So even experienced activists were tackling new questions.

Donny Gluckstein looks at the way the democracy worked in some detail. He correctly puts it in the context of having to defend the Commune against Versailles with its trained army against the much smaller numbers of the rag-tag forces of the National Guard. Prisoners of war were released by Bismarck to help crush Paris. They were bombarded with lies and horror stories about the intentions of the Parisians, whipped into a frenzy of hatred that would be unleashed in the last week of May. But that murderous final stanza was merely the conclusion of growing bombardments and incursions into Paris by the army. These attacks killed scores of Guardsmen, with many others arrested.

Given these conditions, the humanitarian principles the Commune sought to live by often conflicted with the need for defence. For instance, the abolition of the death penalty distanced the idea of revolution from such cruelty. But in the face of massacres and hostages disappearing into the Versailles jails, it was reinstated. Only three were ever executed, but as we subsequently saw following the October Revolution in Russia, there is an unavoidable tension between honourable long-term goals and the immediate question of survival.

Gluckstein shows how the Commune Committee – headquartered in the Hôtel de Ville – related to the network of committees in the arrondissements, the clubs, and myriad other organisations which flourished. He argues that "the main living link between the mass movement and the Communal Council was the clubs".[72]

We cannot understand how democracy functioned in the Commune without grasping the vibrant life of those clubs. They argued for the creation of a stronger leadership in the form of a Committee of Public Safety, which provoked widespread debates. The name invoked the terror of the Great Revolution, which contradicted the image of remaining lawful and pacific which the leaders at the Hôtel de Ville had insisted on. Some women formed their own vigilance committees in spite of reluctance from the Commune Committee. The club Saint-Séverin, possibly where supporters of the International had some sway, asked the Commune to "finish off the bourgeoisie in one blow [and] take over the Banque de France", a point Marx had made on multiple occasions.

A meeting of 3,000 at Louise Michel's *Club de la Révolution* on 13 May, just a week before the final bloody week, unanimously called for the abolition of magistrates, the immediate arrest of priests and the execution of a hostage every 24 hours until the release of political prisoners by Versailles.[73] These are the demands of some of the most radical Communards, which shows both the level of debate and how arguments made by organised militants could get a mass audience. This was partly helped by the indecision in the Hôtel de Ville, which inflamed popular impatience.

Clubs insisted they should oversee the actions of the Commune Committee. Eleven of them formed a federation to produce a bulletin, some summoned the Council members to attend their meetings so there was more of an exchange of views. These chaotic events reflected both the dynamism which had been unleashed, but also much confusion about how to win against the increasingly threatening Versailles troops. Gluckstein concludes that it was the "sections" which included organisations such as the *Union des Femmes* that most effectively worked with the Hôtel de Ville, establishing a "strong and reciprocal" relationship: "In education, for example, much of the momentum came not from the Commune's commission but from the pre-existing bodies of educators". And we have already

---

72. Gluckstein 2006, pp. 46-53.
73. Gluckstein 2006, p. 49.

seen the reciprocal role of the *Union des Femmes* in relation to the Commission of Labour and the Commune Committee.[74]

This issue of how the clubs pressured the Commune Committee, took initiatives and demanded that the Committee inform them of their decisions is important in understanding the role of women in the revolutionary process. Judy Cox correctly challenges Gay Gullickson who, like most historians, downplays the advances for women because they weren't members of the elected Commune Committee. This is doubly mistaken. Firstly, like many feminists, Gullickson assumes that men can't represent women's interests. But support for women's rights is not simply a question of gender, but of politics. As Cox points out, "The Marxist wing of the First International was the only political organisation in France which supported the female franchise. At least four socialist male members of the Commune – Eugène Varlin, Benoît Malon, Édouard Vaillant and Leó Frankel – took initiatives that promoted women's equality in their areas of responsibility".[75]

But it was not simply a matter of principled men standing up against oppression. As already indicated, women's voices were loud and clear in the clubs, on the barricades and in every activity of the Commune. To modern supporters of women's liberation, the fact that women weren't granted the right to vote in the elections seems shocking. But there is no evidence that women demanded it. As Ross says:

> The [Women's] Union showed no trace of interest in parliamentary or rights-based demands. In this its members were, like Louise Michel, Paule Mincke and other women in the Commune, indifferent to the vote (a major goal in 1848) and to traditional forms of republican politics... Participation in public life, in other words, was for them in no way tied to the franchise.[76]

This is true, but the National Committee of the New Guard assumed, when they found themselves at the head of a successful insurrection, that they should operate legally. So the elections for which they got

---

74. Gluckstein 2006, p. 50.
75. Cox 2021.
76. Ross 2016, p. 28.

agreement from the mayors were held under the government's existing law, which only allowed for male suffrage. We don't know what the outcome would have been if prominent women had led a fight for female suffrage, but it is clear that many would have backed them.

Gullickson takes the positions of the right-wing Proudhonists – against whom Marx campaigned relentlessly – as evidence of a general chauvinist male culture which sidelined women. But even the left of the Proudhonists, such as Lefrançais, supported women's rights. And in spite of her feminism, Gullickson does not respect the voice of André Léo,[77] a prominent feminist from well before the Commune and editor of the magazine *La Sociale*. To bolster her case Gullickson quotes an account Léo published of New Guard officers and a physician who acted disrespectfully towards women volunteers. Yet Léo concluded that very article with: "we noticed the very different attitudes present. Without exception the [middle-class] officers and surgeons showed a lack of sympathy that varied from coldness to insults; but from the National Guards came respect and fraternity". And, because she aired the grievance against the officers, Louis Rossel, the Commune's war delegate, asked her for advice about involving more women in the military campaign.[78]

Of course not everyone was immediately convinced of the most radical points described here. The point is that women were challenging backward views, agitating for the reforms they needed, and the Commune endorsed their demands. The majority of Léo's articles in *La Sociale* dealt with issues not specifically about women. But when she did, she emphasised the need *and the potential* for solidarity between the sexes. One of her articles was titled "*Toutes avec Tous*" (all women and men together).[79]

We can add a further point. Gullickson can't recognise the immense advances that women made, and the tradition they left for the working class to learn from because she, like other liberal feminists, focuses on elected leaders. While what happens at that level is not irrelevant, socialists should focus on the changes taking

---

77. This was the pseudonym of Victoire Léodile Béra, under which she wrote several novels, and the name she is known by in the records of the Commune.
78. Gluckstein 2006, pp. 188-90.
79. Gluckstein 2006, pp. 185-91.

place below the surface, where workers were busy establishing democratic structures, raising new ideas and taking incredible initiatives. In the tumultuous events that characterise any revolution, the democratic character of the process cannot be fully understood simply by analysing constitutions or formal structures. It is about the dynamic of that process, and the incipient tendencies that emerge spontaneously through the struggle which can be developed further by conscious political intervention.

Much of the retrospective critiques of the Commune identify their failure to seize the wealth stored in the National Bank as a key mistake. Yet this itself was partly a product of the rigorous democracy that was the norm throughout the Commune. Raoul Rigault, a Blanquist and member of the International, was in charge of the "ex-Prefecture of police". He was a colourful figure with a history of political agitation and organising, dubbed the "professor of barricades" by a magistrate in one of his many trials.[80] He ordered some guards to seize the Bank of France to nationalise the wealth stored there. But prone to the elitism typical of the Blanquists, he did not consult with the rest of the Communal Council, and so the proposal was blocked by the Proudhonists. One of them insisted that the bank "should be respected as private property belonging to the shareholders"! By the time the Communal Council considered Rigault's instruction, the opportunity had been missed.[81]

Engels maintained that "[t]he bank in the hands of the Commune – this would have been worth more than 10,000 hostages". It is debatable whether this would have pushed Versailles to settle for peace as Engels asserted, but it is clear that the money within could have been used to deepen the Commune's achievements. For instance, the Commune had to spend 21 million francs on defence, leaving just 1,000 francs for education, an issue dear to the heart of virtually all who participated. More to the point, such reluctance to take on a bastion of governmental power and the bourgeoisie reflected the constant desire to operate within the bounds of bourgeois legality

---

80. Merriman 2016, p. 16.
81. Gluckstein 2006, pp. 156-57. For an analysis of why Proudhonists were on the right of the Communards, see Gluckstein, pp. 71-76.

and to avoid being cast as responsible for the civil war raging around them.[82] While there are examples of a lack of accountability from some leaders, the weaknesses historians identify have to be seen in the context of the siege, the civil war, and social and economic breakdown. The significant achievement is that which Marx emphasised: the embryo of a workers' democracy, with elected and recallable representatives, plus judges and officials at every level. This historical breakthrough warrants our main emphasis, rather than the understandable shortcomings.

A final point. The structures established by the Commune cannot be taken as a direct model for revolutionaries today. The working class in Paris was the largest group, numbering 900,000, surrounded by 400,000 petty bourgeois running 4,000 greengrocers' shops, 1,900 butchers, 1,300 bakeries. However, Haussmann's reconstruction of Paris had discouraged the establishment of large workplaces. Those that were established were mostly in the outer rim of Paris. The Cail plant in north-east Paris, employing 2,800 to produce steam engines and locomotives, was the exception rather than the norm. Workplaces of over 10 workers were only seven percent of the total, with 31 percent employing between two and ten. Gluckstein concludes:

> The nature of production...had an influence on the organisational structure of the 1871 movement... Trade union action was difficult to mount and broad activities could not easily be built from tiny workplaces. Such units of production could not provide a collective focus for the working class. Instead that came from the National Guard and the clubs which offered a framework for collective expression and organisation.[83]

In the Russian revolution of 1905 workers would take another leap forward and create soviets, reflecting the huge growth of the industrial working class, brought together in workplaces massively larger than anything in Paris in 1871. This meant that the focus of organisation shifted to the workplace, even as the streets remained an important focal point for large and united protests that brought

---
82. Marx et al 2008, p. 71.
83. Gluckstein 2006, pp. 69-71.

workers from across different industries together. This is profoundly important. As Rosa Luxemburg argued, "where the chains of oppression are forged, there they must be broken". Nevertheless the principles of the Commune lived on in the soviets: all delegates and people in places of responsibility to be recallable at any time, accountable to the electors, paid workers' wages and remaining at work where they experienced the conditions about which they made decisions. The Paris Commune is therefore best understood as a premonition, or a *harbinger*, of a future society. In Marx's words:

> The working class did not expect miracles from the Commune. They have no ready-made utopias to introduce *par décret du peuple*. They know that in order to work out their own emancipation... they will have to pass through long struggles, through a series of historic processes, transforming circumstances and men. They have no ideals to realize, but to set free the elements of the new society.[84]

Some aspects of the Commune have been superseded by subsequent developments, and we do not know precisely how the working-class revolution of this century might look. However the basic principles of collectivity and democracy it established remain vitally important to the modern working class.

Ruling class savagery – "la semaine sanglante"

Marx had argued that we make our own history, but not in circumstances of our choosing.[85] The uprising which erupted on 18 March forced the Communards to reorganise society amidst a Prussian siege and a bitter civil war. These factors strongly contributed to the defeat of this heroic uprising.

On Sunday 21 May, troops from Versailles stormed Paris. New barricades went up in street after street, as the population mobilised for a final heroic attempt to maintain their Commune. An eyewitness described how one of the barricades was constructed and defended by "a women's battalion of around a hundred and twenty. At the time that I arrived, a dark form detached itself from

---
84. Marx 1871.
85. Marx 1852.

a carriage gate. It was a girl with a Phrygian bonnet over her ear, a musket in her hand, and a cartridge-belt at her waist. 'Halt, citizen, you don't pass here!'"[86] We see how women have developed from pleading with soldiers not to shoot in March, to now playing a role as proud, fighting combatants in May, prepared to die with dignity and honour.

Just one week later, 30,000 or more people had been murdered by the counter-revolutionaries. The chapter headings used by Lissagaray in his book sum up the experience: "The Versailles fury", "The balance sheet of bourgeois vengeance". The essence of the events is captured in the title of John Merriman's book, *Massacre*.[87] Though there are debates about the death toll, I see no point in quibbling about the precise figures. Many casualties were never recorded, their bodies thrown into mass graves and later incinerated. Countless others disappeared into jails or colonial transportation, where who knows how many died. Others fled to seek sanctuary, and there are few records of who survived wounds inflicted in the fighting. This barbarity was at first cheered on in the respectable bourgeois papers of Europe, whose journalists had followed the army around "like jackals". One journalist had called for "an end to this international democratic vermin" of Red Paris. But faced with "the smell of carnage", swarms of flies on corpses, trees stripped of leaves, the streets full of dead birds, even some of these bourgeois commentators were repulsed. "Let us not kill any more", pleaded the *Paris Journal*, "Enough executions, enough blood, enough victims" lamented the *Nationale*.[88]

But the upper classes who lived off the labour of those being massacred expressed no such limits to their savagery.[89] Respectable women took tours of the dungeons where the arrested were incarcerated, holding their lace-edged handkerchiefs – made by the women at whom they gawked – to their noses against the stench of filth and dying Communards. In particular, they took delight

---

86. Hazan 2010, p. 238.
87. Lissagaray 1976; Merriman 2016.
88. Lissagaray 1976, pp. 307-11.
89. Lissagaray 1976, pp. 146-74; Merriman 2016, chapters 9 and 10. Their accounts give more detail than belongs in an article of this length.

in poking the women with their parasols. Many public figures, including judges and other respectable bourgeois and middle-class types, continued to bay for blood. To justify this frenzy, they invented lies which appealed to the prejudices of this scum. An anonymous Englishman described the Communards as "lashed up to a frenzy which has converted them into a set of wild beasts caught in a trap". This, in his opinion, "render[ed] their extermination a necessity".[90] The ruling class especially hated the women Communards, whom they depicted as "vile", "wild" and sexually depraved.

Their fury was stoked by hysterical stories of the infamous *pétroleuses,* supposedly prepared to burn down the whole of Paris. So the legend of the *pétroleuses* demands our attention. Edith Thomas titled her book on the women of the Commune *Les Pétroleuses,* translated as *The Women Incendiaries.* She examines the evidence and concludes that it's not clear whether there were any *pétroleuses* in the way reactionaries used the term. At the same time, the Communards clearly did use fire as a weapon of war to destroy buildings from which the Versaillese could gun people down. Fire was also used as a form of barricade, a wall of flames to keep the soldiers back, set by the fighters who must have included women and possibly even children.[91] Merriman documents orders given by the war delegate with the National Guard, Charles Delescluze, the ageing Jacobin, and others, including men in the Commune Committee, to blow up or set fire to houses. Delescluze, aware that it had become impossible to muster the kind of military response necessary to repel the soldiers, "adopted a strategy of mass popular resistance". Generals of the National Guard specifically ordered "the burning of a number of monumental Parisian buildings, all in the fancy parts of town", as well as official buildings. One of the Communard generals ordered the Tuileries Palace to be set ablaze. Gustave Lefrançais, the most left-wing Proudhonist, admitted that he was one of those "who had shutters of joy seeing that sinister palace go up in flames". When a woman asked Nathalie Lemel what it was she could see burning in Montmartre, Lemel replied simply, "it's nothing at all,

---

90. Merriman 2016, p. 226.
91. Thomas 1966, pp. 140-59.

only the Palais-Royal and the Tuileries, because we do not want a king anymore".[92]

Marx was right to defend the burning of the city:

> The working men's Paris, in the act of its heroic self-holocaust, involved in its flames buildings and monuments. While tearing to pieces the living body of the proletariat, its rulers must no longer expect to return triumphantly into the intact architecture of their abodes. The government of Versailles cries, "Incendiarism!" and whispers this cue to all its agents...to hunt up its enemies everywhere as suspect of professional incendiarism. The bourgeoisie of the whole world, which looks complacently upon the wholesale massacre after the battle, is convulsed by horror at the desecration of brick and mortar!
>
> ...The Commune used fire strictly as a means of defence. They used it to stop up to the Versailles troops those long, straight avenues which Haussmann had expressly opened to artillery-fire; they used it to cover their retreat, in the same way as the Versaillese, in their advance, used their shells which destroyed at least as many buildings as the fire of the Commune. It is a matter of dispute, even now, which buildings were set fire to by the defence, and which by the attack. And the defence resorted to fire only then when the Versailles troops had already commenced their wholesale murdering of prisoners.[93]

The heroism of children, women and men as they fought to defend their "Communal luxury" would live on in the memory of the socialist movement and workers. Fighting and dying became a sign of revolutionary honour. Memoirs often recall scenes like this one from Lissagaray about the barricade of the Faubourg du Temple:

> [T]he most indefatigable gunner was a child. The barricade taken, all its defenders were shot, and the child's turn also came. He asked for three minutes' respite; "so that he could take his mother, who lived opposite, his silver watch *in order that she might at least not lose everything*". The officer, involuntarily moved, let him go.

---

92. Merriman 2016, pp. 156-59.
93. Marx 1871.

Not thinking to see him again; but three minutes after the child cried, "Here I am!" jumped onto the pavement, and nimbly leant against the wall near the corpses of his comrades.

Lissagaray concluded, "Paris will never die as long as she brings forth such people".[94] And Victor Hugo, who did not originally support the Commune, but responded in solidarity in the face of the massacre, wrote a poem about this incident. He ends with the wishful thought that the officer pardoned the child.[95]

Gustave Courbet recalled:

> The drunkenness of carnage and destruction had taken over this people ordinarily so mild, but so fearsome when pushed to the brink... We will die if we must, shouted men, women and children, but we will not be sent to Cayenne.[96]

Louise Michel became famous for her confrontational stance at her trial:

> Since it seems that every heart which beats for liberty has only right to a little lead, I too demand my part. If you let me live, I shall not cease to cry vengeance... If you are not cowards, kill me.[97]

Out of fear that she would become a martyr around which workers could mobilise, she was condemned to transportation to New Caledonia, where she met Nathalie Lemel. During the defence of Paris, Lemel had taken command of a contingent of the *Union des Femmes*. They marched, red flag in the lead, from a meeting in the *mairie*[98] of the fourth arrondissement to defend Les Batignolles. There, the 120 women held back government troops for several hours. Those who were taken were shot on the spot, one of whom was the dressmaker Blanche Lefebvre, an organiser of the *Union des Femmes* and another member of Marx's circle. Some held a barricade on Place Pigalle for a further three hours, but all were killed on what Lissagaray called "this legendary barricade". Lemel cared for the wounded for hours.

---

94. Lissagaray 1976, p. 287.
95. Tod 2020.
96. The notorious penal colony in French Guiana. Merriman 2016, p. 147.
97. Lissagaray 1971, pp. 343-44.
98. Local town hall.

Her comrade Elisabeth Dmitrieff was at Montmartre with Louise Michel and Léo Frankel in the last hours.[99]

The mass of the poor had few options but to die bravely, which they did with pride. The more educated, if fortunate, found their way into exile. Frankel was smuggled out by a coach driver and escaped to Germany with Dmitrieff. They could be disguised as a Prussian couple because they spoke German fluently. Dmitrieff would return to Russia, only to go into exile in Siberia with a revolutionary with whom she had a genuine marriage. Because of her isolation, she never heard of the amnesty and so lived out the rest of her life in the tundra where so many revolutionaries perished. Michel kept her word and eventually returned to France under the amnesty, was arrested on a demonstration of unemployed workers in 1883 and sentenced to six years of solitary confinement, arrested again in 1890. She returned to France from England, to where she had escaped, and died of pneumonia in January 1905.[100]

A doctor commented on the bravery of the Communards:

> I cannot desire the triumph of your cause; but I have never seen wounded men preserve more calm and sang-froid during operations. I attribute this courage to the energy of their convictions.[101]

And this is how the Commune's supporters interpreted the courageous resistance. It inspired generations, illustrating why the sentiment "it is better to die fighting than to live on your knees" is the most principled response to ruling-class barbarism. If they had meekly surrendered in the name of avoiding violence, there is no evidence that lives would have been saved, and the revolution would surely not have inspired generations of working-class and socialist activists.

Political assessments

"We'll change henceforth the old conditions" runs a line of Pottier's *Internationale*. But how is it to be done? Which politics and theory

---
99. Thomas 1966, p. 132.
100. Merriman 2016, p. 245.
101. Lissagaray 1976, p. 238.

related best to the needs of the Commune? When remembering workers' struggles, assessing the political ideas tested in battle is an important part of honouring their memory. If the suffering of the masses in defeat is to be worth the blood spilled, it is the responsibility of those inspired by them to try to learn the lessons, lest their sacrifices be endlessly repeated. In the last article Rosa Luxemburg wrote before being murdered in January 1919, she made reference to the Paris Commune as a metaphor for the fate of the revolution unravelling around her. But, from the perspective of the historic mission of the working class, such defeats served a purpose:

> Where would we be today *without* those "defeats", from which we draw historical experience, understanding, power and idealism?... [W]e stand on the foundation of those very defeats; and we cannot do without *any* of them, because each one contributes to our strength and understanding.[102]

Again and again, in the intervening 150 years, workers have shown that if only they can take control, they would build a humane society, a socialist world. In every struggle we can celebrate the signs of this, and that inspiration unites those of many different politics on the left. Just think. One hundred and fifty years ago, when the fight for women's rights was in its infancy, the more radical clubs in Paris demanded and got support for the right to abortion.

However, the question which has eluded workers so far is how to win control and hold it, how to defeat the powerful forces of capitalism arrayed against them. Proudhonists, Jacobins and Blanquists were the most influential political groups in the Commune Committee. Marx's International had thousands of members, but was far from cohered around his theory and politics. None of these groups could offer the lead required.

The National Guard had elected a Central Committee only a couple of weeks before the uprising. Though inexperienced, they gathered to consider what to do in light of the spontaneous insurrection. By the end of the day the Hôtel de Ville was occupied as the headquarters of the insurgents. But they lacked the confidence

---

102. Luxemburg 1919.

to assert their authority and organise the necessary defence and reorganisation of the city. In their political confusion, they turned for leadership to the only constitutional body left in Paris, the mayors, who were appointed by the hated central government! The Central Committee of the National Guard insisted that only a newly elected body could take on all the urgent tasks the city confronted. It was eight days before negotiations with the mayors enabled the election of an authoritative body, in which valuable time was lost to the advantage of the Versailles soldiers threatening Paris. Élie Reclus asked on voting day: "What does legality mean at a time of revolution?"[103]

Virtually every historian who has written about it comments on the shambolic nature of the National Guard, which ensured that the Versailles government's victory was easier than it should have been. Similarly, most make a point of discussing the Commune's flat-footed response to the mass uprising. Few, however, draw any political conclusions or seriously explain what went wrong. Edwards sums up the reasons for the disaster: the main concern of the majority of the Committee "was to 'legalize' its situation by divesting itself of the power that had so unexpectedly fallen into its hands". The Blanquists urged a march on Versailles, "a plan which might well have succeeded" following the fraternisation between the army and the Guardsmen.[104] Gluckstein argues that Thiers and Co. would never be weaker than in those first hours and days after 18 March 1871. Military discipline had evaporated, and the French army was yet to be buoyed up by prisoners of war released by Bismarck. Supporting this view is the fact that Thiers rejected a request for troops to set up an anti-Commune outfit inside Paris: "Neither 5,000, nor 500, nor five; I need the few troops still available – and in whom I don't yet have full confidence – to defend the government". A Commune supporter reported that in Versailles the regular troops were not even trusted to patrol the streets.[105]

Auguste Blanqui shared with Marx the expectation that the war would create a situation ripe for revolution. But unlike Marx

---

103. Edwards 1973, p. 26.
104. Edwards 1973, p. 26.
105. Gluckstein 2006, p. 130.

he did not see the working class as the agent to *make* that revolution, only as supporters for a coup. As a result, his supporters had not built roots in working-class organisations or communities, and he languished in jail throughout the revolution due to his involvement in an attempted insurrection just months before. "Blanqui's own account of the debacle [of August 1870] is painfully honest", Gluckstein explains. Blanqui wrote of the response of the workers of Belleville to these gun-toting strangers calling for them to rise up: "[t]he population appeared dumbstruck...held back by fear". And he concluded "We can do nothing without the people!" In spite of their history of organising conspiratorial coups by tiny numbers, the Blanquists participated with great enthusiasm in the mass uprising and the institutions it threw up. Their strength was their preparedness to organise and respond with the necessary violence to defeat the murderous forces arrayed against the Commune.[106] However, lacking their most authoritative leader, the Blanquists were defeated in the debate about marching on Versailles, and a critical moment was missed.

Despite their hostility to organisation, the Proudhonists took many of the leading positions in the Commune Committee. Their tradition had long cultivated a hostility to political organisation of all kinds, which manifested in a reluctance to give elected bodies of the Commune real authority. This then undermined the confidence of those bodies to act decisively, providing Versailles time to get on the offensive. The Proudhonists' respect for private property was also responsible for the decision to leave the enormous wealth of the bourgeoisie safe in the National Bank, and informed a general reticence to take decisive measures in the field of economic and military policy.

Proudhonism today is dead as a political current; however, Proudhon's disciple, Bakunin, still influences some activists. In a typical formulation, Bakunin wrote in his critique of the Commune: "the cause of [humanity's] troubles does not lie in any particular form of government but in the fundamental principles and the very existence in government, whatever form it takes".[107] But this

---
106. Gluckstein 2006, pp. 76-80.
107. Bakunin, "The Paris Commune and the idea of the state", in Marx et al 2008, p. 78.

radical-sounding generality obscures the fact that the Commune's troubles came not from an abstract category, but from the very real power of Thiers' counter-revolutionary army. Only an equally organised power based on working-class democracy could have defended the Commune from the massacre that was to come. Bakunin's abstract slogans – which live on in anarchist milieus today – provide absolutely no guide for what to do in the face of the threat posed by the brutal machine that is the bourgeois state. Workers could not – and still cannot – ignore politics and organisation.

But it wasn't just the question of defence. The demand of the bakers to end night work raised a lot of debate because Commune Committee members, influenced by such ideas as Bakunin articulates, refused to issue a decree to abolish night work, even though they supported it. Bakers had been campaigning for two years, hampered by the tiny size of the bakeries which mitigated against effective organisation. The Committee's response was ludicrous. They opposed any state action on principle, and argued that the workers should "themselves safeguard their interests in relation to the owners". Benoît Malon represented the views of the bakers, 3,000 of whom marched to the Hôtel de Ville demanding a decree: "until now the state has intervened *against* the interests of workers. It is at least fair that today the state intervene for the workers".[108]

Abstract shibboleths against all organisation are no guide to how the left should have related to the radical organisations such as the *Union des Femmes*, the Artists' Federation, and the clubs. If you took these principles seriously you would boycott them, a completely sectarian and destructive attitude which would make you irrelevant, unable to contribute to developing people's consciousness and winning arguments for strategies to win.

It was Marx and Engels who best generalised the lessons of the Commune. Marx had been committed to a view of working-class self-emancipation well before the Commune showed a glimpse of how it could be done. He had witnessed the radical workers' societies and, critically, the Silesian weavers' revolt of 1844, and had subsequently never doubted the creativity and organisational genius of

---

108. Gluckstein 2006, pp. 28-29.

the organised proletariat. His *Theses on Feuerbach* answered the question of how workers could be "educated" for a new society: they educate themselves through their own conscious activity. Marx and Engels developed this idea further in their *German Ideology*, where they argued that to build a socialist society, "the alteration of men on a mass scale is necessary, an alteration which can only take place in a practical movement, a revolution".[109]

Now the Parisian masses had revealed the answer to the question of what to do about the repressive state. Marx had been grappling with this since he concluded in *The Eighteenth Brumaire of Louis Bonaparte* that the problem had been until then that "[a]ll revolutions perfected this machine instead of breaking it".[110] But what could take its place? Two days after *la semaine sanglante*, Marx gave his address to the International, emphasising the achievements of the Commune and its importance to the future of the workers' movement. He had warned against such an uprising in the weeks previous, fearing it was premature, yet did not hesitate to leap to its defence. As with so much of his political work, his writings on the Commune emphasise its fundamental aspects. Unlike the bourgeois revolutions which primarily benefited a minority of capitalist exploiters, the potential of a workers' revolution to liberate the whole of humanity was now shown in practice. He explains how the democratic structures, with the army and police disbanded and the population armed, were the foundation on which workers can be emancipated from the exploitation of their labour. In this way, the practice of the workers of Paris actually broke new ground; their heroism created the conditions for Marx and Engels to clarify and concretise their previous ideas regarding the self-emancipation of the working class. Overall, Marx's writings on the Commune stand in sharp contrast to the abstract shibboleths in Bakunin's work.

But it would be Lenin who brought all these elements together, transcending what is usually assumed to be a contradiction between spontaneous revolts and organisation.[111] The counterposition between spontaneity and organisation abounds in Bakunin's

---

109. Marx and Engels 1932, p. 60.
110. Marx 1845.
111. For my assessment of Lenin, see Bloodworth 2013.

critique, and is taken for granted by many activists today. The issue is particularly fraught when women are involved. Women's activities in rebellions like this are often portrayed as elemental, unplanned and not very political. This emphasis on spontaneity is often sexist and downplays the role of leadership, foresight and planning by the women themselves. The Commune perfectly illustrates Lenin's arguments. To begin with, there can be no revolution without spontaneity. The radicalisation sufficient to generate the Paris Commune did not develop incrementally, it exploded and shocked the world. It's true that the uprising that seized the cannon in Montmartre emerged in a context of rising discontent and bitterness, but the rebellion in turn radicalised and transformed the situation decisively.

The Commune shows how there is not some barrier between a revolutionary upsurge itself and the activities and politics that exist beforehand. For instance Eugène Varlin and Nathalie Lemel were involved in workers' campaigns for women's rights and equal pay in the 1860s. In the growing number of strikes before 1871, some workers had learnt from their experiences. A strike by 5,000 bronze workers in 1867 won with support from the International, which organised funds from workers in other countries. The lesson of international solidarity was not forgotten. And other workers – significantly in textiles from where women participated in Dmitrieff's *Union des Femmes* – began to see the value of organisation and strikes in a number of cities. In a strike by miners in the Loire region workers' wives had fought bravely against the gendarmes during a strike at Le Creusot in 1870. Ideas promoted by the Proudhonists, who argued that "women should stay indoors and avoid the physical and moral dangers of workshops", were now rejected by working-class men. They declared that women should exercise their independence and "will march alongside us in the exercise of democratic and social cooperation". Those ideas could most effectively be kept alive and popularised if taken up by organisations, rather than being left to the whimsy of individual happenstance.[112]

Lenin's most significant theoretical breakthrough was to see

---

112. Gluckstein 2006, pp. 68-71 for details of strikes and the maturing of working-class activists.

that the task for revolutionaries is to prepare for the spontaneous outbursts before they happen. This preparation is not a purely intellectual exercise, but entails participating in every struggle, raising ideas which challenge participants to reject the ideas of capitalism. Not all workers will develop class consciousness at the same time; consciousness will always be uneven, as it was in the Commune. This means revolutionaries need to build a party which organises the most class-conscious and militant workers, the "vanguard" as Lenin called them. Such a revolutionary party needs to raise the level of class consciousness generally, by which Lenin meant the degree to which workers understand the role of their own class, and that of all other social layers, and how much they understand their class power. They need to understand that their class can and must lead other classes in a revolution if capitalism is to be overthrown. The party needs a history of participating in and leading struggles so they gain a wide understanding of the momentum of struggle, how to judge different strategies and the arguments of different political organisations. Only this offers the best chance that the arguments of those who always support compromise and moderation will be defeated.

The vanguard must have burned into their consciousness that if our side seriously challenges the ruling class and their state, there is no limit to their "undisguised savagery and lawless revenge", in Marx's words. Revolutions have time and again crashed against the seemingly timeless existence of the state, and the mistake of seeking to remain within the "rule of law". Lenin's solution was to organise the vanguard to be prepared to repeat the first acts of the Commune: to disband the police and army, and to arm the working class and poor. It must not shrink from responding to ruling-class violence in order to defend the revolution.

The Commune's legacy

In the Paris Commune, the ruling class saw the shape of a new society. They understood that such a world of equality and justice could only be built on the ruins of capitalism. So they sought to systematically obliterate its memory.

In the Louvre today, images of the royal family overthrown in the Great Revolution are sympathetically portrayed. But a small collection from the Commune is hidden away in the basement. A collection of artefacts, documents and the like is included in the museum dedicated to the art of Paul Éluard in Saint-Denis. Ironically it is housed in an old Carmelite convent. It was originally set up by the Communist council of Saint-Denis.

In the 1870s the bourgeoisie set out to refashion Paris with monuments to the Republic. The last quarter of the nineteenth century has been referred to as "a golden age of monument building" as part of the effort at "self-definition" following the trauma of 1870-71. Restoring the Vendôme column was, of course, a huge priority. Sometimes the purpose of new monuments or buildings was made explicit. The church of Sacré-Coeur was built on Montmartre. When laying the foundation stone, architect Charles Rohault de Fleury declared that Sacré-Coeur reclaimed for the nation "the place chosen by Satan and where was accomplished the first act of that horrible Saturnalia".[113]

It is easy to see the negation of the Commune in the grotesque splendour of the Sacré-Coeur. But a lot of the reconstruction was not so explicit. Much of the art which was promoted and the spaces reorganised were merely presented as celebrations of the Republic. But try as they may, the memory often reverberated in what was not said or built. One space allowed to socialists was the *Mur des Fédérés* (Wall of the Federals),[114] located in the *Père Lachaise* cemetery where the blood of unknown numbers was spilled in the last days of the Commune. Presumably authorities thought this the most fitting memorial: calculated to sear our souls and to signal that attempts at anti-capitalist rebellions will always be drowned in unimaginable savagery. But they were mistaken. Visitors leave a constant sea of red roses, and leave with a renewed hatred of the bourgeoisie and a desire to fight for the promise of the Commune. In 1907, the Parisian municipal council planned to install Paul Vautier-Moreau's *Monument to the Victims of Revolutions*, sculpted from the stones of the barricades, on which was engraved Victor Hugo's clarion call to end the "vengeance". There was such an outcry from supporters of the Commune,

---

113. Eschelbacher 2009.
114. As the Guardsmen were often referred to.

who preferred to keep that space simply for the Communards, that it had to be placed outside the wall of the cemetery.[115]

William Morris paid homage to the destruction of the Vendôme column in his novel *News from Nowhere*, published in 1890. The apricot orchard which replaces Trafalgar Square, dominated by the statue of Admiral Nelson is, as Ross says, a "symbolic revisioning [of] both the Place Vendôme and Trafalgar Square...their aesthetic of nationalistic and timeless monumentality become supra-national space".[116]

In spite of the efforts of the descendants of the butchers who saturated Paris in blood, the memory of this first workers' revolution cannot be completely suppressed. So a social history of Paris, published in English in 2010, revisits some of the accounts by its participants and supporters. Eric Hazan, the author, reminds us how modern day charlatans, rather than obscure the history completely, cynically attempt to co-opt the inspiration of the Commune for their own opportunistic reasons. A plaque in Paris has inscribed on it: "The last barricade of the Commune resisted in the Rue de la Fontaine-au-Roi. A hundred and twenty years later, the Socialist party and its first secretary Pierre Mauroy render homage to the people of Paris who sought to change their lives, and to the 30,000 dead of the Time of the Cherries". Hazan, who documents the truth of those days, reminds us: "This trumpery makes short work of history, for Louis Blanc, the Mauroy of his day, maintained that 'this insurrection is completely to be condemned, and must be condemned by any true republican'."[117] *Le temps des cerises* to which the inscription refers is a song written in 1866. It became popular during the Commune, with verses added as it was sung on the barricades and in the clubs. The title is a metaphor for the hope for a new life after a revolution, making the hypocritical inscription by the reformist party even more galling.

For decades workers remembered the Communards' courageous defiance. On May Day 1901, thousands of mourners joined the funeral procession for Paule Mincke through the streets of Paris.

---

115. Eschelbacher 2009.
116. Ross 2016, p. 60.
117. Hazan 2010, p. 291.

They chanted "Vive la Commune!" and "Vive l'Internationale!" as more than 600 police, 500 soldiers and 100 cavalry guarded the streets against any possibility of a repeat of 1871.[118] More than 100,000 attended Louise Michel's funeral in Paris in 1905. Socialists and anarchists celebrated the Commune every March. The ghastly images of tortured women beamed around the world by the bourgeois press could not undercut the sense of pride and solidarity that their courage inspired. In the NSW outback mining city of Broken Hill, for at least a decade into the twentieth century, the Socialist Sunday School organised the annual anniversary commemoration of the Commune. In another piece I concluded that "[it] certainly was not portrayed as a celebration of male achievements, as is often claimed by feminist historians: 'What greater and grander sublimity can be depicted than that of men and women who are prepared to sacrifice their lives for even a dream?'" An article in the socialist paper in the town "emphasised female bravery", telling the story of when soldiers tried to force Communards to kneel before their guns: "one woman with a child in her arms refused to do so, shouting to her companions: 'Show these wretches that you know how to die upright'."[119]

An historian of the annual events which continued for decades writes:

> They drew on the Commune as an example of international cooperation, drawing on their shared class identity. The Commune was rewritten annually, creating a palimpsest. Speakers drew on the Commune as a symbol of working-class government, or of revolution, a symbol of warning and hope, of past, present and future, something to learn from, and revere.[120]

In spite of so many efforts to obscure its history, the Commune is still invoked as a reference point for the idea of revolution, or challenges to authority to this very day. As I write, a post by *Buzzfeed*, "Stormings of History Ranked from Best to Worst", appeared in response to the invasion of the Capitol by far-right Trump supporters. The Commune is their second-best example, second only to the

---
118. Cox 2021.
119. Bloodworth 2005.
120. Landrigan 2017, p. 78.

October Revolution.[121] Even the prestigious *Lancet* in the year of the one hundred and fiftieth anniversary pays homage to the Commune with an article about Mary Putnam Jacobi. The conclusion is a tribute to the power of the Commune to inspire hope for a better world: "The origins of her philosophy, a philosophy that provides the seed for an American renaissance today, lay in the blood spilt on the streets of Paris 150 years ago".[122]

Conclusion

We began with the image of the "sphinx" conjured by Marx to convey how the Commune terrified the bourgeoisie and their hangers-on. We leave it as the world descends into ever more horrifying chaos which creates catastrophes one after the other. The World Bank warns governments around the globe to avoid making premature cuts to measures taken to prevent the economy from completely collapsing. This advice is not driven by humanitarian concern for those who would suffer from the cuts, but by fear of revolt. The sphinx haunts them still.

The Paris Commune reminds *us* of what Walter Benjamin said, that the fine and spiritual aspects of life we hunger for can only be won by the struggle for the rough, material things which make them possible. And that "they are present as confidence, as courage, as humour, as cunning, as steadfastness in this struggle". That is why the Paris Commune still commands our attention, and is worthy of serious study. And why it still has the power to inspire our confidence in the working class to create a "Communal luxury" for humanity to this day.

---

121. Buzzfeed 2021
122. Horton 2021.

References

Benjamin, Walter 1968, "Theses on the Philosophy of History" in *Illuminations, Essays and Reflections*, Schocken Books.

Bloodworth, Sandra 2005, "Militant spirits: the rebel women of Broken Hill". https://sa.org.au/interventions/rebelwomen/militant.htm.

Bloodworth, Sandra 2013, "Lenin vs 'Leninism'", *Marxist Left Review*, 5, Summer. https://marxistleftreview.org/articles/lenin-vs-leninism/.

Buzzfeed 2021, "Stormings of History Ranked from Best to Worst", January. https://www.buzzfeed.com/tessred/stormings-of-history-ranked-from-best-to-worst-dogxsiwtv3?utm_source=dynamic&utm_campaign=bfsharefacebook&fbclid=IwAR0Bm0V61HcfuBZsc6jth8J51i6z-enf8-N_WefnVp1pITFqvlRQoAa9_kI.

Cox, Judy 2021, "Genderquake: socialist women and the Paris Commune", *International Socialism*, 169, 5 January. http://isj.org.uk/genderquake-paris-commune/.

Edwards, Stewart (ed.) 1973, *The Communards of Paris, 1871* (Documents of Revolution series, Heinz Lubasz, general editor), Thames and Hudson.

Eschelbacher, Andrew 2009, "Environment of Memory: Paris and Post-Commune Angst", *Nineteenth Century Art World*, 8 (2), Autumn. https://www.19thc-artworldwide.org/autumn09/environment-of-memory

Gluckstein, Donny 2006, *The Paris Commune. A Revolution in Democracy*, Bookmarks.

Hazan, Eric 2011, *The Invention of Paris. A History in Footsteps*, translator David Fernbach, Verso.

Horton, Richard 2021, "The Paris Commune and the birth of American medicine", *The Lancet*, 397, (102070), 16 January. https://www.thelancet.com/journals/lancet/article/PIIS0140-6736(21)00086-6/fulltext

Landrigan, Aloysius Judas 2017, *Remembering the Commune: Texts and Celebrations in Britain and the United States*, MA thesis, University of Melbourne. https://minerva-access.unimelb.edu.au/handle/11343/198112

Lissagaray 1976 [1876], *History of the Paris Commune of 1871*, translator Eleanor Marx, New Park Publications.

Luxemburg, Rosa 1919, "Order Prevails in Berlin", *Die Rote Fahne*, 14 January. https://www.marxists.org/archive/luxemburg/1919/01/14.htm

Marx, Karl 1845, *Theses on Feuerbach*. https://www.marxists.org/archive/marx/works/1845/theses/theses.htm

Marx, Karl 1852, *The Eighteenth Brumaire of Louis Bonaparte*. https://www.marxists.org/archive/marx/works/1852/18th-brumaire/

Marx, Karl 1871, *The Civil War in France*. https://www.marxists.org/archive/marx/works/1871/civil-war-france/index.htm

Marx, Karl and Friedrich Engels 1932 [1846], *The German Ideology*. https://www.marxists.org/archive/marx/works/1845/german-ideology/index.htm

Marx, Karl, Friedrich Engels, Mikhail Bakunin and Peter Kropotkin 2008, *Writings on the Paris Commune*, Red and Black Publishers.

Merriman, John 2016, *Massacre. The Life and Death of the Paris Commune of 1871*, Yale University Press.

Ross, Kristin 2016, *Communal Luxury. The Political Imaginary of the Paris Commune*, Verso.

Thomas, Edith 1966 [1963 as *Les Pétroleuses*], *The Women Incendiaries*, Secker and Warburg.

Tod, MK 2020, *Poetry about the Paris Commune*, blog, 10 September. https://awriterofhistory.com/tag/poetry-about-the-paris-commune/

JORDAN HUMPHREYS

Capitalism, colonialism and class: A Marxist explanation of Indigenous oppression today

Jordan Humphreys is a socialist activist in Sydney and a regular contributor to the Marxist Left Review.

THE CONTINUED OPPRESSION of Indigenous people is one of the most potent expressions of the brutal nature of Australian capitalism. Despite all the talk about reconciliation, the reality is that unemployment, poverty and police brutality are rife. In 2018 the Indigenous employment rate was around 49 percent as compared to 75 percent for non-Indigenous Australians – almost the same as it was a decade previously.[1] Racist policing and incarceration rates remain devastating. Since the Royal Commission into Aboriginal Deaths in Custody ended in 1991 at least 434 Aboriginals and Torres Strait Islanders have been killed in custody. Not a single one of these deaths – or more accurately murders – has resulted in a successful prosecution of a police officer.[2] This oppression is reinforced for each new generation by the racist structures of Australian society. Aboriginal children are only 6 percent of 10-17-year-olds in Australia, yet in 2019 they made up 54 percent of the juvenile detention population. Indigenous kids also made up nearly 65 percent of children under 14 in detention, and according to a 2016 report 94 percent of children in detention aged 10-12 will

1. Closing the Gap report 2020.
2. Russell and Cunneen 2018.

end up back in prison before they turn 18.[3]

Recognition of the lack of any real progress for Indigenous people, despite establishment claims to the contrary, has led to growing popular concern over the issue. Ten years ago, the Invasion Day marches around the country were defiant but isolated events attended by at most a few hundred people. Today tens of thousands of Indigenous and non-Indigenous people flood the streets every January 26 demanding justice. The spectacular Black Lives Matter rebellion against race and class in the United States has had reverberations here, reinforcing this shift in popular consciousness. For broad layers of people, this has raised the issue of how we can end Indigenous oppression.

On the Australian left, the dominant explanation for Indigenous oppression is that we are still living in a settler colonial society. Often this is meant in a vague and general way to link anti-Indigenous racism to the continent's invasion in 1788. It also serves as a rebuttal to right-wing commenters who argue that Australia either has – or will soon – resolve Indigenous oppression by progressing into a post-racial society. However, as a serious analysis, settler colonial theory is both an inaccurate portrayal of the present nature of Indigenous oppression and has had a disorienting impact on attempts to develop a strategy for liberation. There are two key, and interlocking, problems with settler colonial theory that I want to explore in this article. The first is the nature of the relationship between Indigenous oppression and the capitalist system. The second concerns the relationship between the oppression of Indigenous people and the non-Indigenous working class.

Settler colonial theorists argue that the relationship between Indigenous people and "settler society" in contemporary Australian capitalism is a colonial relationship. This means that it is an exploitative relationship in which "settler society" as a whole, ie including migrants of all backgrounds, non-Indigenous capitalists and workers alike, all gain material privileges from the dispossession of the Indigenous population. Core to settler colonial theory is the belief that even working-class "settlers" benefit from Indigenous oppression.

---

3. Allam and Murphy-Oates 2021.

Sai Englert puts forward the common sense view:

> If settler workers are exploited as workers within the settler colony, they remain settlers. As such they participate in the processes of accumulation by dispossession through the occupation of lands, the elimination or exploitation of indigenous peoples, and the extraction of expropriated resources. For example, at a very basic level, their houses, workplaces, and basic infrastructure such as roads, railways, etc., are all premised on the capture and control of indigenous land. Settler workers are both exploited by settler bosses and their co-conspirators in the dispossession of indigenous peoples. As such, class struggle within a settler society has a dual character: it is waged over the distribution of wealth extracted from their labour as well as over the colonial booty.[4]

The term "settler" is defined by Sarah Maddison in her book *The Colonial Fantasy: Why White Australia can't solve Black problems*:

> I use the terms "settler" and "non-Indigenous" in relation to any individual or group of people who came to Australia at any time after the first invasion in 1788. The term "settler" is intended to be discomforting, deliberately underscoring the nature of non-Indigenous people's relation to this territory and its peoples as a further impetus towards decolonial transformation.[5]

Maddison does acknowledge that "the extent to which settlers benefit from colonisation is modified to varying degrees by their skin colour and cultural background (not all settlers are white or Anglo), and by class, gender, sexuality and physical ability". However, she is also very clear that settlers "are all complicit in sustaining colonial relationships... We are none of us outside or above these relationships. Migrants are still settlers, white progressives are still settlers".[6] This analysis is backed up by most left-wing writers on Indigenous issues. Sai Englert is more explicit, arguing in a recent issue of *Antipodes: A Radical Journal of Geography* that "even if working-class settlers

---

4. Englert 2020.
5. Maddison 2019, pxii.
6. Maddison 2019, pxiii.

are exploited by their ruling classes, overthrowing the settler state would mean overthrowing a system in which they share, however unequally, in the distribution of the colonial loot".[7] In activist circles Clare Land, in her book *Decolonizing Solidarity*, and the self-described "Aboriginal nationalist" group Warriors of the Aboriginal Resistance (WAR) are prominent advocates of the settler colonial argument.[8]

However, this is predicated on a highly misleading analysis of the relationship between Australian capitalism, Indigenous oppression and the working class. It is particularly disorienting to argue that the relationship between Australian capitalism and Indigenous people *today* is "colonial" in nature, with its implication that all of "settler society" is bound up in a colonial exploitation of the Indigenous population. This is to attribute the continuation of Indigenous oppression to the population as a whole rather than Australian capitalism and those who run it.

Even in the early period of colonisation proper, it is one-sided to present all non-Indigenous people as benefiting from the genocide of Indigenous people. This position becomes more problematic when discussing the period from the late 1800s onwards, when the last major frontier battles ended in defeat for the Indigenous population. This moment marked the dominance of industrial capitalism over the political economy of the continent, decisively ending the colonisation process as the core dynamic shaping society. Indigenous oppression of course didn't end at this point, but it did undergo an important shift as Indigenous people's control over the land was broken, and they were forced to find a space within the implanted capitalist system. From this point on it was the capitalist system that structured Indigenous oppression, albeit in ways that reflected the colonial origins of Australian capitalism.

Some aspects of settler colonial theory resemble black nationalist ideas popular in leftist circles during the 1960s and '70s. The contemporary settler colonial theorists, however, are profoundly shaped by the rise of identity politics and privilege theory to hegemonic status on the broad left, as well as the shift in academia to

---

7. Englert 2020.
8. Land 2015 and Warriors of the Aboriginal Resistance 2014.

post-colonial approaches to history. Many of the general problems with identity politics are reflected and heightened in settler colonial theory.[9] Like identity politics more broadly, settler colonial theory developed as an alternative to Marxism, often taking up the criticisms of socialist politics that had already been raised by post-colonial theorists.[10]

This article will argue that it is Marxism which can best illuminate the contemporary causes of Indigenous oppression and help develop a strategy capable of ending it. Indigenous oppression continues today because it is in the interests of Australian capital, rather than the non-Indigenous population as a whole. This argument has important implications for any strategy seeking not just to mitigate oppression but uproot and eliminate it. So in this article, I will discuss the limitations of "decolonisation" theory and explore an alternative strategy based on solidarity and working-class revolutionary agency.

Theorising the roots of Indigenous oppression as capitalist in nature rather than as the result of some separate colonial relationship in no way means downplaying the reality of Indigenous oppression, nor does it mean ignoring the specific dynamics of the Indigenous situation that make it different from other forms of racism. My analysis also has nothing in common with the strain of economic reductionism that has marked some socialist, and in particular reformist socialist, thinking on the question of oppression.[11] Economic reductionists end up oversimplifying the complexity of the relationship between class, capitalism and oppression in a crude way that often downplays the importance of tackling questions of oppression for the development of socialist class consciousness. Instead the development of a genuinely Marxist strategy on this question must take as its starting point the horrific reality of Indigenous oppression and the prevalence of racism within the non-Indigenous working-class and white liberals, even among those who might sympathise with the plight of Indigenous peoples. Given all that, it is even more urgent to accurately understand the causes of that oppression so

---

9. For a classic Marxist critique of identity politics see Smith 1994.
10. Foster et al 2020.
11. See Garnham 2018 for a critique of economic reductionism.

we can clarify the importance of destroying the racist structures of Australian capitalism.

Colonisation

The colonisation of the continent that would become Australia was bound up in the development of the global capitalist economy and the rise of modern imperialism. Following the American War of Independence the British empire faced two interrelated problems. Further economic expansion into the Americas and the Atlantic was now blocked by the newly established republic and other European rivals. On top of this Britain could no longer use the vast American colonies as a dumping ground for its ever increasing convict population. The establishment of the colony in New South Wales helped in both these respects. A more permanent base in the Pacific could help the British empire make a turn towards expansion into Asia, an area already home to the vast colonial empires of the Spanish, Portuguese and the Dutch, while the creation of a penal colony, with significant room for expansion, would help to relieve the constant pressure on Britain's prisons. Another factor pushing Britain to colonise the continent quickly was competition from other imperialist rivals. The French for instance were already investigating the landmass: shortly after the British First Fleet arrived, the French explorer La Perouse appeared on a mission to survey Botany Bay.

This colonial project was founded on the dispossession of the Indigenous people and a genocidal offensive against them. Initially, this offensive was confined to the areas surrounding the early colonies. But as the outpost morphed into centres of capitalist expansion in the 1820s, the war against Indigenous people spread throughout the continent.

Henry Reynolds notes that "the documentary evidence left behind all over Australia of these frontiers wars is various and voluminous".[12] The Indigenous population waged a heroic war of resistance against the destruction of their communities. This war of resistance began within a few weeks of the arrival of the First Fleet. It continued, through ebbs and flows, for the next 140 years, with most historians

---

12. Reynolds 2013, p. 26.

concluding it reached its endpoint in the 1928 police massacre of a group of Warlpiri people at Coniston in Central Australia.[13] After that, Indigenous resistance would continue but in new forms and a vastly different context. Despite this continued resistance to further intrusions by the colonial authorities, the struggle over the grasslands in the 1840s and '50s revealed that the Indigenous population was not in a position to organise the kind of military power necessary to successfully defeat the British invaders.[14]

While this genocidal war was organised by the colonial authorities and primarily carried out by their military and police forces, some members of the working class, both convicts and free labourers, also participated in massacres. Probably the most infamous incident of this was the Myall Creek Massacre of 1838. This involved the murder of at least 28 Indigenous people by a group of eleven stockmen, including assigned convicts, former convicts and even a black African, and was led by the squatter John Henry Fleming. However, as this example suggests, many instances of working-class participation in violence against Indigenous people were organised by figures in authority.

However, most convicts and free settlers were never directly involved in massacring Indigenous people – particularly as the colony started to attract newcomers by the tens of thousands. The convicts rotting away in the prison hulks on the Thames didn't decide to establish a colony in 1788. The vast majority of convicts would have happily complied with the Aboriginal people's demand that they leave the country and never come back. In fact this is what convicts tried to do wherever they were given half a chance. Convicts in the First Fleet tried to convince sailors in La Perouse's fleet to smuggle them back to Europe. In 1791 Mary Bryant and a crew of convicts managed to steal a boat and escape to Timor in what was at the time the second-longest open boat journey in the world. When escape back to Europe wasn't possible convicts also fled into the bush and some lived with Aboriginal communities for some time. Further complicating the settler colonial narrative is the existence

---

13. Reynolds 2013 for an overview of both the genocide by the colonial authorities and the resistance to it by the Indigenous population.
14. Goodall 2008, pp. 25-39.

of the Native Police, a force made up of Indigenous troopers under the command of white officers. In Queensland the Native Mounted Police were involved in some of the worst massacres of Indigenous people. Aboriginal trackers were used to hunt down escaped convicts, bushrangers, and Indigenous people resisting colonisation.

There were also important tensions within colonial society from the outset. The convicts had been brought to the colonies against their will, and suffered under the lash of their colonial overlords. Once free settlers directly experienced the reality of colonial life with its corruption, poverty and brutality, they found much to be discontented with. There were repeated disturbances, riots and clashes. In 1804 200 convicts led by a veteran of the Irish Rebellion of 1798 escaped from a prison farm and fought a defiant battle with the British colonial authorities. By the 1820s early trade unions had begun to form in Sydney and Hobart. The historian Michael Quinlan has documented 5,047 instances of organisation by convict workers and 1,379 by free workers prior to 1851.[15] It was the same colonial state overseeing the oppression of both the European workforce and Indigenous people: "From the moment of the first occupation, force was applied on two fronts, against convicts and blacks – controlling the white workforce by the lash and the gallows, and creating the space within which the settlement could grow".[16]

The overall context did set very definite limits on the possibility of solidarity between the two groups struggling under the oppression of the early colonial state. The reality of an ongoing colonial war made it almost unthinkable that any sort of serious alliance between them could be constructed. There were some colonial liberals, humanitarians and clergymen who expressed supposed sympathy for the plight of the Indigenous people and even condemned some of the massacres, particularly those not directly organised by the colonial state. For instance, though the settler Fleming escaped justice and became a respected farmer and churchwarden despite leading the Myall Creek massacre, seven of the stockmen involved in Myall Creek were hanged for murder. However, even these early critics never rejected the central logic behind the genocide. After all,

---
15. As quoted in Fieldes 2019.
16. Connell and Irving 1980, p. 32.

to do so would mean going against the whole colonial project upon which they had accrued their relative wealth and authority. For example, the young liberal barrister Richard Windeyer joined the Aboriginal Protection Society in the wake of the Myall Creek massacre. While he campaigned for the right of Aborigines to give evidence in colonial courts he also "disagreed with the sentiments that the natives had been usurped by fraud and violence by the Europeans... Nor could he entertain the ridiculous notion that we had no right to be here".[17]

From settler colony to industrial capitalism

The colonisation process constructed a settler colonial state, however it also laid the basis for this settler colony to be superseded by a more developed industrial capitalism. Throughout the 1800s the colonial project underwent an enormous transformation. As the frontier wars ended in defeat for Indigenous people across the continent, the colonisation process reached its completion. This is not to say that Australia at this point began developing into a post-racial society. However the context of Indigenous oppression did change as the primitive accumulation of the land in the hands of a small minority was accomplished and the intensive development of industrial capitalism began. This shift would have important consequences for Indigenous people, non-Indigenous workers and Australian capitalism more generally. This shift from a settler colony to an industrial capitalist nation went through several stages but was essentially complete by the late 1800s.

From the 1830s, the colonial project underwent a significant change. Until then, the end goal of the Australian colonial project had been somewhat ambiguous. Was it just to be a penal dumping ground for Britain's convicts? Or a self-sustaining colonial economy? Two mutually reinforcing processes pushed the colonial project towards

---

17. Windeyer's views are quoted in Keneally 2009, p. 407. Windeyer's comments do raise the question of whom he was arguing against. This is also raised by a 1844 letter from Henry Mort, who was living on the frontiers of settlement in Queensland, that describes a debate amongst stockmen over whether a nation has the "moral right... to take forcible possession of a country inhabited by savages". The majority of the stockmen agreed that they do, but who disagreed? And why? See Keneally 2009, p. 406.

the second option. On the one hand, there was the development of a domestic capitalist economy. On the other, there was an influx of capital from Britain as the economic opportunities on offer in the young colonies became clear. Underpinning and further spurring on these developments were the commodification of landed property and the expansion of a market in free labour-power, which were two sides of the same economic process reshaping class relations. This further transformed the colonial economy into the beginnings of an industrial capitalist economy.[18]

These changes had important implications for the nature of Australian society. First of all it laid the economic basis for the development of a distinctive Australian capitalist class, with its own class and imperialist interests, which weren't always in accordance with those of the British ruling class. Secondly while the colonies had been capitalist from their inception,[19] the class lines of society became more precise as the early colonial system gave way to industrial capitalism and the struggle between the capitalists and the working class sharpened. By the end of the 1800s this had resulted in the creation of an independent Australian capitalism which had developed beyond a settler colonial state. This would have important implications for the relationship between Indigenous people and the non-Indigenous working class.

As we have noted, some convicts and free labourers had been involved in the violent struggle over the land with Indigenous people during the early colonial period. We must be careful in unpacking the actual relationship between the different classes in colonial society and the land itself. This is because there has been a strong tendency among Australian left historians to either romanticise the democratic nature of the frontier (as in Russell Ward's once-classic *The Australian Legend*) or else to exaggerate the effect that land ownership had on holding back the development of working-class consciousness and in particular entrenching racist attitudes (for instance in Humphrey McQueen's *A New Britannia*). Often these historians were influenced by US theorists who explored the role of

---

18. This is a summary of the detailed studies of the transformation of the colonial economy by Wells 1985 and Connell and Irving 1980.
19. See Humphrys 2012 and Hillier and O'Lincoln 2013.

the frontier in blocking the development of class organisations in America.

However the relationship between colonialism, the land and popular consciousness was quite different in Australia compared to the United States. The American westward expansion involved over 7 million settlers by 1840. This mass migration campaign was driven by the American government, which granted 600,000 white families farmland almost for free. These settlers were absolutely vital to entrenching the American government's control over the newly conquered territory that they gained through a series of wars from 1812 to 1867 against the Native Americans, Mexicans and European rivals. Many American settlers had to engage in armed confrontations with Native Americans and Mexicans in order to secure control over their newly acquired land.

In Australia settlement outside the main urban areas involved a significantly smaller proportion of the population, and after the initial invasion there was little serious possibility of the colonial government losing control over its territory. The struggle over control of the land in colonial Australia could at times be an intense political issue, but it was overwhelmingly a debate carried out between different factions of the colonial elite, with limited space for interlopers from the lower classes. As we shall see, from quite early on the majority of the population was concentrated in urban city centres.

In the early colonial period the key site of the struggle over land was within the colonial state organisations. This often expressed itself in conflicts between the governor and the system of magistrates that expanded from the 1820s onwards to oversee the convict system. By its very nature this institution excluded most of the colonial population. As Connell and Irving note, "only gentlemen could be made magistrates, and in much of the countryside the only gentlemen available were pastoralists".[20] Attempts to limit the power of pastoralist-magistrates via stipendiary magistrates, who were often decommissioned army officers, failed, and at any rate, simply involved the empowering of a different section of the colonial

---

20. Connell and Irving 1980, p. 34.

elite. In his time, Governor Macquarie had appointed a few wealthy ex-convicts as magistrates, to the wrath of the country gentlemen. However, the convicts (who from the 1820s onwards were no longer directly controlled by the government but assigned to private settlers) and free settlers did not have the wealth or power to exert significant influence over the land policies of the state.[21]

By the 1820s "practically all the usable land in the Sydney region had passed into private hands".[22] The overwhelming majority of this land was in the hands of the already wealthy. By 1821 about 80 men controlled 60 percent of all alienated land in New South Wales, and by the 1830s there were around 400 gentry estates in New South Wales and 250 in Van Diemen's Land.[23] From 1830 onwards colonial policy shifted to the sale of Crown land to private persons rather than the granting of land primarily by political patronage. However, this still excluded the vast majority of the population from access to land. Ex-convicts or free settlers who enriched themselves and established an important place in the colonial economy could now buy land, but this was only a small minority of the population.

The struggle over control of the land continued throughout the 1800s, culminating in the Free Selection Acts of the 1860s. A minority of workers were able to establish themselves as small landholders or independent miners, although many still engaged in waged labour periodically. By the end of the 1800s, the space in Australian society for such a social layer rapidly declined as an economic crisis, the concentration of large pastoral and mining capital and the introduction of new, and expensive, technologies drove many off the land and back into the waged labour force.[24]

Land ownership continued to have some attraction in the imagination of the working masses, but for the vast majority, it remained an unattainable utopia. As Humphrey McQueen notes, despite the ideological importance of the land "Australia had a greater percentage of its population in towns than almost any other country: more

---

21. See Connell and Irving 1980, pp. 33-35.
22. Connell and Irving 1980, p. 35.
23. Connell and Irving 1980, pp. 51-2.
24. Markey 1988, pp. 56-86.

than 50 percent in 1891, more than America".[25] Even those who were able to take the risk often found that land ownership on a small basis quickly turned into an unprofitable trap and either sunk into isolated poverty or returned with broken spirits to the cities after a few years.

Many historians have focused on colonial discussions about the need for a "yeoman" community of small peasant farmers that would create social, economic and moral stability.[26] As interesting as the ideology of this might be, the problem is by focusing on it, writers can end up ignoring the reality that no such community ever came into existence in Australia. The "yeoman" project, which would supposedly reduce class conflict by tying together capitalists and workers as joint landowners, failed against the reality of minority capitalist control over the land.

These economic changes also had implications for the relationship between these workers and Indigenous people. As Heather Goodall explains:

> The mainland Australian colonies had now diversified. In the longest settled colonies of New South Wales, Victoria and South Australia conflict with Aboriginal landowners had ended, abruptly, in the 1850s, and had only been reactivated sporadically in the following decades... This was in great contrast to the colonies of Queensland and Western Australia, where frontier brutality was flaring violently in the more remote pastoral areas.[27]

The commodification of the land led to greater wealth for those at the top of society. Meanwhile, the expansion of the market in free labour entrenched the mass of the colonial population in waged labour. This was particularly the case after the ending of the convict system throughout the mid-1800s.[28] With the pastoral boom of the 1830s the demand for labour substantially increased and the colonial government "swung from a policy of encouraging rich immigrants whose capital would absorb convict labour, to a policy of encouraging, indeed subsidising, working class immigrants".

---
25. McQueen 1976, p. 151.
26. See for instance Goodall 2008, pp. 47-48.
27. Goodall 2008, pp. 124-25.
28. The following summarises Connell and Irving 1980, pp. 36-44.

By 1851, when the population of the eastern colonies was approaching 450,000, more than 100,000 immigrants had been subsidised. Most of the men who came, up to the time of the gold rushes, were labourers, and most of the women were domestic servants. A minority had trades and hence had a chance of setting up on their own, but most were unskilled (many being from Irish agricultural districts) and dependent on finding employment when they arrived in the colony.[29]

By the mid-1800s then the mass of the colonial population were propertyless wage workers, mostly concentrated in urban centres. They had little to no direct experience of fighting the Indigenous population, particularly as the frontier wars continued only on the edges of the colonies. Many had little to no direct experience with the Indigenous population on any level whatsoever due to the genocidal effects of colonisation and racist segregation.

After colonialism – explaining the persistence of anti-Indigenous racism

How did the shift from settler colony to industrial capitalism reshape Indigenous oppression? Once the Indigenous population were dispossessed of control over their land, their racist oppression continued through the structures set up throughout the 1800s by, and in the interests of, the Australian capitalist class. The Protection Board, the prison-house, the missions, the courts, the stations, and later the urban slums, welfare departments, shipyards, factories and mines became the vehicles through which Indigenous people's lives were subordinated to the needs of capital.

The establishment of the first major Aboriginal missions in NSW during the 1830s and 1840s was in accordance with the needs of the colonial elites to find a place to put the dispossessed Indigenous population to make way for pastoral expansion. The colonial and then state-based Aborigine Protection Boards were set up to ensure both that Indigenous people remained in a situation of structural discrimination unable to reassert their rights to the land, and that when possible their labour could be drawn upon

---

29. Connell and Irving 1980, p 38.

to help the capitalist work process. The courts, police and prisons backed up this oppression with brute force. The latter-day welfare departments, urban slums and Aboriginal government departments simply updated these projects for the contemporary needs of the capitalist class. All of these institutions, which are at the heart of Indigenous oppression, were set up, maintained and defended by the capitalist class, its political parties and ideologues. The treatment of the Stolen Generations, Indigenous children who were stolen from their families by federal and state government agencies and church missions, was a particularly barbaric example of the capitalist logic behind Indigenous oppression. While so-called "full-blooded" Indigenous people were mostly condemned to segregation from Australian society, government authorities sought to integrate "half-caste" Indigenous children into the capitalist system by removing them from their communities and training them to be unpaid – and often abused – domestic servants and workers. Many government and church officials gained personal profits from the exploitation of the Stolen Generations while clothing their activities with the ideology of "assimilation".

Racist oppression is often an expression of the various aspects of the competitive capitalist system. Sometimes, as in the case of the post-war migrant workforce in Australia, this oppression could be expressed very directly in the structure of a segregated workforce with bosses using divisions between workers to cement their control, as well as around the broader political issue of migration. However this isn't always the way the connection between capitalism and oppression develops. Anti-Muslim racism in Australia is very much linked to the question of imperialism and general political issues rather than industrial relations. One of the historic divisions within the Australian working class was the sectarian divide between Catholics – particularly the Irish Catholics – and Protestants. This divide shaped the development of Australian working-class politics and intersected with questions of class, British imperialism and religious bigotry.

The situation Indigenous people faced, particularly initially, was exclusion from the capitalist labour market and a high degree of government control over many aspects of their lives. For the ruling class the key objective was to stamp out any possibility of an Indigenous challenge to capitalist control over the land and – when that possibility dramatically receded – to ensure that Indigenous people could not stand in the way of capitalist expansion. Over time though, as we shall see later in this article, Indigenous people were drawn into the labour market. However only in particular situations did they form an identifiable and distinct section of the workforce, despite almost always being in a subordinate position. So this situation was quite different from that of post-war era working-class migrants or historically African Americans who formed a significant and very visible section of the blue-collar workforce concentrated in strategically important sections of the economy, such as the auto industry.

Indigenous oppression is constantly reinforced by the capitalist state through the police, the courts, the media, the education and the political system. These institutions both express the oppression produced by capitalism and entrench it further. These are not independent processes but different expressions of the multifaceted nature of Indigenous oppression under capitalism, all of which endures because it is in the interests of Australian capitalism that it continue.

Settler colonial theorists disagree with this analysis, instead arguing that Indigenous oppression endures because of the continuation of colonial structures and "settler logics". What precisely these colonial structures are, and what their relationship is to class and capitalism is left unclarified. So Sarah Maddison argues that the reason why control over the land is at the heart of Indigenous and non-Indigenous tensions is because of the "need for new territory in order to create an economic base for settler society",[30] without explaining why this is in the interests of settler society as a whole or what the nature of the economic base of settler society is. Maddison also presents the "failures" of the Northern Territory Intervention, attempts to reduce Indigenous incarceration rates and the Closing the Gap strategy as being rooted in the dominance of the ideology of the "colonial fantasy" on policymakers. On this basis, she then

---

30. Maddison 2019, pp. 75-76.

argues that "Australia may yet be capable of decentring colonial power and making space for Indigenous resurgence in the justice system, but first it must relinquish the colonial fantasy".[31]

However, this is to ignore the real material interests that underlie Indigenous oppression and shape all of these policies. To say that the Northern Territory Intervention "failed" because it was motivated by a paternalist settler colonial logic is to accept at face value the establishment's self-justification for its actions. As Diane Fieldes has argued in a previous issue of this journal, while paternalistic racism was mobilised by sections of the liberal middle class to justify the Northern Territory Intervention, "'underlying these attitudes was something more fundamental: the long-term hostility of pastoralists, mining companies, other capitalists and governments – the Australian ruling class, in other words – to Aboriginal rights".[32] The demonisation of remote Aboriginal communities was promoted to undermine their legitimacy and justify the expansion of the rights of mining and tourist capitalists over that land rather than some general and amorphous desire of "settler society". This doesn't mean that the Northern Territory Intervention was purely about the narrow economic interests of the mining and tourism bosses. Many of the Indigenous communities affected sit on land that isn't particularly useful from a profitability standpoint.

However the Intervention can only be fully understood in terms of the broader desire by the Australian ruling class to roll back the gains Indigenous people have made to have some control over their land, and to promote racist lies that have always been politically important for the right. Reinforcing this is the centrality of mining for Australian capitalism as a whole. As Martin Upchurch has argued in the *International Socialism* journal, a number of Global North countries such as Canada and Australia are highly dependent on fuels and minerals. The share of mining in the Australian economy "has grown from around 5 percent of GDP in 2005 to just under 10 percent in 2019".[33] This provides a strong justification for the Australian ruling class to defend the interests of the mining industry against

---
31. Maddison 2019, p. 153.
32. Fieldes 2010.
33. Upchurch 2020.

the claims of Indigenous communities, with a recent example being the extinguishing of an Aboriginal land rights claim in Queensland by the state Labor government to make way for the Adani coal mine.

Similarly, programs to reduce Indigenous incarceration or poverty fail not primarily because of the paternalistic liberal worldview that surrounds them but because there is a strong structural basis to racism broadly, and Indigenous oppression particularly, rooted in the needs of capitalism. To seriously address these issues you would have to confront the underlying problems of structural inequality and the role of the police, the legal and welfare systems in Australian society, all of which bring us back to the logic of industrial capital accumulation, not settler colonialism.

There are more left-wing settler colonial theorists who at least discuss capitalism. However, even the most radical settler colonial theorists rarely clarify the relationship between colonialism and capitalism. Sometimes colonialism is seen as a process that has little to do with questions of class power or capitalist society.[34] Others refer to capitalism without explaining if colonialism is an outgrowth of capitalism, a separate but related structure or something entirely distinct. Even those theorists who have explored how the competitive logic of capitalist accumulation drove the dispossession of Indigenous peoples often end up positing a related but separate colonial structure as being the cause of Indigenous oppression today. So some theorists discuss what is called "colonial-capitalism",[35] but this suffers from the same problems US writers have identified in the term "racial capitalism".[36] It avoids trying to grapple with a unified theory of Indigenous oppression and capitalism by presenting colonialism as an external – even if related – phenomenon to capitalism. Just because capitalism oppresses both Indigenous and non-Indigenous workers this doesn't mean that their lives and experiences are the same. However, you don't have to theorise a separate "colonial" structure of oppression to account for this difference. Instead, by taking as your starting point the development of capitalism, you can

---

34. So Sarah Maddison doesn't even refer to capitalism or class in The Colonial Fantasy.
35. Fiedler 2018.
36. Post 2020.

explain why certain groups are held down in structurally oppressive conditions.

To say that Indigenous oppression today is rooted in Australian capitalism doesn't mean that the origins of that oppression in the settler colonial period are irrelevant. Quite the contrary. If the Indigenous population had been entirely killed, such as happened in parts of the Caribbean, or if there had been no Indigenous population to begin with, then there would be no Indigenous political question in Australia today. Many Marxists have fruitfully explored how the context of Australian capitalism developing as a settler colony shaped, and continues to shape the politics of race, immigration and imperialism. The point though is we have to explain why Indigenous oppression endured even once the colonisation of the continent was completed. Here we have what are in the end two competing explanations. On the one hand Indigenous oppression can be seen as another facet of the oppressive and exploitative capitalist system, alternatively it can be rooted in an ongoing colonising process. As settler colonial theory has cohered into a more developed challenger to Marxism, this requires socialist writers to more accurately clarify the relationship between settler colonialism, capitalism and the working class, whereas in the past unqualified references to Australia's settler colonial nature would have been less problematic.

Indigenous oppression and working-class consciousness

If Indigenous oppression is rooted in capitalism then this has important ramifications for the relationship between the Indigenous population and the non-Indigenous working class. Settler colonial theorists argue that the "settler" working class is, in the words of Englert, "complicit in sustaining colonial relationships". This is only true in the sense that you can be complicit in any injustice by refusing to acknowledge or rebel against it, for whatever reason. However in this sense the working class was – and still is, everywhere in the world – complicit in every injustice and social problem. This list would have to include their own exploitation and oppression, which most workers do little to resist most of the time. This is not complicity in any meaningful sense of the word.

Yet the argument of settler colonial theorists goes well beyond complicity. It is that settlers *benefit* from the oppression of Indigenous people, and are in fact part of the cause of that oppression. But if non-Indigenous workers did benefit from Indigenous oppression then it is hard to understand the development of Indigenous and non-Indigenous working-class relations over the next hundred years. If the working class were beneficiaries of Indigenous oppression, then as workers developed a greater understanding of themselves, their interests, and the strategies they needed to overcome the exploitative nature of the capitalist system, through the class battles over the last several decades, they would undoubtedly have become *more* hostile to the Indigenous population. However, as we shall see, history shows that they became more open to Indigenous claims and desires.

We previously explained how by the mid- to late 1800s the mass of the colonial population were propertyless wage workers, concentrated in urban centres, who had little direct experience in oppressing Indigenous people. Of course, the working class did not all spontaneously adopt progressive opinions on the Indigenous population. Racism in general was rife, and even workers who had some sympathy for the plight of Indigenous peoples often accepted the dominant idea that they were a "dying race". However Englert's assertion that "settler labour movements fought for the intensification of settler expansion and racial segregation through colour bars, boycott campaigns and demands for expulsion" is not an accurate portrayal of the Australian labour movement's approach to the Indigenous population.[37]

In the early years of the Australian working class it is true that some groups of workers expressed concern over Aboriginal "cheap labour" from time to time, however this was not a prominent issue among the class overall. This is largely due to the fact that Indigenous people were so oppressed and excluded from Australian society that they rarely competed with non-Indigenous workers for jobs. Even when Indigenous workers were able to enter the workforce in relatively large numbers, compared to their overall population the

---

37. Englert 2020.

numbers were still tiny. In South Australia, for instance, a layer of Indigenous workers managed to become skilled tradesmen in the shearing industry by the end of the nineteenth century. However in 1901 the total Indigenous population in South Australia was only 3,888 (as compared to 354,001 non-Indigenous people) and there were only 6,000 workers, Indigenous and non-Indigenous alike, employed in the shearing industry, so any competition in this this field would have been marginal in relation to the working class as a whole.[38]

So the question of Indigenous workers was not posed in the same way as migrant workers in Australia or African Americans in the US, that became a key strategic and political question for the labour movement from very early on. It is also different from the question of migration and the White Australia policy, which was a widely accepted idea by the Australian labour movement. In fact most union leaders, when the issue was raised at all, made a distinction between Indigenous people and migrant workers, arguing that as Indigenous people were "native" to Australia they shouldn't be excluded in the same way as non-white migrants. So the Amalgamated Shearers' Union of Australasia and the General Labourers Union excluded non-white migrant workers such as Asians, but "were not prepared to advocate discrimination against Aborigines (and some 'coloured' aliens)". A trade unionist and early leader of the Queensland Labor Party stated in 1897 that Indigenous workers "have the right to be employed; a right to the first show to get a living, and if the aborigine does a day's work on a station, or on a farm, or anywhere else he is entitled to a fair wage the same as a white man or anyone else".[39]

If it was mostly in rural communities that tensions between Indigenous and non-Indigenous workers arose, it is also here that we find some of the earliest examples of sympathetic working-class attitudes and even joint action. Both of these elements are expressed in the history of the Australian Workers Union (AWU), which had its base among the working class in rural communities. While provisions against the union membership of Chinese and "South

---

38. Elton 2007, p. 36.
39. All quotes from Markus 1978.

Sea Islanders" were present in the formative years of the AWU, these were not extended to include Indigenous workers (or for that matter Maori workers who would travel to Australia during the shearing season). As Judith Elton has explained in her detailed PhD thesis, the different treatment of Indigenous workers by the AWU was due to three factors.[40] Firstly there was "little perceived danger of Aboriginal workers undermining wage rates in shearing related occupations".[41] Partly this was because they were a small section of the workforce but it was also because where Indigenous workers did form a more substantial part of the shearing workforce, for instance in South Australia, there was no legislation preventing Aboriginal workers from being paid the same as non-Aboriginal workers. In fact Aboriginal workers had started to become increasingly assertive in claims for higher wages as some became skilled shearers working among non-Aboriginal workers. Elton writes: "in these circumstances, employers could not have used Aboriginal shearers and shed hands as a group to undercut the wages of other shearing related workers".[42] Secondly, the number of Indigenous workers was so small that it was difficult for bosses to generate fear that they were going to seriously take over the jobs done by non-Indigenous workers. Thirdly, the nature of shearing work emphasised the importance of skill and experience. In the context of a mixed workforce Indigenous workers could "prove" their shearing skills in practice and in front of non-Indigenous workers. There is ample evidence that many non-Indigenous workers respected the shearing abilities of Indigenous workers, with the latter winning local shearing prizes as early as the 1870s and 1880s, and Indigenous workers from the Poonindie mission becoming high prized and valued shearers across South Australia and beyond.[43]

Now this doesn't mean that every AWU member had progressive ideas about Indigenous people. Attitudes could range from supportive to antagonistic, depending on a range of factors. The debate at the 1891 conference of the Australian Shearers Union (ASU) that would

---

40. Elton 2007, pp. 70-72.
41. Elton 2007, p. 70.
42. Elton 2007, p. 70.
43. Elton 2007, p. 34.

later be amalgamated into the AWU, however, reveals that there were unionists grappling with the issue of Indigenous oppression.

At this conference the Creswick (Victoria) branch of the ASU moved a motion that would allow all Indigenous workers to be admitted as life members of the union without paying any union fees, as long as they refused to work in non-union sheds like other ASU members. They were partly influenced to move the motion based on the work of the shearers' unions in New Zealand in recruiting a highly militant Maori workforce. The ASU general secretary supported the motion with the argument that "It is a graceful act to those from whom the country has been taken. No liberal minded man could surely object to this concession to the original owners of the soil". Cook, a delegate from South Australia concurred making the point that it would be a graceful act to allow Indigenous workers to join without having to pay union fees considering "their circumstances were not the same as white men, and their earnings were not the same". Some unionists argued against the motion on the basis that Indigenous workers were less committed to unionism and so shouldn't get special treatment for their lack of interest. Supporters of the motion however pointed to the loyal character of many Indigenous union members:

> Watkins (Adelaide), said "it was a mistake to say the aboriginals were ignorant" and McInerney (Young, NSW), stated that "he wished all the white men were as good as the Australian darkies... – they were fine fellows as far as he saw. He knew a number who had cleared out of the shed when it was found "non-union". Percy (Cobar, NSW), concurred, "In one shed in Cobar an aboriginal was the only one of twenty who walked away for unionism".[44]

In the end a compromise motion was adopted which waived the entrance fee for "full-blooded aborigines", and the requirements of Indigenous members was left to individual union branches to decide. These issues were then put to the test during the economic depression of the 1890s. As unemployment skyrocketed some non-Indigenous workers did start to demand that Aboriginal workers be fired

---

44. Elton 2007, p. 74.

instead of them. However the ASU officials publicly rejected these demands. Even when Aboriginal workers signed on to non-union agreements at lower pay the ASU refused to specifically criticise Aboriginal workers, arguing that it was unfair to target them as many more non-Indigenous workers had signed such agreements than Indigenous workers. When scabbing by Aboriginal workers helped contribute to the defeat of shearers' strikes in South Australia, the ASU response was to investigate ways they could better recruit and maintain Aboriginal membership, not to blame them as a group.[45]

There was a gap between the formal positions and actual practice of the AWU, as well as a high degree of unevenness across different sections of the union. In 1920 the Queensland branch of the AWU left the federal award in favour of a state award, with the consequence that in that state Aboriginal station hands were no longer covered.[46] This might have been an issue more of neglect than conscious discrimination. However in 1919 the Queensland AWU leadership, pastoral capitalists and the Chief Protector of Aborigines did collaborate on fixing a minimum wage for Indigenous shearers that was only two-thirds of the official shearers award. In the Northern Territory cattle industry the AWU collaborated with other unions to promote the interests of white workers at the expense of Aboriginal workers, although in the end the result was declining conditions for both.[47] Attitudes towards Indigenous membership also varied across the country. So the Indigenous activist William Ferguson joined the AWU in 1909, becoming a union representative in the Riverina, and found the shearers "free-and-easy" in regard to him being Indigenous. In rural New South Wales, Victoria and South Australia Indigenous workers seemed to be welcomed into AWU membership with few tensions. However at the same time branches of the AWU in Western Australia had local autonomy over whether or not to exclude Indigenous members, with the Broome branch excluding them while Port Hedland admitted small numbers. In the Northern Territory the Northern Australia Workers Union (NAWU) excluded Indigenous members unless they had one parent of European

---

45. Elton 2007, p. 74-76.
46. Elton 2007, p. 133.
47. Elton 2007, p. 171.

descent. This decision was shaped by the fact that it was illegal for "full-blooded aborigines" to be covered by union award wages in the Northern Territory at the time. The gains of the AWU were also whittled away over time. While the 1917 award included Aboriginal workers, by 1920 these gains had been undermined by the decisions of the Arbitration Court, and then they were lost completely by 1932 when working-class organisation and confidence collapsed in the wake of the Great Depression.[48]

It is worth comparing the relationship between the non-Indigenous working class and Indigenous workers in Australia to that between the Israeli and Palestinian working classes. This is because many settler colonial theorists draw a comparison between these two situations in order to argue that the Australian working class benefits from Indigenous oppression.[49] And as Israel is still a settler colonial state the comparison can also help to draw out the similarities and differences between countries which are presently settler colonial in nature and those which still have Indigenous oppression but are industrial capitalist nations with completed colonial processes.

In Israel the colonising process is ongoing, with Israel's expansionist desire to claim more Palestinian land coming up against the armed resistance of the Palestinians, resulting in sections of land still under at least the formal political control of Palestinian authorities.[50] In Israel there is compulsory military service, so significant sections of the Israeli working class have some direct experience in oppressing Palestinians. There is also a sizeable minority of Zionist settlers who are involved in recurring violent struggles with the Palestinians over land control on the borders of the Israeli state. The question of the expansion of the Zionist project and the subjection of the Palestinians is the major question of Israeli politics. Even most of what passes as the left and the socialist movement in Israel supports the continued oppression of the Palestinians.

---

48. See Chapter 4 in Elton 2007.
49. See for instance Englert 2020, who argues that the Australian working class benefits from Indigenous oppression without using a single example of this occurring in Australia. Instead he references union attitudes towards migration and then asserts a comparison with the Israeli working class.
50. Thier 2018.

By contrast there is no real equivalent to the Zionist settler population among the Australian working class. While some racist workers have acted in appalling ways towards Indigenous people, the vast majority of the working class has never been involved in violent conflicts with Indigenous people over control over their land. The battle over Indigenous rights in Australia is still very much a politically contested one, however hegemonic support for oppressing the Indigenous population does not exist to the same degree in Australia as in Israel. For instance there is no serious discussion, even among liberal-minded Israelis, about moving the date of Israel's Independence Day or acknowledging the harm done to the Palestinians, even symbolically.

It could be argued that non-Indigenous workers in Australia benefit not because they are directly involved in the colonisation of land but because without the dispossession of Indigenous people the whole economy and society in which they live wouldn't exist. This is the implication of the arguments of many settler colonial theorists. It also bears some similarity to the theory of the labour aristocracy that is popular with some sections of the socialist left.[51] In fact it has the most in common with the most extreme versions of the theory of the labour aristocracy, such as the Japanese-American Maoist J Sakai, who argues that the white working class of the US forms a privileged and reactionary social layer incapable of uniting with any section of the oppressed.[52]

The problem with this argument is that it can't explain why non-Indigenous workers have supported Indigenous struggles. In fact it generally suffers from a lack of historical analysis. Englert argues that class conflict in settler colonial societies can be "resolved… by intensifying the dispossession of indigenous populations in order to improve the material conditions of settler workers".[53] But this is not a dynamic within the history of the Australian labour movement. No government has ever seriously attempted to resolve a period of intense class conflict by increasing the dispossession of Indigenous

---

51. For a critique of the theory of the labour aristocracy in the context of Australian history see Bramble 2012.
52. Sakai 2014.
53. Englert 2020.

people and somehow passing on better material conditions to the non-Indigenous working class. This was not a feature of the great strikes of the 1890s, the 1917 general strike, the militancy of the inter-war years or the 1960s and '70s. In fact the main dynamic shaping the intensification of attacks upon Indigenous people has been the changing interests of Australian capitalism. So the increased assault upon land rights throughout the 1990s wasn't driven by an attempt to resolve class conflict by giving out benefits to the working class, rather it was shaped by the needs of mining capitalists to stop any serious expansion of Indigenous land rights in a period of an expanding market for raw minerals, bolstered by a conservative cultural offensive by a new generation of emboldened right-wing politicians in the Liberal and National parties. And the mining companies driving attacks upon land rights could hardly be called friends of the working class. CFMEU mining division President John Maitland made the connection between the exploitation of non-Indigenous workers and the mining companies' campaigns against land rights in the aftermath of the 1992 Mabo High court decision which granted some Aboriginal people land rights:

> What is driving CRA, BHP, MIM and the rest in their campaign of vague and dreadful threats about withdrawing investment is exactly the same pressure that drives them to lecture the United Mineworkers' Union about "unreasonable wage claims" and "restrictive work practices" – the lust for profit. The blackmail is the same, only the targets differ.[54]

The settler colonial argument that non-Indigenous workers and bosses are simply fighting over the spoils they have stolen from Indigenous people also doesn't capture the actual dynamics of class struggle and exploitation. The reality is that where bosses are able to get away with a deeper exploitation of Indigenous workers, the rest of the working class suffers, rather than benefits. The Communist novelist Frank Hardy noted that where unions in the Northern Territory allowed bosses to get away with paying Indigenous workers little or nothing at all, white workers' wages were also the lowest in

---

54. Quoted in Bramble 2012.

Australia.[55] Conversely, as we shall see later in this article, joint struggle by Indigenous and non-Indigenous dock workers in Darwin led to workers there having the highest wages in any tropical port. More broadly the capitalist society that has been created on the dispossessed lands of the Indigenous peoples is one filled with exploitation, oppression and cruelty. It is not the interests of the non-Indigenous working class that this society continues as it currently exists, rather it is in their interests to overthrow this society and build a radically different one based upon workers' democracy and socialist liberation.

Just because the non-Indigenous working class in Australia doesn't benefit from the oppression of Indigenous people doesn't mean that many workers can't accept bigoted ideas about Indigenous people. And even after the end of the frontier wars, anti-Indigenous racism has remained a constant feature of Australian society. Settler colonial theorists would argue that such racism continues to have a hold over significant sections of the non-Indigenous population because of the privileges they receive as settlers. Here I will map out an alternative explanation.

Marxists have always argued that workers can and do accept ideas that are contrary to their interests, from right-wing conservatism and fascism through to social-democratic reformism. These ideas can be promoted by various capitalist institutions, from political parties to the education system. However the extent to which they are taken up depends upon the state of working-class organisation and consciousnesses. When the working-class movement is weak then the reality of alienation and the pressures of capitalist ideology are felt more deeply by the working class. This opens up workers to reactionary ideas rooted in oppression such as sexism, racism and homophobia but also to all sorts of sectional ideas, such as the divisions between blue-collar and white-collar workers, or casual and permanent employees. Given that, it's not particularly surprising that workers accept some racist ideas about Indigenous people that are pushed by the racist media and produced by structural oppression.

However as workers begin to fight, they can gain more confidence

---

55. Quoted in Bramble 2012.

in themselves and their class, and can begin to see through the lies and divisions fostered by the ruling class's propagandists. It is not surprising then that, as with the example of the AWU explored above, it was during the periods of working-class combativity and union growth that anti-Indigenous ideas receded greatly. In fact this was strong enough to even survive the depression of the 1890s. However the containment of working-class advancement and the incorporation of union leaderships within the arbitration system started to undermine these advances throughout the 1920s. During the Great Depression of the 1930s the utter collapse of the AWU throughout much of the country and ensuing decline in working-class confidence opened the space for the strengthening of anti-Indigenous ideas across the class.

These dynamics are even clearer in some of the history explored in the rest of this article, which shows how opportunities for anti-racist action emerged in parts of the working class, and the key role played by left-wing minorities within the broader union movement. In this way, non-Indigenous workers are very different from politicians, government officials, middle-class professionals or business people. Whatever backward ideas they might believe about society, workers genuinely have no interest in the continued oppression of Indigenous people, unlike those classes that draw their power and authority from the structures of capitalism. This distinction is rarely discussed by settler colonial theorists.

At any given moment there is a significant gap between the objective possibilities of opposition to Indigenous oppression and its concrete realisation. The same is true of all aspects of class consciousness, which does not develop in a linear process. It is the product of a complex interaction of objective circumstances, social struggle, historical experience and political intervention. It emerges in fits and starts, develops unevenly across different sections of the class, and moves only by a series of approximations. Even then there are periods of retreat in which lessons are lost and consciousness recedes. Unsurprisingly, the struggles of Indigenous people for self-determination have been crucial in driving the development of mass opposition to their oppression. These struggles have been deeply shaped by the transformation undergone by the Indigenous population in the aftermath of the frontier wars, and in particular by the formation of an Indigenous working class.

In the second half of this article, we will look at just how this played out through the development of Indigenous and non-Indigenous working-class relations throughout the twentieth century.

The Indigenous working class and capitalism

Reconstructing the history of the Indigenous working class, particularly in its early years, is a difficult task. First of all, Indigenous people were often excluded from regular participation in the labour market, and due to the effects of colonisation and racism, formed a very small percentage of the working class as a whole. Added to these difficulties has been the lack of interest in Indigenous workers, even by anti-racist theorists. Elements of settler colonial theory often end up reinforcing the impression that while Indigenous people were exploited by colonial society, they shouldn't be considered as a part of the working class. This is rooted in the emphasis settler colonial theorists place on what they call the "logic of elimination".[56] This logic meant that settler colonial societies sought to violently remove Indigenous people from their land and replace them with white settlers rather than transforming the Indigenous population into a mass exploited workforce. This is compared to colonial, but in the view of these theorists, non-settler colonial societies, such as South Africa, which did focus on developing the original population into a mass exploited workforce. A dichotomy is set up between the "bodily exploitation" of some populations and the "territorial dispossession" of others.[57] However this rigid distinction between settler colonial and other colonial societies is at odds with the actual history of colonisation.

While the "logic of elimination" might appear to explain the situation in Australia and the United States, the situation was quite different in other countries also considered settler colonial by these theorists. In New Zealand, the Maori population began to be dispossessed by settlers following its formal annexation in 1840. However Maori labour was significant for the colonial project from

---
56. Wolfe 2016.
57. Wolfe 2016, p. 17.

very early on and they were never as excluded from the economy as Indigenous people in early Australia. From 1840 to the late 1850s Maori "competed vigorously with settlers in the grain and vegetable produce as well as the labour markets".[58] The colonial government also made use of Maori labour in public work gangs. In the late 1850s the collapse of produce markets and the introduction of steam-powered ships undermined the economic power of the Maori community, however for a whole period the settler and Maori economies were interdependent. Following Maori defeats in the wars of the 1860s land was rapidly transferred to the colonialists. Most of the Maori population tried to eke out an existence on what little land was left, but they often had to supplement their incomes by working as farm labourers, road builders and meat workers. As the rural economy developed they also started to work as shearers and station workers. By the late 1800s Maori workers were essential for shearing in Wairarapa, Hawke's Bay, the East Coast and Poverty Bay. This tendency increased over time, with one writer arguing that "by the early twentieth century the completely self-sufficient Maori family was rare. The most fundamental and characteristic feature of Maori life was casual employment".[59] Close to 90 percent of stations in Hawke's Bay and the East Coast employed Maori shearers and on the large East Coast stations the coverage was 100 percent.[60] Maori workers also played an important role in the timber industry. From the 1930s onwards Maori workers also increasingly played an important role in the urban economy. The urbanisation and further proletarianisation of Maori in the post-war boom concentrated them in the blue-collar working class, of which they were a militant section.[61]

Even in South Africa things aren't as clear cut as sometimes presented. While the labour of Africans was indeed key to the economy, the white settlers needed to dispossess them of vast swathes of profitable land for their farms and mines. Expropriating the African population from the land was also essential for creating

---

58. Nightingale 2007, p. 77.
59. Nightingale 2007, p. 81.
60. Nightingale 2007, p. 84.
61. Roper 2011, p. 27.

an African labour force to use in the gold-mines.[62] There is a growing body of academic work on Africa, South America and Asia criticising the rigid distinctions often taken for granted by settler colonial theory.[63] What all this work reveals is that different colonial regimes almost always had to use some combination of "bodily exploitation" and "territorial dispossession". This is also true of Australia.

The focus that settler colonial theorists have on the purely territorial aspect of Indigenous oppression ends up distorting their understanding of the relationship between Indigenous people and capitalism. For while they acknowledge that there have been changes in the nature of Indigenous oppression over time, they argue that the "logic of elimination" is the constant driving force behind settler colonial societies' relationship with Indigenous people. In so far as this means that racism, oppression, and a lack of control over the land is a constant feature of Indigenous oppression, this is accurate. As an explanation of what is driving that racism and oppression, however, it is ambiguous, unclear and not rooted in any serious discussion of the changing dynamics of Australian capitalism.

The result of this is a strong tendency to treat Indigenous people as totally divorced from the rest of the working class, and indeed capitalist society. Instead, they are presented as being dispossessed by an amorphous colonial power structure whose relationship with capitalism is always nebulous. When settler colonial theorists do discuss Indigenous labour relations, they often refer to it as "colonial" labour relations, even well into the twentieth century. This can appear to be justified because Indigenous labour often had specific features such as the non-payment of wages, or the payment of goods or welfare instead of wages, and systems of extreme exploitation or even slavery such as "black-birding" which involved the use of Aboriginal workers as enslaved labourers in the early Western Australian pearling industry and Pacific Islanders in

---

62. Callinicos and Rogers 1978, p. 18. This book also contains an important critique of the "internal colonisation" theory in South Africa that influenced an earlier strain of left-wing Australian analysis of Indigenous politics. Many of Callinicos' and Rogers' critiques apply to the Australian version of this theory. See Goodall 2008, pp. 76-77.
63. See Englert 2020 for an overview of this work.

Queensland. However, as Marxist historians have shown in regard to the persistence of "unfree" labour, such particular forms of exploitative work are not incompatible with capitalism. They do not constitute a separate structure within the capitalist mode of production but rather are one of the many forms that capitalist labour relations can take.[64]

It is true that during the initial colonisation process in Australia the motivation of the capitalist class wasn't to incorporate Indigenous people into the workforce but rather to continue the process of driving them off profitable land. As one study of the early South Australian economy puts it, "when the colony of South Australia was planned, the possibility that Aboriginal people might be a significant source of labour was never seriously contemplated... It was Aboriginal land that the colonists wanted; if Aboriginal labour proved valuable, then this was a bonus, but it was not an expectation".[65]

While Aboriginal labour came to play an essential role in the pastoral industry, particularly in the less populated states and territories, this was exceptional. In New South Wales and Victoria, Indigenous workers were a small minority of the population, and their labour wasn't in particular demand for any sections of the capitalists, so they often had to suppress or obscure their identity to enter into the predominantly white workforce. Patterns of Indigenous employment also shifted over time:

> By the early years of the twentieth century, increasingly segregationist government policies began to force Kooris out of the workforce. Furthermore, as the huge sheep stations were broken up, Kooris had to move their makeshift homes to reserves. The 1930s Depression reinforced this trend, as Kooris who had supported themselves all their lives were forced onto settlements to get unemployment relief.
>
> During World War II Aborigines were drawn back into the labour force and for the first time moved in significant numbers from rural areas to the cities. Hundreds came to Sydney to work in munitions factories at St Marys or crowded into the slums of

---

64. See Banaji 2010, in particular chapter 5.
65. Foster 2000, p. 1.

South Sydney. This trend was reversed in the immediate post-war years, as housing shortages and a slump in employment drove many from the cities back to camp on reserves and riverbanks.[66]

The general pattern is that where capitalists were able to find an exploitable use for Indigenous labour then they used them. Where they couldn't, Indigenous people either had to try their luck on the labour market or else were condemned to live in the ever-expanding network of missions.

Some Indigenous people entered the workforce not because capitalists found a use for their labour in a particular context but because they moved to urban areas and found that there was no way to survive except as a waged worker. There is some evidence that some Indigenous people purposefully moved to the cities in the belief that they would be able to have a better life for themselves or at least for their children, than what they could eke out on the missions.[67]

The waterfront became one such place that attracted Indigenous workers. From the early 1920s, a vibrant multi-racial workforce of white, Indigenous and migrant wharf labourers emerged on the Darwin waterfront, many of whom were the descendants of Indigenous and migrant pearl divers. Industrial port cities like Wollongong and Newcastle also attracted Aboriginal workers from local missions and reserves into the expanding and interlocking maritime, steel manufacturing and coal mining industries. The railways were also an important place of employment. Torres Strait Islanders who had originally been involved in the marine industry and cane cutting started to work on railways in northern Australia after the Second World War, with several hundred laying railway tracks by the 1960s.[68]

Those Indigenous people who found themselves being drawn into the capitalist labour market strove to adapt to their new conditions of life while holding on to what aspects of their traditional culture they could. In the process, their lives, conditions and

---

66. Armstrong 2005, p. 4.
67. See Scrimgeour 2020, p. 5.
68. Lui-Chivizhe 2011.

consciousness underwent an enormous upheaval. As Scrimgeour explains in regard to Aboriginal workers in Western Australia:

> Some of the people who went on strike in 1946 were the children of desert migrants, while many had themselves undertaken the long journey and made the profound changes involved in the transition from a hunter-gatherer economy to life in the settler-dominated Riverline region. They remembered living as children at the desert waterholes of their home country, the long journey they had made with their families... It seems likely that these cultural adjustments...resulted in a dynamic Aboriginal culture accustomed to adaptation and change, which would serve as the bedrock of the Aboriginal industrial and political action in the 1940s.[69]

While Indigenous life was still dominated by racism, poverty and violence, here and there Indigenous people were able to start to carve out spaces to live and then resist. In Sydney, the waterfront became an important site in the development of a political consciousness for a minority of Indigenous workers. Given the extremely limited options for them, this was an important route towards being able to fight for their rights in the new situation. To combat the structural racism integrated into the state – a particularly vicious and oppressive outcome of the colonial settler origins of Australia – Indigenous workers needed to find allies who could offer serious solidarity. The mixing together of left-wing trade union activism, socialist politics and the influence of overseas black nationalist ideas, for instance Garveyism, through foreign sailors,[70] made the waterfront an essential site in the development of political consciousness for a minority of Indigenous workers such as the future founder of the Australian Aboriginal Progress Association and active member of the Waterside Workers Federation, Fred Maynard. Later generations would undergo similar changes through their experiences on the waterfront. Many of these Indigenous working-class activists would either be influenced by or become members of the Communist Party

---

69. Scrimgeour 2020, pp. 5-7.
70. For the influence of Garveyism on Aboriginal waterside workers see Maynard 2005.

of Australia (CPA), as we shall explore later in this article. In 1940, Chicka Dixon left Wreck Bay Aboriginal Reserve on the NSW South Coast, aged 14, to work as a casual labourer at Port Kembla. Later he moved to Sydney, getting involved in union activism as a builders' labourer and then on the Sydney waterfront, before becoming an organiser for the Waterside Workers Federation and later a leading Aboriginal activist during the 1960s and '70s.

Kevin Cook, who also went on to become an important Aboriginal and trade union activist, was born in Wollongong and his early life was shaped by the militant working-class culture that had developed there. One account of his life explains that he grew up

> hearing stories from his uncles about the work on the local farms, picking beans and other crops as well as the long days in the heavy iron and steel works of the towns, and about the work in coal mining in the surrounding escarpments. That meant he was hearing from an early age about the unions on the South Coast, where working people, black or white, had often been able to work together across colour lines to gain better conditions.[71]

When the government pushed Aboriginal children out of public schools during the 1920s and '30s, Aboriginal communities on the South Coast fought back and won the support of local trade unions.[72]

In Darwin during the 1930s, initial opposition to the employment of Indigenous and migrant workers on the waterfront gave way to significant struggles for equal wages.[73] These struggles produced a culture of solidarity on the docks. In 1932 Johnny Ah Mat, the son of a Malay pearl-diver and a Torres Strait Islander woman, was elected as a union delegate for the Sorting Shed Section in Darwin, and one writer explains:

> The NAWU (Northern Australian Workers Union) organised the casual labourers into three semi-permanent gangs. There was no "racial" division within the gangs – each had a mixture of workers. There is no evidence to suggest that "half-caste" workers were

---

71. Cook and Goodall 2013, p. 14.
72. Cook and Goodall 2013, p. 12.
73. The following section on Darwin is drawn from Martinez 1999, pp. 188-210.

forced to take on the more physically taxing jobs such as working in the ship's hold, nor that they could not hold positions of seniority. Certainly, the union did not judge its workers according to "racial" stereotypes. There were over one hundred unemployed men in Darwin in 1937. On the list of Relief Workers each worker was judged by the union as fair, good or poor, but there was no correlation between this assessment and the worker's "race". Furthermore, there were capable white workers on the unemployed list while "coloured" workers remained employed as waterside workers. This suggests that white workers were not given preferential treatment.[74]

The strong bonds of solidarity forged in Darwin benefited all workers. The 1937 Payne and Fletcher report found that Darwin waterside workers were paid almost double the wages of wharfies in Brisbane and higher than any other tropical port. For Indigenous workers, this meant getting paid more in a month than they could hope to earn in an entire year while employed by the Aboriginal Department.

There were also broader cultural ramifications. Indigenous and non-Indigenous workers played in mixed-race football teams. Indeed the Buffaloes, who won the 1936 premiership, were captained by Johnny Ah Mat's brother, a tradition continued for many decades with Robert Ah Mat, Johnny's grandson, playing for the Sydney Swans in the 1990s. The NAWU newspaper championed the Buffaloes, making them into heroes for its working-class readership. Football games also included mixed-race afterparties and unions fought for the right of Indigenous workers to drink at Darwin pubs. When racists banned Indigenous players in 1927 it led to a community boycott and attendance at the games fell from several hundred to a small handful.[75] Police Paddock, an area set aside for the "coloured" community just outside Darwin, became an important space for developing this culture of solidarity. Unemployed white men who emigrated to Darwin made their camps near the area and appreciated the help they received from the community. The Ah Mat family organised social events and music nights for the unemployed men

---

74. Martinez 1999, p. 194.
75. Martinez 1999, pp. 196-98.

to welcome them into the city. In return, the Unemployed Workers Movement organised their own mixed-race social events and invited the Police Paddock community.

The culture of class struggle and solidarity created in Darwin during this period highlights one of the problems with settler colonial theory – its tendency to treat the non-Indigenous population as a homogeneous bloc. As Julia Martinez argues, "there has been a tendency, in discussing Darwin, to depict the white population as colonial masters, ignoring the role of white workers". However, as she points out, it is "only within a working class perspective of Darwin that one can find images of worker solidarity to act as a counterpoint to colonial elitism".[76]

There were real limits to the anti-racist working class culture in Darwin at this time. While the rights of so-called "half-castes" were championed, those deemed to be "full-blooded" Aborigines were excluded from the union movement. The union campaigns to support Aboriginal workers on the docks did accept much of the assimilationist framework promoted by the government. However, it is worth noting that while the official assimilation policy entrenched the division between Indigenous and non-Indigenous workers, union policy in Darwin challenged this division, even if not in a consistent way. Interestingly, the division between "half-castes" and "full-blooded" Indigenous people was also widely accepted by early Aboriginal activist organisations. Both these organisations and non-Indigenous anti-racist activists would change their views on this question over the coming years.[77]

Even though many Indigenous people often found themselves excluded from or a small section of the workforce, some industries did find a specific use for Indigenous labour. In her research into the use of Aboriginal labour in Western Australia's north, Anne Scrimgeour found that:

> As early as 1879, for example, all of the 18,000 sheep on the large coastal station of Mundabullangana were shepherded by *marrngu*, and a newspaper report stated in 1883 that on De Grey Station,

---

76. Martinez 1999, p. 204.
77. Martinez 1999, pp. 204-8.

which ran 40,000 sheep and 6000 heads of cattle, all the work was "done by natives, sheep shearing, washing wool, fencing, tank making, bullock and horse driving, in fact all the work required on and about the station".[78]

A similar process took place in South Australia. While Aboriginal labour had been used during the gold rushes of the 1850s, a new wave of European migration had pushed them out of the workforce. But in the less populated northern and western parts of the colony, Aboriginal labour was still needed for the stations to function.[79]

As capitalist expansion penetrated ever deeper into the far reaches of the continent and the frontier wars suppressed resistance, Aboriginal groups often had little choice other than to move closer to areas settled by whites. As traditional Aboriginal society collapsed in the face of colonial violence, the attraction of moving closer to white settlements increased, particularly as the spread of flour, tea, sugar and tobacco seeped into Aboriginal communities. As they did so, local bosses worked out that they could benefit from incorporating them into their exploitative system. As Scrimgeour puts it, the requirement for Aboriginal people to live in designated "native camps" near the stations left "the country free for pastoral activity while simultaneously creating a pool of labour for the stations".[80] Indigenous labour proved useful for a number of purposes: women were widely used as domestic servants, while pearl fishing was extremely profitable for a lucky few. But it was the pastoralists who were most reliant on their talents.

The role that Aboriginal labour played in the Western Australian pastoral industry was often deliberately obscured by the bosses. To justify the lack of payment in wages and other discriminatory practices, these pastoralists often argued that they only allowed Aboriginal people to work on their stations out of charity. They argued that their labour was in effect costly because they would have to give provisions not just for the individuals working but for their extended family as well. Many pastoralists complained about "lazy"

---

78. Scrimgeour 2020, p. 1.
79. Foster 2011, p. 1.
80. Scrimgeour 2020, p. 11.

Aborigines who had to be constantly overseen. In reality, through a combination of outright violence and their control over rations, the pastoralists disciplined Indigenous workers into a highly profitable workforce that could be paid well below what other workers would accept.

The testimony of Frank Gare, an officer of the Department of Native Affairs in the 1950s, is interesting for the light it throws on the importance that pastoralists held Aboriginal labour:

> Most of the station people you talk to, the employers, spoke very well of their stockmen. They usually had criticisms in a general way of Aborigines in general, but they usually said, "Oh, but I've got good men here, they're good stockmen. I couldn't do without them". It was rather an odd attitude that their employees were well above average. But if you went to each station in turn they all had the same idea.[81]

Charles Baxter, a Country Party MP, told the Western Australian Legislative Assembly in 1943 that if the government was given too much control over Aboriginal labour it would "render the position of the pastoral industry impossible inasmuch as those engaged in that industry will not have labour available from the native race".[82] In South Australia, similar views were expressed in the late nineteenth century. In 1892 the Sub-Protector for Aborigines found that most cattle and sheep stations employed up to a dozen Aboriginal workers. When a station manager from the MacDonnell Ranges was asked if the stations could be worked without Aboriginal labour he replied "No, probably not". A telegraph officer responded to the same question: "I don't know what they [the squatters] would have done without them".[83]

Perhaps no further proof of the importance of Aboriginal labour for the pastoralists in Western Australia is needed than the fact that when Aboriginal groups or individuals tried to leave the station, they were forcefully brought back by the local police force. Similarly, if Aboriginal people camped near a station where their labour was

---

81. Quote from Scrimgeour 2020, p. 16.
82. Quote from Scrimgeour 2020, p. 11.
83. Quotes from Foster 2011, p. 2.

not needed or was deemed by the pastoralists as harming the "work ethic" of those already being used as labour, they were driven away. Like so many others, Aboriginal people's lives and experiences were organised according to the needs and desires of capitalism and the labour market.

The left wing of the workers' movement and early Indigenous activist organisations

Sarah Maddison argues that contemporary progressive thought on Indigenous oppression remains trapped within what she calls the "Australian colonial fantasy", in particular the belief that "colonialism was something sad but inevitable" which would be resolved through a process by "which colonialism would come to be supplanted by a modern, unified nation" backed up "by the misplaced belief that public policy would provide the means of resolving the colonial problem".[84] While this is an accurate criticism of much middle-class liberal thinking on racism in Australia, a very different tradition emerged within the radical wing of the workers' movement and the Australian left in the early 1930s. This tradition started to reflect the changing objective possibilities for solidarity between non-Indigenous workers and Indigenous people. It built on some of the earlier attitudes taken by more progressive trade unionists, but also went beyond them.

Unsurprisingly, the most significant advances in solidarity with Indigenous people were made by the most radical wing of the workers' movement at the time. During the 1920s and the first half of the 1930s, the Communist Party of Australia took a radical stand against Australian imperialism and nationalism.[85] This put them in a good position to reject the founding myths of the Australian state, arguing instead that Australian nationalism was reactionary. The CPA's strong opposition to nationalism and racism were also deeply influenced by the anti-colonial and anti-racist positions of the international Communist movement.

---

84. Maddison 2019, pp. 218-19.
85. For the early CPA's analysis of Australian capitalism see Kuhn 1986, pp. 14-18. It is worth noting that this analysis would undergo significant change during the Popular Front period from the mid 1930s.

Articles criticising the ALP's racist policies towards Indigenous people appeared in the Communist Party's press by the mid-1920s. In 1931 they published *Communist Party Fight for Aborigines: Draft Programme of Struggle Against Slavery* which included:

> a call for the abolition of all forms of forced labour; equal wages; abolition of the Aboriginal Protection Boards – "capitalism's slave recruiting agencies and terror organisations"; release of all Aboriginal prisoners and the empanelment of Aboriginal juries to hear cases involving Aborigines; the restoration of Central, Northern and N-W Australia to form independent Aboriginal republics; and the development of Aboriginal culture.[86]

These positions were built upon throughout the 1930s. The 1934 issue of *The Proletariat* put out by Communists in the Melbourne University Labor Club carried an article called "Towards the Emancipation of the Aborigines". The article declared that "It is no exaggeration to state that there has been a great awakening of interest in the Australian Aborigines during the last two or three years". After describing the "slave-labour" which Indigenous people are forced to carry out for "colonial super-profits of the Australian bourgeoisie" and the robbery of "all political rights", the author proceeded to demolish the idea that colonisation benefited Indigenous people, arguing that "the aborigines have been brought very close to total annihilation at the hands of the imperialists". Notably, the article also takes aim at the idea that they are simply a "dying race", arguing that:

> Bourgeois scientists who predict the extinction of the aborigines, also reckon without the broad sections of the population who are vigilantly watching the treatment of the aborigines, and who are exposing and resisting the worst of the attacks upon being launched against the natives... [W]e must...then reject decisively the bourgeois theory that aborigines are doomed to extinction. Even without Socialism, they may be saved from extinction.[87]

This article wasn't an exception. The Communist Party press carried

---
86. Boughton 1999.
87. All quotes from GR 1934.

articles throughout the 1930s on the economic exploitation and political oppression of Indigenous workers. These were not just words: in 1933 the Communist Party played a key role in preventing a massacre of Indigenous people in Arnhem Land.[88]

There isn't space here to critically engage in-depth with the development of the Communist Party's analysis and practice concerning Indigenous oppression and its relationship to the Communist Party's Stalinist politics. It is sufficient to say that a new generation of anti-Stalinist revolutionaries can learn much from their contributions to the struggle for Indigenous liberation, while critically examining how the evolution of their Stalinist politics undermined their approach to this vital question.

Alongside this development on the left, the first modern Indigenous activist organisations were being formed. In NSW, Aboriginal communities had taken disputes with the Protection Board to the public and the press since the early twentieth century. In 1915, on the Hasting River, Aboriginal protesters confronted an inspector with spears and shields in defiance of legislation taking away their children. In 1919, returned Aboriginal servicemen from the north coast protested against segregation and presented a petition demanding civil rights to the state government.

In the early 1920s this activity culminated in the formation of the first state-wide Aboriginal political organisation in NSW. Fred Maynard founded the Australian Aboriginal Progressive Association (AAPA) in response to the growing segregation of rural towns, and it quickly spread, building an initial base among Aboriginal farmers, carpenters and boat builders on the Macleay, Nambucca and Bellinger rivers.[89] The Association engaged in a tireless campaign against the Protection Board, fighting against the separation of Aboriginal families, government restrictions and segregation laws. By August 1925 the AAPA had eleven branches on the north coast, with a membership of 500. In 1926 the organisation formed links with similar struggles on the south coast and in Sydney. Unfortunately, by 1927 the organisation was broken up after two years of ceaseless harassment by the Protection Board, but many took the lessons from

---

88. Gibson 2019.
89. The following is from Goodall 2008, pp. 178-87.

these battles as they went on to play a role in other organisations.

William Ferguson was another important early Indigenous activist.[90] He had strong links to the workers' movement, the AWU in particular, from his many years working as a shearer. In 1916 Ferguson and his family settled in Gulargambone, a small town in the central west of NSW. In Gulargambone he led a campaign to reform the local branch of the ALP and helped establish a new Trades and Labour Council in the town, which then elected him as its secretary for two years. During this time he was also a leading local campaigner against the use of conscription in the First World War. Ferguson was clearly trusted as an important working-class leader in the region by workers, non-Indigenous and Indigenous alike. During the 1930s Ferguson launched the Aborigines Progressive Association (APA), one of many Indigenous activist organisations formed around this time. The APA itself was divided into two wings, with Ferguson's wing drawing on support from left-wing trade unionists and socialist activists.

There was also important activism by Torres Strait Islanders throughout the 1930s and '40s. In 1936 a strike of 400 Torres Strait pearl divers broke out in response to increased controls over the ownership of boats and lack of payment in wages by the Queensland government. After six months of the strike, the government sacked the local government Protector, leading to a "jubilant atmosphere" on the Islands.[91] This strike laid the basis for a series of stay at home strikes by Torres Strait Islander soldiers during the Second World War. In 1947 white Communist activist Gerald Peel published *Isles of the Torres Strait* which detailed the exploitation and oppression on the islands. Peel had been inspired to write the book after meeting a Torres Strait Islander at the Communist Party offices in Sydney. The Islander explained to him that he had had political discussions with American and Australian Communist seamen who were stationed in the Torres Strait during the war. One seaman encouraged him to read historical and political books, and while mixing with them the Islander told Peel it felt "like back home".[92] Peel's book championed

---

90. See Stanbrook and Fieldes 2019.
91. Wetherell 2004.
92. Jordan 2011, p. 254.

the rights of Torres Strait Islanders and recognised them as a distinct identity long before other organisations, with the Federal Council for the Advancement of Aborigines only changing its name to the Federal Council for the Advancement of Aborigines and Torres Strait Islanders in 1964.

The CPA developed a distinctively radical approach to the question of Indigenous oppression that emphasised working-class solidarity against racism. The fruits of this approach would become clear in a number of important Indigenous struggles in the post-war period.

Indigenous struggles and working-class solidarity

Contemporary discussions of the possibility of Indigenous and non-Indigenous solidarity are fraught and overwhelmingly pessimistic. In *Decolonizing Solidarity* Clare Land argues that there "are limited scenarios in which non-Indigenous people or institutions in settler colonial contexts are motivated to engage with Indigenous people out of a concern for their own immediate material self-interests".[93] When Sarah Maddison discusses the possibility of non-Indigenous people supporting Indigenous struggles she is exclusively concerned with the role of "progressive settler scholars".[94] This dovetails with much mainstream history, which emphasises the role played by progressive clergy, students or middle-class humanitarians and either downplays or ignores the role of workers. Land to her credit does discuss examples of working-class solidarity with Indigenous struggles, however her reliance upon settler colonial theory prevents her from explaining why some sections of the working class support Indigenous struggles while others don't. After all, according to her framework, they're all equally "settlers".

The general pattern is that when workers are well organised, benefits flow to the whole class, whereas when bosses have their way, fragmentation and inequality reigns. In this section I will examine the post-war era, where the full ramifications of the changing relationship between Indigenous struggle and working-class action previously described become clearer. This was an uneven

---

93. Land 2015, p. 216.
94. Maddison 2019, pxxxvii.

and contradictory process, and the high points of struggle shouldn't be taken as expressing the average view of workers at this time. Of course, a detailed account of all the post-war Indigenous struggles and the solidarity they did or did not receive is beyond the scope of this article. Instead my goal is to present some vignettes that point to possibilities. Fuller accounts of these struggles can be found in the books and articles referred to in the footnotes. A notable absence in this section is the Gurindji strike which has been well documented elsewhere.[95]

Some of these struggles were Indigenous working-class campaigns that drew upon non-Indigenous working class support. Others are examples of left-wing working-class activists who had gained confidence through their own struggles and were then motivated to take an anti-racist stand. The point of this section is to establish that solidarity between Indigenous and non-Indigenous workers is possible and to explore the reasons why it can emerge. By examining these events, we can begin to understand the dynamics that make possible solidarity between Indigenous and non-Indigenous workers and activists.

A key role was played in all of these struggles by members of the CPA and other working class-orientated activists who were often influenced by the Party. Communist activists used their influence with the working-class movement to educate workers in the politics of class solidarity, internationalism and opposition to racism. This approach was vital for the success of many of the struggles I will be discussing, because of the complex way class consciousness develops and the constant pressures against the development of solidarity due to the influence of the capitalist system on the working class.

As Sandra Bloodworth has argued against critics who want to emphasise the weaknesses of the working-class movement and the hegemony of racist ideas, focusing just on the low points of struggle and the limitations of working-class activists even when they are acting in solidarity with Indigenous struggles misses the point. She writes:

> The significance of struggle is the potential for ideas and attitudes

---
95. See McConvell 2018.

to be challenged. And the stronger the confidence engendered by the struggle, the more likely it is that racist and sexist ideas (to name just two) will be challenged. Trade unions and their willingness or otherwise to engage in industrial struggle are central. And the historical records (as opposed to academic histories) indicate that the left wing trade unions, most of which were heavily influenced by Communist Party activists, were of great importance in laying the basis for the developing radicalism of the Aboriginal rights movement during the sixties.[96]

The Pilbara strike 1946-49[97]

The roots of the Pilbara strikes lie in the clash between the intensification of discrimination against Aboriginal workers in Western Australia during the Second World War and growing anti-racist sympathy within a section of the workers' movements and left-leaning society. The exodus of white workers from the pastoral industry and into the army, combined with the importance of continued wool production for the war effort, led to a hardening of the exploitation of Aboriginal workers on the stations. Despite many Aboriginal workers volunteering to help with the war effort, authorities were suspicious about their loyalty, and so military personnel carried out surveillance of Aboriginal communities to detect subversion. Stricter segregation was also put in place across the state to keep Aboriginal people away from soldiers over concerns about "sexual misconduct".

At the same time, the 1940s was a period of growing sympathy for the plight of Aboriginal people among an important minority of the Western Australian population. A weekly radio broadcast on human rights issues hosted by Edward Beeby, a Communist and founder of the Anti-Fascist League (AFL) regularly discussed the oppression of Aboriginal people. The broadcast was the basis for discussion groups of the AFL which by 1943 had 2,700 members and 72 branches holding weekly meetings across Western Australia. Anti-racist working-class communities had started to emerge in some areas in the state. In Port Hedland, a community of mixed European

---

96. Bloodworth n.d.
97. This section draws heavily upon Scrimgeour 2020.

and Aboriginal descent established a "Euralian Association" which campaigned for decent housing, education, employment and equal status with the non-Aboriginal community. Some of the Association's members were employed on the wharves or the railway line and were members of the AWU. The Association won a considerable degree of support in the town, leading to a significant undoing of segregation within Port Hedland. This changed in November 1942 when the authorities clamped down, and the Euralian community was declared a prohibited area, before being forcibly segregated and a pass system established.

A campaign against the pass system started to take off. One link between the Euralian Association and the Anti-Fascist League was white activist – later Communist – Don McLeod, who would go on to play an important role in the Pilbara strikes. McLeod attended a "big half-caste meeting" in Port Hedland called to discuss how to organise against the pass system. He helped promote the struggle through the AFL's radio program and articles written for the *Fremantle Districts Sentinel*. Through this work, he came into contact with a vibrant community of communists and left-wing anti-racist activists in Perth, including the writers Katharine Susannah Prichard and Mary Durack, the anthropologist Fred Rose and Edward Beeby. This community connected McLeod with a broader network of communist activists who were involved in the struggle for Aboriginal rights across the country. It was during this time that McLeod read communist literature on Aboriginal rights. The plan for a strike of Aboriginal workers started to become more concrete through discussions between McLeod, Aboriginal men who worked with him sinking wells and local Aboriginal Lawmen. Also playing a central role was Clancy McKenna (Warntupungkarna) the son of a white pastoralist and a Nyamal woman, who had recently resigned from his job in protest over discriminatory wages.

While there was rising anger in the Aboriginal community about their conditions before McLeod got into contact with them, there was also underconfidence about how to fight. The key ideas McLeod promoted were that Aboriginal labour was essential to the pastoral industry, that because of this strike action was key, that if they fought then working-class allies across the state could be mobilised to support them, and that it was unlikely that the police and pastoralists would just murder them all – a widespread and understandable fear amongst Aboriginal station workers at the time. As Scrimgeour, who generally takes a rather critical view of McLeod's influence at this time, argues, "although he played down his role in instigating the strike, McLeod clearly took an active role in sowing the seeds of the strike idea. Among a disempowered Aboriginal population seeking a way 'to help ourself', his ideas found fertile soil".[98]

The idea of a strike of Aboriginal workers was discussed in large Aboriginal meetings at Nullagine, Moolyella and Marble Bar. McKenna and the Lawman Dooley Bin Molyullah travelled across the state visiting far-flung stations to promote and organise the strike. At the same time, McLeod started to popularise the idea in Communist Party circles, writing to leading party members about the development of plans for the strike and seeking advice about the way forward. By 1945 the idea of a strike had spread widely, and while McLeod might have been its inspiration, it quickly became driven by the Marrngu people themselves. As McKenna put it, "McLeod gave us a hint about the strike, and we took it up".[99]

After years of preparation, the strike began on 1 May 1946. Hundreds of Aboriginal workers took part, and strike camps were organised across the Pilbara. Strike action was also taken by hotel workers, domestic servants and miners in Marble Bar on 1 May. One large coastal station on the De Grey River had already gone on strike before 1 May in order to take action just as the mustering began, revealing that the workers were thinking about how best to use their power.

The strike immediately came up against all the racist institutions of Western Australian capitalism, who had previously been sceptical about the organising capacities of Aboriginal workers. Many employers simply sacked the Aboriginal workers who went on strike and expelled them from their properties. The police went station to station threatening the workers with exile if they joined the strike. Then McKenna and Dooley were imprisoned and McLeod arrested.

---

98. Scrimgeour 2020, p. 78.
99. Scrimgeour 2020, p. 94.

The leaders of the Pilbara strike knew that for their campaign to be successful, they needed what McLeod called "power behind us", ie, solidarity action from workers in industrial cities. Following the arrests of McKenna, Dooley and McLeod, a vigorous campaign broke out in the south of the state. Trade unions, civil liberties and women's groups campaigned against the imprisonment of the strike leaders and in support of the strike movement. Open meetings were held, and protests organised in Perth. Encouraged by the growing show of support from the south the strike movement spread and in Port Hedland strikers marched on the jail in which McLeod was imprisoned, leading to him being freed. As it became clear the strike was going to continue, support flowed in from around the country. Nineteen unions in Western Australia, seven national unions and four Trades and Labour Councils supported the strike and sent money.

The decisive moment came in August 1949 when the Seamen's Union banned the shipment of wool from the Pilbara. After three days the government caved in and substantial gains were made in wages and conditions.

While the strikers garnered significant union support, this wasn't universally the case. The leadership of the Australian Workers Union worked with the Department of Native Affairs to oppose the strike.[100] For the AWU this sprang from a combination of its poor record on the Aboriginal issue and its vicious anti-communist stance. While the AWU didn't deny Aboriginal membership, it left the final decision to local union representatives. So the AWU in Port Hedland welcomed members of the Euralian community into the union, while they were barred from well-paid employment in Broome. When Pilbara strikers tried to find temporary employment on the docks during the long strike, the AWU refused to give them union tickets.

The AWU state secretary Charlie Golding is reported as believing the Pilbara strike

> had been inspired by the Communist, Donald McLeod, and because he did not favour the tactics of this individual he proposed to telegram the Union representative at Port Hedland

---

100. Scrimgeour 2020, pp. 255-70.

stating that Union tickets were not to be issued to persons deemed to be natives according to the Native Administration Act.[101]

The AWU also campaigned against the employment of strikers on the Port Hedland railway and joined in an anti-communist crusade against the white stationmaster who allowed them to be employed. These attitudes within the AWU didn't go totally unchallenged. At an AWU members' meeting on 19 February, the decision to refuse membership to the Pilbara strikers was overturned, and the meeting said they would refuse to work on the wharves if Aboriginal men were not given equal opportunity for jobs.[102] The attitudes of the AWU leadership also stand in contrast to railway workers, who helped Aboriginal strikers board trains after police had attempted to ban them.[103]

How do we explain the differences between the AWU and other unions? The settler colonial perspective doesn't offer a useful explanation. Don McLeod was as much of a "settler" as Charlie Golding. The difference was politics. The AWU was a right-wing bureaucratic union hostile to the Communists and rank-and file-democracy and deeply embedded within the Australian Labor Party, with its racist policies towards Aboriginal people. On the other hand, McLeod, the Seamen's Union and the left-wing activists who rallied to support the Pilbara strikers had a commitment to working class action around political and social issues. It is this that allowed them to close the gap between the objective possibilities of solidarity and its realisation, while the AWU remained trapped within the conservatism of ruling-class ideology.

The Darwin Aboriginal workers' strikes 1947-1951[104]

In February 1947 a strike broke out among Aboriginal workers as a result of poor pay and living conditions in Berrimah Compound outside Darwin. In December 1950 and January 1951 Aboriginal workers employed as cooks, gardeners, painters and general

---

101. Scrimgeour 2020, p. 258.
102. Scrimgeour 2020, p. 261.
103. Scrimgeour 2020, pp. 265-66.
104. The following account comes from Middleton 1977, pp. 99-101 and Day 2019.

labourers on the Bagot Aboriginal reserve went on strike. These strikes were organised by the Aboriginal workers themselves, who held mass meetings to decide the course of strike action. Serious repression was unleashed to break up the strikes. One of the strike leaders, Fred Waters, was banished to Haasts Bluff, a desert area about 1,000 miles from Darwin, for "organising the natives to strike". Another strike leader who "neglected to obey a lawful instruction" during the strike was imprisoned for four months.

Two important factors shaped these strikes. The first was the contradictory effects of the Second World War on the consciousness and situation of Indigenous and non-Indigenous workers in the Northern Territory, which left a legacy after the war was over. The war broke down the isolation of northern and central Australia, with railways and airports being built to facilitate travel and communication to the military base in Darwin. At least 1,000 Aboriginal workers were recruited to work in food production, the Civil Construction Corps and as labour aids to the military base. Middleton writes that "these measures made a considerable contribution to the breakdown of the Aboriginal traditional hunting and gathering economy" which were "destroyed and replaced by new, wider affiliations".[105]

The experiences of these Aboriginal workers both stirred greater desire in the possibilities of equality and frustrated those desires. Aboriginal workers were paid in cash wages, and despite not being paid the same as white soldiers they were paid many times even the nominal amount that station owners "paid" them in rations. Some Aboriginal workers received training in semi-skilled industrial trades, drove trucks and were housed in the military barracks. They also interacted with white soldiers and workers in a far less segregated environment than during peacetime. Middleton describes the effects on both Indigenous and non-Indigenous workers and soldiers at the time:

> They were the first white Australians in contact with the Aborigines who were not involved or interested in exploiting them. The experience of living and working with such people, the

---

105. Middleton 1977, p. 78-79.

contrast between army conditions and the ways in which they were exploited and treated by the pastoralists, and the observation of the Black soldiers all had important ideological consequences for the Aborigines. Their world view was expanded, particularly their consciousness of support and sympathy among a section of the white population and their shared experiences and aims with other groups of Aborigines. The basis was laid for the unity which was developed and for organisations and campaigns which were begun after the war.[106]

One expression of the growing consciousness of at least some white workers of the plight of Aboriginal people was the novel *No Sunlight Singing* by Joe Walker. The novel details the exploitation of Aboriginal workers in the 1930s and '40s in Darwin. Walker published the book in 1960 but it was based upon what he learned first from Aboriginal people he worked with during the war in the Civil Construction Corps in Darwin, and then, after the war, in his role as a left-wing union organiser and editor of the union newspaper *The Northern Standard*, which openly supported the Aboriginal strikes in Darwin.[107]

At the same time though, the war increased the destruction of what remained of the traditional Aboriginal communities in the areas around Darwin, resulting in the further integration of Aboriginal workers into the exploitative capitalist economy and in greater numbers than before.

Middleton argues that "Communist Party of Australia members particularly used these experiences as the basis for the development of their theoretical policy and practical support for Aboriginal people". She goes on to make an important point that there was a "reciprocal process" in which the consciousness of the exploitation and oppression of Aboriginal workers "was raised in both the Aborigines themselves and in the white population".[108]

The other important factor then was the role of the Communist Party. The North Australian Worker's Union (NAWU) in Darwin

---
106. Middleton 1977, p. 80.
107. Thanks to the excellent website run by Joe Walker's son Alan Walker which is dedicated to keeping alive No Sunlight Singing.
    https://www.nosunlightsinging.com
108. Middleton 1977, p. 81.

organised financial and legal support for the striking workers and their families. This was only possible because in 1946 the NAWU had been taken over by a group of Communist activists led by George Gibbs, who had defeated the right-wing AWU-aligned leadership of the union.[109] The NAWU went to the High Court of Australia in an attempt to challenge the Aboriginals Ordinance that was used to deny Aboriginal workers the right to strike. The Aboriginals Ordinance was a constant source of complaint by the NAWU. It made it illegal for Aboriginal workers to either go on strike or join a union in the Northern Territory. At a conference in 1947, a request that Aboriginal workers be allowed to join the NAWU was denied by the Labor government.

There is also some evidence that Communists in the NAWU helped the Aboriginal strikes in more direct ways. In his memoirs Murray Norris, a Communist Party activist in the NAWU, recalls:

> Early in 46 the first of the Aboriginal strikes took place. I can't remember the date now, but it was after the first strike that took place on the wharf. I had come up from the Centre to report, which I generally did about every four months, and was sitting in the union office when I heard a stone drop on the roof. I had a look around and couldn't see any kids about. A little later I heard another one on the roof so I figured that I had better take a better look. As I walked all around the buildings and at the back I heard the familiar sound "Eh", the sound that an Aborigine makes when he wants to get your attention. I walked over to some long grass and hidden there were seven Aborigines. They told me that they wanted to talk to the union about striking. They wanted assistance and advice what to do. As I am tone deaf I have great difficulty in translating broken English and they had to keep repeating what they were saying. I told them to hold on and went back to the union office. Frank Whiteoak, the Darwin Organiser, was there so I told him about it and took him back down. Some of them knew him and he was the bloke they had really come to see. They were too polite to tell me that they didn't know me. Frank took over and formed a strike committee with himself as adviser in the

---

109. See Townsend 2009, p. 27.

background. I still have a photo of this first strike committee with Frank.[110]

This support shown by the NAWU was then reciprocated by the Aboriginal workers themselves. During a six-week-long hospital strike in 1948 wealthy women attempted to scab on the strike. In response Aboriginal domestic workers who were employed by these wealthy women went on strike, refusing to do the laundry and clean the house. As Norris puts it in his memoirs, "as soon as the 'silver tails' found that there was nobody at home to do all the dirty work, they quickly turned tail and went home".[111]

The 1957 Palm Island strike[112]

Palm Island has a long history as the "Alcatraz" for Indigenous people in Queensland. Established in 1918 as a "reserve" to send particularly "rebellious" Indigenous people to, including the leaders of a strike at the Taroom reserve in 1916, it became a horrifying prison island. It was also a key part of capitalist strategy to control Indigenous people more generally by segregating Indigenous workers considered unsuitable for labour while simultaneously being used as a threat to intimidate the rest of the Indigenous workforce. As Peggy James of the Boulia region put it, "they only had to mention Palm Island and we were quiet".[113]

As more and more Indigenous people spoke out against discrimination on the mainland the numbers of explicitly political and activist Indigenous workers sent to Palm Island increased. The conditions on the island were absolutely appalling. Under the virtual dictatorship of the ex-police officer Roy Henry Bartlam, Indigenous "inmates" were forced to salute all white people, work without pay, and labour for the personal gain of Bartlam and his friends. Resistance to any of this was met with extreme brutality and imprisonment in solitary confinement without pause for weeks on end. Repression was particularly harsh in terms of labour relations, with Bartlam

---

110. Norris 1982.
111. Norris 1982.
112. The following section draws heavily on Watson 1995.
113. Watson 1995, p. 151.

enforcing strict segregation and punishing the most minor misdemeanours in the workplace. The building trade was a particular focus for Bartlam's brutality and desire to squeeze whatever labour he could out of his workforce. Indigenous workers started meeting in private to discuss the possibility of strike action on the island.

In June 1957 these issues came to a head when Bartlam tried to have Albie Geia, a Palm Island native, deported from the island for demanding his correct wage. In response the Palm Island community declared a general strike and the Indigenous population rallied to support Geia. The strike quickly raised the general issues affecting the Indigenous community, demanding better wages, housing and for Bartlam to leave the island. The strike ground the island to a halt, with even members of the police force joining, leaving Bartlam to barricade himself in his house with his remaining supporters. Eventually Bartlam called for reinforcements from the Queensland police to help put down the revolt. After five days the strike was eventually crushed, with many Indigenous workers deported from the island with machine guns pointed at them.

While the mainstream press painted the strikers as ungrateful natives and the Queensland state Labor government sent in the police, it was the Communist Party and their supporters who campaigned to support the Indigenous strikers. The Communist newspaper *Tribune* defended the strike as "thoroughly justified", denounced Palm Island as a "penal colony" and called for a public inquiry staffed with trade union representatives in order to stop a whitewash by the police and the government. The Townsville Trades and Labour Council, which was led by Communist Party members at the time, campaigned against the repression of the strike. They also tried to use the strike and its repression as a chance to educate workers across the state about why it was important to stand in support of the Indigenous workers.

More broadly the historian Joanne Watson has made the point that you can't understand the actions taken by the Indigenous workers on Palm Island without placing them in the context of industrial struggle and left-wing working-class politics at the time.[114]

---

114. Watson 1995.

Many of the "rebellious" Aboriginal workers sent to the island had experience with trade unions and the Communist Party. In 1942 a group of non-Indigenous miners in north Queensland, likely influenced by the Communist Party, called for the payment of award wages for Aboriginal station workers. This action inspired Aboriginal stockmen at Woodleigh station to walk off the job in protest. In response the police cracked down and the ringleaders were deported, likely some to Palm Island. In the early 1950s the Communist Party raised the issue of Aboriginal rights at rank-and-file workers' conferences across the state, and organised research teams to visit Indigenous workers at Weipa and Yarrabah, which then reported back to union meetings on the exploitative conditions faced by Aboriginal workers.[115] Indigenous workers native to Palm Island also had links to trade unions and left-wing activists, some of which dated back to connections made during the Second World War.

The South Coast Aboriginal Advancement League[116]

In November 1961 the South Coast Aboriginal Advancement League was founded by a number of white Communist trade unionists and local Indigenous activists. The formation of the League was inspired by a conversation between white Communist Joe Howe and Aboriginal activist Joe McGinness, who met while working on the Cairns waterfront. Upon returning to Wollongong Howe got in touch with local Communist trade unionists. The Illawarra had a strong left-wing trade union tradition that had been spearheaded by Communists during the 1930s and then consolidated during and after the Second World War in the coal mines, docks and briefly at the steelworks. The South Coast Labour Council (SCLC) was notable for its radical positions and its interventions into local unions to back up left-wing challenges to right-wing union bureaucrats.

Prior to establishing the League, the SCLC organised a survey of the conditions of Indigenous seasonal pickers who worked for white farmers on the South Coast. Despite resistance by reserve managers, they travelled south and documented not only widespread exploitation and poor housing conditions but also the political aspirations of

---
115. May 1994, p. 161.
116. The following section draws heavily from Donaldson, Bursill and Jacobs 2017.

Aboriginal people. When Howe introduced the survey to a meeting of the SCLC he noted that Aboriginal people had been "deliberately kept in a humiliating condition" by both Liberal and Labor governments:

> Through bitter experience they see governments and employers as their enemies. They are unionists, some of them, they are part of the Australian Labour movement. We in our Unions, do not practice discrimination. Our Aboriginal people are fighting for freedom in common with the African people, American negroes and others. Greet our Aborigines as friends. Your co-operation will end discrimination.[117]

The report also noted the desire of Illawarra Aboriginal communities for land rights and an end to the abuses of the Welfare Board and the desecration of sacred sites. Once the League was formed, it set about campaigning against discrimination across the Illawarra. The focus of the League was on the everyday racism and segregation that Aboriginal people faced. The League worked with the Waterside Workers Federation to win the right of Aboriginal people to drink at the Port Kembla and Wollongong pubs. Throughout the rest of the South Coast discrimination was even more entrenched, particularly in the rural towns. Aboriginal people were excluded from pubs and faced segregation in schools, pools, shops and cinemas.

In March 1962 a branch of the League was set up in Nowra. Fred Moore, a longstanding trade union activist from Wollongong, spoke at its inaugural meeting and was particularly impressed by the involvement of young women. For the new branch's first action, an Aboriginal woman, Norma Sherman, some of her friends and Moore entered a café that refused to serve Aboriginal people. Moore explains what happened next:

> Well, we sat there and sat there and they wouldn't serve us. So I got up and said "What's your problem mate?" The man said he did not want the custom of the women because if he served them he'd get no more business from other people. He said he would serve us if we moved to the back of the café, out of sight. We refused. Racism was pretty rampant in Nowra then. Well, we left and put out the

---
117. Donaldson et al 2017, p. 59.

word that if anyone refused to serve an Aboriginal person again we would ban all deliveries of food to their business.[118]

A week later the women returned and were served, and by 1964 segregation had been defeated in Nowra. This was a year before the far more famous Freedom Rides organised by Charles Perkins and the student activists at Sydney University. The activism of the League also laid the basis for future struggles in the Illawarra such as the campaign during the 1967 Referendum and the fight for land rights at Wreck Bay. A layer of Indigenous working-class activists was formed out of these struggles in the Illawarra and would go on to play important roles throughout the rest of the country.

The events in the Illawarra are a particularly strong refutation of the settler colonial thesis. Here we have mostly non-Indigenous working-class activists leading a struggle for Indigenous rights. Why these "settlers" took up the fight against segregation in the Illawarra will forever remain a mystery to most contemporary academic writers on Indigenous issues. No wonder then that it has almost been entirely forgotten from history.

The NSW Builders Labourers Federation and Aboriginal rights 1967-1975
The radical and class struggle-oriented NSW Builders Labourers Federation (BLF), with members of the CPA playing a leading role, formed a strong alliance with the struggle for Aboriginal rights and the emerging Black Power movement. This alliance built upon earlier work that the BLF had done to build solidarity with Indigenous struggles. In 1967 Dexter Daniels, an Indigenous organiser for the North Australian Workers Union and leading figure in the Gurindji strike, spoke at a BLF meeting in Sydney. The building workforce at the time was very ethnically mixed, and so the lines of racial segregation were less rigid. The BLF took a strong stand against anti-migrant racism by the bosses and argued against anti-migrant attitudes among workers. This put them in a strong position to discuss the issue of Indigenous rights with the union's membership, which included a number of Indigenous members. The relationship built up between migrant and Indigenous BLF members at the time

---
118. Donaldson et al 2017, pp. 62-63.

goes some way in showing what is wrong with the emphasis of settler colonial theorists on the "privileges" of settler migrants.

Kevin Cook, Aboriginal activist and BLF organiser, explains how the racism of the bosses helped them build an opposing culture of solidarity:

> I think the bosses played right into our hands, because, on a building site, most of the bosses, whether they be foremen, leading hands, thought they were a cut above everybody else and they'd go along and say, "Get out of here you wog bastards" and all of that, and the Builders Labourers' union got onto that, and started pulling the bosses up and in fact sacking the bosses for being racist.
>
> So that built the migrant people up too, no longer could the boss come up and call an Italian a wog, in a detrimental way. He might say, "Hey you wog bastard" if he was a mate of his, but on no account could he do that if he was angry or had the shits, he just couldn't do it, because he'd get the sack. That made it a lot easier when you were talking about black issues, it was a social issue the same as not calling migrants "wogs" on the site. And the bosses done that a hell of a lot and the migrants got very, very angry.[119]

BLF activist Bobby Baker remembers Greek and Italian BLF members joining the land rights marches. They formed links with left-wing migrant organisations such as the Greek Communist Party and the Federation of Italian Migrant Workers and Families (FILEF) that would continue for many years, including participation in the 1988 anti-bicentennial marches.

From the late 1960s onwards an Indigenous urban militant activist milieu started to emerge in Redfern that quickly embraced the politics of Black Power.[120] This younger generation of Indigenous activists were open to more confrontational methods of social change. As Gary Foley writes, "when the high expectations created by the 1967 referendum were dashed by government inaction, the younger activists felt a strong sense of betrayal and cynicism at

---

119. Cook and Goodall 2013, p. 41.
120. Foley 2001.

the more non-confrontational methods and tactics of the older generation".[121] A new attitude was reinforced by nightly clashes with the NSW police who patrolled Redfern and inspired by the general radicalisation of the 1960s and development of Black politics in the United States.

These activists formed strong links with the radical left organisations and movements flowering in Sydney at the time, and in particular with BLF leaders Jack Mundey, Bob Pringle and Joe Owens and the Indigenous BLF activist Kevin Cook. The BLF saw its role as a democratic workers' organisation that used its industrial power to take stands on broader social issues. Both the BLF and the Black Power activists in Redfern played a key role in the anti-apartheid protests during the 1971 Springbok tour, with Bob Pringle arrested for trying to saw down a goalpost at the Sydney Cricket Ground.

Perhaps the most important intersection between the BLF and the Black Power activists was in Redfern itself. In the early 1970s building developers began to circle "The Block", two streets of semi-derelict houses near Redfern Station that had become an important social and political centre for the Indigenous community in Sydney. With the building boom at its height, the developers wanted the houses torn down and replaced with new high-rise housing and offices. Here we have the perfect test case for the settler colonial thesis. "Settler" building workers were being asked to demolish Indigenous housing by their bosses. If they refused their jobs, and "privileges", would be at stake.

The BLF immediately banned any demolition or construction work on the Block, essentially ending plans by developers to purchase the land. The pressure brought to bear on the Whitlam government by the Black Power activists in Redfern and the BLF led the government to fund the purchasing of the land by an Aboriginal-controlled organisation, the Aboriginal Housing Company, in the first urban land rights claim in the twentieth century.[122]

Clare Land can acknowledge the "longevity" of the BLF's engagement with Indigenous struggles, and can even point to important reasons why this was the case: the union's industrial strength

---
121. Foley 2001, p. 7.
122. Cook and Goodall 2013, p. 50.

and radical politics.[123] However, she never engages with how this fits in with her broader commitment to settler colonial theory. The classic Marxist strategy of uniting the oppressed and exploited in a common struggle against the conditions produced by capitalism is not some pie in the sky dream or a dogmatic scheme forced onto social movements. The history presented in this section shows that it is a viable strategy grounded in the actual relationship between Indigenous and non-Indigenous workers under Australian capitalism. Settler colonial theory can not explain these struggles. Its lack of a class analysis and assertion that all non-Indigenous people are privileged as "settlers" makes it impossible for settler colonial theory to appreciate the possibilities of solidarity.

Decolonisation, revolution and the working class

The analytical problems with settler colonial theory have repeatedly been expressed in more concrete debates over how we can build a movement to challenge Indigenous oppression today, and what kind of movement we want to build into the future. Supporters of the settler colonial argument often point to the genuine failures of paternalistic approaches to solving the so-called Indigenous "problem". But their correct criticisms of middle-class liberal racism often spill over into scepticism about genuine displays of popular support for Indigenous justice by non-Indigenous people. It often seems that the central point for these theorists is to aim their fire at those seeking to show solidarity with Indigenous struggles rather than the exploitative system that oppresses both Indigenous people and non-Indigenous workers. A particularly noxious example of this recently was the attacks on young African migrants in Melbourne who sought to organise a solidarity rally with the Black Lives Matter movement in the US. Members of WAR demanded that these young African migrants cancel their demonstration on the basis that they are "settler Africans" whose experience of racism is fundamentally different to that of both African Americans and Indigenous people. This ignores the fact that African youth in Melbourne are a constant target for racist police harassment. After a strident online campaign

---

123. Land 2015, pp. 63-65.

backed by hysterical white liberals, the demoralised African youth abandoned their plans for a protest.

The weaknesses of settler colonial theory are also present in the political strategy of "decolonisation". Originally decolonisation referred to the process by which the colonially dominated nations of the global south achieved national independence. Today it is a more amorphous term that refers to the process of deracialising oppressive structures, societies and cultures. It can encapsulate any number of mutually contradictory political practices and strategies. The more moderate strands of decolonisation bear a striking resemblance to traditional liberal strategies for social change, with a focus on education, cultural representation and individual empowerment.

More left-wing proponents do look to transform the racist structures of society. However, without clarifying the relationship between Indigenous oppression and capitalism, let alone the question of solidarity between Indigenous and non-Indigenous workers, it is difficult for settler colonial theorists to develop a strategy for defeating racism that doesn't fall back into a liberal or reformist framework.

Take, for example, this guide for how white "allies" can help the struggle for decolonisation:

To engage with decolonisation you can:

- value Indigenous knowledge and scholarship. In Australia, this can mean listening to Indigenous people on their knowledge about bushfire management
- encourage and insist on teaching about Indigenous people and cultures in schools
- support restitution efforts, such as programs which are revitalising Indigenous languages
- call on institutions – including across education, the arts, media and politics – to hire Indigenous people throughout the organisation and in positions of leadership
- look for ways people in your workplace might face

> discrimination and unconscious bias, and speak up against these structures
>
> - fight for justice arising from Indigenous guidance, by walking alongside Indigenous people at rallies and placing their voices front-and-centre at events.[124]

These might all be worthwhile activities in and of themselves, but they don't add up to a strategy for liberation. The analysis of Indigenous oppression as rooted in the nature of Australian capitalism outlined in this article lays the basis for the elaboration of genuine revolutionary strategy. The united struggles that both Indigenous and non-Indigenous workers were able to forge during the post-war years show that such solidarity isn't some utopian dream. Despite such a working-class culture of solidarity being beaten back during the decades of the neoliberal offensive, it remains a broken thread to be remade on a deeper, broader and stronger basis.

There are, however, significant obstacles to the recreation of such a united movement. These obstacles are reflected in the trajectories of Indigenous politics over the last four decades. The forging of solidarity between sections of non-Indigenous and Indigenous workers from the post-war years to the heights of the late 1960s and early '70s was rooted in the strength of the working-class movement. The retreat of the workers' movement from the mid-seventies onwards reversed this process, although not totally. The gains of that period couldn't be entirely obliterated, either from the consciousness of working people or society in general, and lived on in various ways. However, the forward momentum was definitely checked, as revealed by the pushback against land rights from the late seventies. While important struggles continued to attract significant levels of sympathy from unionised workers, they generally weren't able to mobilise the kind of social power necessary to win.

This relative decoupling of the workers' movement and Indigenous activism reinforced the growing sense of pessimism of much of the left and the retreat into the beginnings of what we would today call identity politics. Separatist arguments emphasising the

---

124. O'Dowd and Heckenberg 2020.

autonomy of different struggles gained a stronger foothold. This kind of destructive politics simply served to further the fragmentation of the solidarity and unity that had emerged in the sixties and seventies. Struggles didn't just disappear; from the 1988 anti-Bicentennial marches to the Invasion Day rallies today people continued to be mobilised around the issue of Indigenous justice. However, they generally suffered some of the same weaknesses as those in the late seventies and eighties, the lack of some form of economic or political power to begin to challenge the roots of Indigenous oppression.

A new development reinforced these trends – the slow emergence of an Indigenous middle class. It is important not to overestimate the size of this social layer. Indigenous people are extremely oppressed, and historically have been more excluded from any toehold in mainstream middle-class society than African Americans in the United States. However, from the mid-seventies onwards, and speeding up at the beginning of the twenty-first century, there is a development of class differentiation with the Indigenous population of Australia.

In 2016 20 percent of Indigenous men and 27 percent of Indigenous women who live in major cities and were working, were employed as either managers or professionals.[125] This compares to 15 percent and 24 percent respectively in 2006.[126] While this category does include some white-collar workers it also embraces roles within what Marxists have called the new middle class in education, human resources, psychology, medicine, law and the media. This Indigenous middle class is a small social layer. However, it can have a disproportionate weight within Indigenous circles and society at large due to the access the middle class has to the media and political power and the convergence between its aims and that of the liberal non-Indigenous middle class. A stark example of the emergence of this class differentiation within the Indigenous community was on display during the battle over the "redevelopment" of the Block in Redfern which pitted the local Indigenous community and activists like Jenny Munro against Mick Mundine, CEO of the Aboriginal Housing Company.

---
125. Venn and Biddle 2018, p. 10.
126. Gray et al 2013, p. 12.

This Indigenous middle class has different elements within it. There is a small, but vocal, extremely conservative wing represented by the likes of Noel Pearson, Mick Mundine and Jacinta Price. The dominant current though is a liberal progressive wing which in turn has various shades of more moderate opinion. There is a strong identification with the Indigenous middle class by the non-Indigenous liberal middle class. The politics of settler colonial theory suit both these social layers. Their strategy is rooted in the traditional liberal ideas of cultural representation, education and individual empowerment and based upon an alliance between the progressive non-Indigenous middle class and the emerging Indigenous middle class. The radical Gumbaynggirr activist Gary Foley pointed almost two decades ago to the dangers of the emergence of an Indigenous middle class and its links to the incorporation of community services into the public service, with the resulting changes of consciousness even for well-meaning Indigenous activists.[127] For both the Indigenous and non-Indigenous middle class there can be a convergence around criticism of some of the failures of government policy and mainstream liberalism, combined with an elitist cynicism towards working-class politics.

The history of anti-racist struggles explored in this article point towards an alternative strategy for Indigenous liberation. The starting point for this strategy is an understanding that Indigenous oppression is unambiguously rooted in the nature of Australian capitalism. It cannot be overcome without the Australian ruling class being overthrown. The only social layer capable of doing this is the working class, which includes within it both non-Indigenous and Indigenous people. Because Indigenous oppression is rooted in capitalism, the working class has an interest in challenging Indigenous oppression, even if significant sections of the working class are not always aware of that interest. Through the complex interaction of working-class struggle, the development of an anti-capitalist layer of workers through that struggle, and the creation of strong revolutionary working-class organisations, the possibility for a sustained movement in solidarity with Indigenous struggle can emerge. As the

---

127. Foley 2019.

history of the NSW BLF shows, such a movement, while rooted in the industrial power of the working class, would not be counterposed to mass street protests or militant actions by minorities. These actions can play a vital role in giving confidence to the oppressed, publicising their issues and politicising the working class. Such a movement could, in the immediate sense, challenge many of the expressions of Indigenous oppression and in the long run, contribute to the formation of a revolutionary movement that could end Indigenous oppression forever.

The formation of a layer of radical Indigenous activists and the rebuilding of a militant and socialist workers' movement are then necessarily prerequisites for the construction of a sustained movement for Indigenous liberation. An essential part of this process is the growth of the revolutionary Marxist left. The objective possibilities for forging a culture of united working class struggle are in many ways greater today than in the past. Consciousness of Indigenous oppression among the population is much greater today, thanks to the legacy of the struggles during the 1960s and '70s and recent Indigenous activism. The development of this consciousness is made easier by the greater urbanisation of the Indigenous population which has both helped to generate and sustain Indigenous activism while also making the possibility of unity among Indigenous and non-Indigenous working-class people more feasible. The emergence of a radical layer of Indigenous activists, a significant left-wing class struggle current within the workers' movement and a revival of the revolutionary left will not appear overnight. Clarity about the political basis upon which such a movement could be constructed will be a vital part of its emergence.

References

Allam, Lorena and Laura Murphy-Oates 2021, "Australia's anguish: the Indigenous kids trapped behind bars", *Guardian Australia*, 18 January. https://www.theguardian.com/australia-news/2021/jan/18/australias-anguish-the-indigenous-kids-trapped-behind-bars

Armstrong, Mick 2005, "Aborigines: problems of race and class", *Class and Struggle in Australia*, Pearson Education.

Banaji, Jairus 2010, *Theory as History: Essays on Modes of Production and Exploitation*, Haymarket Books.

Bloodworth, Sandra n.d., *Aboriginal rights & trade unions in the 1950s and 1960s*. https://sa.org.au/interventions/kooris_unions.htm

Boughton, Bob 1999, *The Communist Party of Australia's involvement in the struggle for Aboriginal and Torres Strait Islander People's Rights 1920-1970*. https://ro.uow.edu.au/cgi/viewcontent.cgi?article=1012&context=labour1999

Bramble, Tom 2012, "Is there a labour aristocracy in Australia?", *Marxist Left Review*, 4, Winter. https://marxistleftreview.org/articles/is-there-a-labour-aristocracy-in-australia/

Callinicos, Alex and John Rogers 1978, *Southern Africa after Soweto*, Pluto Press.

Closing the Gap report 2020. https://ctgreport.niaa.gov.au/employment

Connell, RW and TH Irving, 1980, *Class Structure in Australian History: Documents, Narrative and Argument*, Longman Cheshire.

Cook, Kevin and Heather Goodall 2013, *Making Change Happen: Black and White Activists talk to Kevin Cook about Aboriginal, Union and Liberation Politics*, Aboriginal History Monographs. https://press-files.anu.edu.au/downloads/press/p245561/pdf/book.pdf

Day, William 2019, *A brief history of the strikes by aboriginal workers in Darwin, 1947-1951*. http://www.drbilldayanthropologist.com/resources/NadpurAKAFredWaters%26PrinceofWales1951BD.pdf

Donaldson Mike, Lee Bursill and Mary Jacobs 2017, *A History of Aboriginal Illawarra, Volume 2: Colonisation*, Dharawal Publications.

Elton, Judith 2007, *Comrades or competition?: Union relations with Aboriginal workers in the South Australian and Northern Territory pastoral industries, 1878-1957.* Unpublished PhD thesis, Flinders University, Australia.

Englert, Sai 2020, "Settlers, Workers, and the Logic of Accumulation by Dispossession", *Antipode: A Radical Journal of Geography*, 52 (6). https://doi.org/10.1111/anti.12659

Fiedler, Lauren 2018, "Colonial-capitalism and the shrinking possibilities for achieving Aboriginal equality and agency in Australia: a critical study of 'economic' strategy for social and political advancement", *NEW: Emerging Scholars in Australian Indigenous Studies*, 4, pp. 33-38.

Fieldes, Diane 2010, "The Northern Territory Intervention and the liberal defence of racism", *Marxist Left Review*, 1, Spring. https://marxistleftreview.org/articles/the-northern-territory-intervention-and-the-liberal-defence-of-racism/

Fieldes, Diane 2019, "Review: The making of the Australian working class", *Marxist Left Review*, 17, Summer. https://marxistleftreview.org/articles/review-the-making-of-the-australian-working-class/

Foley, Gary 2001, *Black Power in Redfern 1968-72*, PhD thesis, Victoria University. http://vuir.vu.edu.au/27009/1/Black%20power%20in%20Redfern%201968-1972.pdf

Foley, Gary 2019, "The Black Middle Class". https://www.youtube.com/watch?v=TRGFTvvj5Ps

Foster, Robert 2011, "Rations, coexistence, and the colonisation of Aboriginal labour in the South Australian pastoral industry, 1860-1911", *Aboriginal History Journal*, 24, ANU Press. http://press-files.anu.edu.au/downloads/press/p72891/pdf/article0118.pdf

Foster, John Bellamy, Brett Clark and Hannah Holleman 2020, "Marx and the Indigenous", *Monthly Review*, 71 (9), 1 February. https://monthlyreview.org/2020/02/01/marx-and-the-indigenous/

Garnham, Sarah 2018, "Against reductionism: Marxism and oppression", *Marxist Left Review*, 16, Winter. https://marxistleftreview.org/articles/against-reductionism-marxism-and-oppression/

Gibson, Paddy 2019, "Socialists and the fight to end the frontier massacres", *Solidarity*, 24 January. https://www.solidarity.net.au/highlights/socialists-and-the-fight-to-end-the-frontier-massacres/

Goodall, Heather 2008 [1996], *Invasion to Embassy: Land in Aboriginal Politics in New South Wales, 1770-1972*, Sydney University Press.

GR 1934, "Towards the Emancipation of the Aborigines", *Proletariat*, Melbourne University Labor Club, August.

Gray, Mathew, Monica Howlett and Boyd Hunter 2013, *CAEPR Indigenous Population Project 2011 Census Papers: Paper 10 Labour Market Outcomes*, Centre for Aboriginal Economic Policy and Research. https://openresearch-repository.anu.edu.au/bitstream/1885/119281/1/2011CensusPaper10_LbrMktOutcomes.pdf

Hillier, Ben and Tom O'Lincoln 2013, "Five hundred lashes and double irons: the origins of Australian capitalism", *Marxist Left Review*, 5, Summer. https://marxistleftreview.org/articles/five-hundred-lashes-and-double-irons-the-origins-of-australian-capitalism/

Humphrys, Elizabeth 2012, "The birth of Australia: Non-capitalist social relations in a capitalist mode of production?", *Journal of Australian Political Economy*, 70, Summer. https://www.ppesydney.net/content/uploads/2020/05/The-birth-of-Australia-Non-capitalist-social-relations-in-a-capitalist-mode-of-production.pdf

Jordan, Douglas 2011, *Conflict in the Unions: The Communist Party of Australia, Politics and the Trade Union Movement, 1945-1960*, PhD thesis, Victoria University. http://vuir.vu.edu.au/16065/1/Douglas_Jordan_PhD.pdf

Keneally, Thomas 2009, *Australians: Origins to Eureka*, Allen & Unwin.

Kuhn, Rick 1986, *Paradise on an instalment plan: the economic thought of the Australian labour movement between the depression and the long boom*, PhD thesis, ANU. https://openresearch-repository.anu.edu.au/bitstream/1885/7450/1/Kuhn_PhDThesis2nded1986.pdf

Land, Clare 2015, *Decolonizing Solidarity: Dilemmas and Directions for Supporters of Indigenous Struggles*, Zed Books.

Lui-Chivizhe, Leah 2011, "Making history: Torres Strait Islander railway workers and the 1968 Mt Newman track-laying record", *Aboriginal History Journal*, 35, ANU Press. http://press-files.anu.edu.au/downloads/press/p148271/html/Text/G02%20Lui-Chivizhe.html?referer=&page=

Maddison, Sarah 2019, *The Colonial Fantasy: Why White Australia can't solve Black problems*, Allen & Unwin.

Markey, Raymond 1988, *The Making of the Labor Party in New South Wales: 1880-1900*, New South Wales University Press.

Markus, Andrew 1978, "Talka Longa Mouth", *Who are our enemies? Racism and the working class in Australia*, Hale and Iremonger.

Martinez, Julia 1999, *Plural Australia: Aboriginal and Asian labour in tropical white Australia, Darwin, 1911-1940*, PhD thesis, University of Wollongong. https://ro.uow.edu.au/cgi/viewcontent.cgi?article=2437&context=theses

May, Dawn 1994, *Aboriginal Labour and the Cattle Industry: Queensland from White Settlement to the present*, Cambridge University Press.

Maynard, John 2005, "'In the interests of our people': the influence of Garveyism on the rise of Australian Aboriginal political activism", *Aboriginal History Journal*, 29, ANU Press. http://press-files.anu.edu.au/downloads/press/p73931/pdf/ch0153.pdf

McConvell, Tanya 2018, "Big things at Daguragu: Remembering the Gurindji Strike", *Red Flag*, https://redflag.org.au/gurindji/

McQueen, Humphrey 1976, *A New Britannia: An argument concerning the social origins of Australian radicalism and nationalism*, Penguin Books.

Middleton, Hannah 1977, *But now we want the land back: A History of the Australian Aboriginal People*, New Age Publishers.

Nightingale, Richard Beresford 2007, *Maori at Work: the Shaping of a Maori Workforce within the New Zealand State 1935-1975*, PhD Thesis, Massey University. https://mro.massey.ac.nz/bitstream/handle/10179/1422/02_whole.pdf?sequence=1&isAllowed=y

Norris, Murray 1982, *Rebuilding the North Australian Workers Union, 1942-1951*. http://roughreds.com/rrone/norris.html

O'Dowd, Mary Frances and Robyn Heckenberg 2020, "Explainer: What is decolonisation?" *The Conversation*, 23 June. https://theconversation.com/explainer-what-is-decolonisation-131455

Post, Charlie 2020, "Beyond 'Racial Capitalism' – Towards a Unified Theory of Capitalism and Racial Oppression", *Brooklyn Rail*, October. https://brooklynrail.org/2020/10/field-notes/Beyond-Racial-Capitalism-Toward-A-Unified-Theory-of-Capitalism-and-Racial-Oppression

Reynolds, Henry 2013, *Forgotten War*, NewSouth Books.

Roper, Brian 2011, "The fire last time: the rise of class struggle and progressive social movements in Aotearoa/New Zealand, 1968 to 1977", *Marxist Interventions*, 3. https://openresearch-repository.anu.edu.au/bitstream/1885/12557/1/Roper%20The%20fire%20last%20time%202011.pdf

Russell, Sophie and Chris Cunneen 2018, "As Indigenous incarceration rates keep rising, justice reinvestment offers a solution", *The Conversation*, 11 December. https://theconversation.com/as-indigenous-incarceration-rates-keep-rising-justice-reinvestment-offers-a-solution-107610

Sakai, J 2014 [1983], *Settlers: The Mythology of the White Proletariat from Mayflower to Modern*, Kersplebedeb Publishing.

Scrimgeour, Anne 2020, *On Red Earth Walking: The Pilbara Aboriginal Strike, Western Australia 1946-49*, Monash University Publishing.

Smith, Sharon 1994, "Mistaken Identity – or can identity politics liberate the oppressed?", *International Socialism*, 2:62, Spring. https://www.marxists.org/history/etol/newspape/isj2/1994/isj2-062/smith.htm

Stanbrook, Gavin and Fieldes, Diane 2019, "William Ferguson: The life of an Aboriginal rebel", *Marxist Left Review*, 18, Winter. https://marxistleftreview.org/articles/william-ferguson-the-life-of-an-aboriginal-rebel/

Thier, Daphna 2018, "What's the matter with the Israeli working class?", *International Socialist Review*, 110, Autumn. https://isreview.org/issue/110/whats-matter-israeli-working-class

Townsend, Terry 2009, *The Aboriginal Struggle & the Left*, Resistance Books. https://socialist-alliance.org/sites/default/files/aboriginal_struggle_the_left.pdf

Upchurch, Martin 2020, "Is there a new extractive capitalism?", *International Socialism*, 168, October. https://isj.org.uk/extractive-capitalism/

Venn, Danielle and Nicholas Biddle 2018, *2016 Census Papers: Employment Outcomes*, Centre for Aboriginal Economic Policy Research, ANU. https://caepr.cass.anu.edu.au/research/publications/employment-outcomes

Warriors of the Aboriginal Resistance 2014, *Manifesto*. https://issuu.com/brisbaneblacks/docs/war_manifesto_d91595ceee8754

Watson, Joanne 1995, "'We Couldn't Tolerate Any More': The Palm Island Strike of 1957", *Labour History*, 69, November.

Wells, Andrew David 1985, *A Marxist Reappraisal of Australian Capitalism: The Rise of Anglo-Colonial Finance Capital In New South Wales and Victoria, 1830-1890*, PhD thesis, ANU. https://openresearch-repository.anu.edu.au/handle/1885/121712

Wetherell, David 2004, "The Bishop of Carpentaria and the Torres Strait Pearlers' Strike of 1938", *The Journal of Pacific History*, 39 (2).

Wolfe, Patrick 2016, *Traces of History: Elementary Structures of Race*, Verso.

MICK ARMSTRONG

Between syndicalism and reformism: Founding the Communist Party of Australia

Mick Armstrong has been actively involved in socialist politics since the late 1960s. He is the author of numerous pamphlets and articles on revolutionary organisation and the Australian labour movement, including *The Industrial Workers of the World in Australia*, and *The Labor Party: A Marxist analysis*.

IN OCTOBER 1920, inspired by the successful workers' revolution in Russia, a group of radicals with a history in a variety of socialist and syndicalist organisations came together to found the Communist Party of Australia (CPA). The party was only tiny to begin with – perhaps 750 out of an Australian population of around 5 million at the time – but it had great hopes and expectations for a revolutionary challenge to capitalism.

Unfortunately it had been formed late, past the peak of the radical wave that had swept Australia during World War I and its immediate aftermath. Its initial years were difficult ones as it tried to come to grips with the revolutionary ideas of the Russian Bolsheviks and build a base in the working class. Indeed it was flat out even surviving the 1920s.

Nonetheless it was to go on in the 1930s and 1940s to build a powerful presence in the trade union movement. For decades committed rank and file Communist activists played leading roles in a vast array of workplace struggles, street protests, student politics and innumerable campaigns. Consequently the party built an influence that went well beyond the ranks of its formal membership. From the Popular Front years of the mid-1930s onwards, the party had a powerful impact on intellectual, artistic and broader small-l liberal circles, including even some Protestant religious groupings. While never in a position to seriously challenge the ALP as the leading force in the working-class movement, the CPA became per head of population the largest Communist party in the English-speaking world.[1]

The tragedy was that the politics that dominated the CPA from the 1930s onwards were those of Stalinism. The Stalinist vision of "socialism" was a dull grey authoritarian dictatorship in which working-class people had absolutely no control over their lives. This represented a total abandonment of Karl Marx's vision of socialism as a society of genuine human freedom. Though rank-and-file worker Communists undoubtedly played a positive role in many struggles, the overall impact of the Stalinist politics of the CPA and its fellow parties around the world was disastrous. They condemned the working-class movement internationally to decade after decade of needless defeats. The fact that they championed the murderous regimes in Russia, Eastern Europe and China as workers' paradises eventually served to help discredit the very idea of socialism among vast sections of the working class and the oppressed.

By the early 1930s the CPA had been turned into a rigid bureaucratic machine to serve the foreign policy goals of the Russian state. Then from the mid-1930s onwards the party advocated a class-collaborationist popular front approach which sacrificed workers' interests to the pursuit of alliances with assorted capitalist and middle-class forces that Russia's rulers were seeking to cultivate. For the next 50 years the Stalinist politics of the CPA and its various offshoots, such as the Maoist Communist Party of Australia (Marxist-Leninist) and the pro-Moscow Socialist Party of Australia (SPA), dominated left-wing politics in Australia. It came to ideologically hegemonise the outlook of much of the ALP left: reflected in the fact that when the pro-Moscow loyalists of the SPA split from the CPA in the early 1970s the NSW Labor left split along similar lines. The CPA's class-collaborationist approach ultimately culminated in the 1980s in the pivotal role prominent Communist union officials

---

1. For an overview of the history of the CPA see O'Lincoln 1985.

such as Laurie Carmichael, head of the then powerful Metalworkers Union, played in drafting the Prices and Incomes Accord used by the Hawke/Keating Labor government to undermine rank-and-file union organisation and impose some of the harshest cuts in wages in Australian history.

But this Stalinist class collaborationism was far from being the outlook of the rank-and-file worker militants and socialist activists who assembled together one hundred years ago in Sydney to found the CPA. They stood for working-class self-emancipation and an end to capitalist tyranny.

The political background

The context of the formation of the CPA was an enormous rupture in Australian society brought on by World War I.[2] Australia suffered one of the highest casualty rates of any of the combatant nations. At the third battle of Ypres alone, there were 38,000 Australian casualties. These statistics are manifested in every tiny country town, with the long list of names on the local war memorial of those who died for "King and country". These hypocritical memorials do not include the far greater numbers who suffered shattering injuries and lasting trauma (recognised today as PTSD) that destroyed their lives.

The Anglo-Australian ruling class was determined to make workers pay the cost of the imperialist war effort. They imposed the harsh War Precautions Act to crush dissent, and unleashed hysterical mobs of middle-class patriots and drunken soldiers to deal with "disloyalists" and leftists. Six thousand eight hundred and ninety people were interned in concentration camps. However the slaughter on the Western front, combined with savage attacks on living standards and democratic rights and the obscene profits of capitalist war profiteers, provoked a profound working-class radicalisation. A tremendous upsurge in strikes rocked the country during the war and its immediate aftermath.

The war provoked rebellions in country after country – two of which had major repercussions in Australia. First came the Easter 1916 Dublin rebellion. The murderous British reprisals against the

---

2. For an overview see Armstrong 2015.

rebel leaders and the subsequent war of Irish national liberation invoked enormous bitterness among Irish Australian workers, then about a quarter of the working class. These feelings were intensified by a wave of persecution of Irish Australians as traitors to the nation. This in turn entrenched anti-imperialist sentiments. Australian empire loyalists glorified the British Empire as the empire on which "the sun never set", but for a large section of Irish Australian workers and left-wing workers more generally it was the empire on which "the blood never dried". This polarisation led to a domination of ALP membership by Irish Australians which persisted for 50 years.

The October 1917 revolution in Russia was initially welcomed by virtually all wings of the labour movement. It was to have a transformative impact on the left as more information about the revolution gradually seeped through to far away Australia, whose isolation from international political developments had been compounded by harsh wartime censorship. By 1919 all the existing radical currents were being profoundly challenged ideologically. Among the broad masses the revolution inspired the hope of an alternative world in which working-class people called the shots. As one account put it: "Apocalypse was in the air in 1918 as workers, daily expecting peace, read ecstatic accounts of 'Russia's stupendous historic achievement'".[3]

Up until late 1915 the federal Labor governments of Andrew Fisher and then Billy Hughes, in cohorts with pro-war union officials, had largely held the line against working-class dissent. But then the dam began to burst with a spectacular series of predominantly victorious rank and file-led strikes: waterside workers in Melbourne, miners in the radical centre of Broken Hill, shearers in Queensland and NSW, Newcastle BHP steelworkers, Queensland meatworkers and most importantly NSW coal miners. Army enlistments collapsed. In Queensland, one of the most turbulent states, they fell from 3,890 in January 1916 to only 280 in January 1918.[4]

The attempt by the Hughes Labor government to impose conscription brought all the tensions to a head. Up until this point any public display of "disloyalty" had been assaulted by right-wing

---

3. Kennedy 1978, p. 155.
4. Penrose 1993.

mobs. Now the tables began to turn. A bitterly fought campaign of riotous public meetings, strikes and mass mobilisations, which saw the formation of worker militias to repulse attacks by right-wing mobs, led to the narrow defeat of conscription in the October 1916 referendum. The ALP was torn apart by the crisis. Formerly moderate union leaders, under pressure from an outraged rank and file, and fearing they would be outflanked by genuinely revolutionary forces, expelled pro-conscriptionists from the ALP, including Prime Minister Billy Hughes, NSW Premier William Holman and a host of other MPs. The tide was shifting sharply to the left.

On 2 August 1917 the Great Strike started in Sydney's tramway and railway workshops. Though centred in Sydney, it rapidly swept much of the country, drawing in up to 100,000 workers and lasting in all for 82 days.[5] This was no bureaucratic, top-down affair. It was a mass rank-and-file upsurge, with most workers walking out either in direct defiance of their officials or without their support. However no democratically controlled leadership emerged to propel the Great Strike forward to victory. There was no central leadership body to organise key tasks such as mass picketing to bring out more workers, the formation of worker defence squads to combat attacks by police and armed strike breakers, to produce daily strike bulletins, and above all to politically cohere workers in this direct confrontation with state power.

The revolutionary syndicalists of the Industrial Workers of the World (IWW or Wobblies), who had grown significantly on the basis of opposition to the war, proved incapable of playing this role. This failure in part reflected the IWW's inability to cope with harsh police repression. The more fundamental weakness, however, was that the IWW's syndicalist approach meant it did not see its role as fighting for the *political* leadership of the working class in a direct challenge to the power of the capitalist state. That would have entailed politically, and not simply industrially, challenging the reformist ALP and union officials. Tragically, no sizeable socialist party had emerged to fill the breach and to galvanise opposition to the union leaders and provide political direction to the insurgent

---

5. See Bollard 2013.

movement. This eventually enabled the officials, despite furious opposition from an outraged rank and file in numerous unions, to break the strike by forcing individual groups of workers back to work.[6]

So the greatest mass strike movement in Australian history went down to defeat, with widespread victimisations of militants. But this was far from the end of the story. Billy Hughes, installed after his expulsion from the ALP as the head of a conservative government, immediately attempted to take advantage of workers' demoralisation with another attempt to introduce conscription. He badly miscalculated.

Peace sentiment was growing and the 1917 second conscription referendum was defeated even more decisively than the first. It was particularly bitterly contested in Victoria, where young women and men in Melbourne's inner working-class suburbs repeatedly rioted and attacked ruling-class pro-conscription speakers. Meanwhile a huge crowd of 100,000 out of a total Melbourne population of 700,000 rallied at the old Richmond racecourse to cheer on defiant anti-conscription speakers.

Nineteen eighteen witnessed an industrial lull but in 1919 and 1920 workers won a series of stunning victories in a renewed surge of strike action. The Seamens Union, under new socialist leadership, openly defied the Arbitration Court with an illegal strike to win major gains in wages and conditions, despite the jailing of union secretary Tom Walsh, later a founding member of the CPA. In the radical centre of Broken Hill the 8,000 members of the syndicalist-led Amalgamated Miners Association (AMA) won an incredible victory, including a path-breaking 35-hour week for underground miners, after the 18-month-long "Big Strike" from May 1919 to November 1920.[7]

In Western Australia, after a bitter clash with armed police in May 1919, which saw one worker killed and seven badly wounded, Fremantle waterside workers backed by large crowds of working-class women succeeded in driving out the scabs brought in during the 1917 Great Strike. They went on to seize Fremantle and force the

---

6. Armstrong 2015, pp. 104-6.
7. For the Broken Hill "Great Strike" see Kennedy 1978.

conservative Colebatch government to resign. "Within the year", as historian Justina Williams writes,

> a goldminers strike was being fought out bitterly with armed "specials", and other strikes came thick and fast as mass discontent rose with unemployment, hunger and broken promises in the aftermath of the war. Transcontinental railway line workers, civil servants in Perth, miners at Collie, butchers, hotel and restaurant employees and many others were striking.[8]

In Townsville, an important centre of syndicalist strength and subsequently of the Communists, striking meatworkers in 1919 were fired on by police as they attempted to storm the police lock-up to free jailed strike leaders. In response, workers raided hardware stores to arm themselves and seized the city. In Charters Towers railworkers struck in solidarity to try to prevent police reinforcements sent by the state Labor government reaching Townsville.

Moderate and right-wing union officials were swept from office in union after union, including the powerful Waterside Workers' and Seamens' unions as well as the Ironworkers, Miscellaneous Workers and numerous smaller unions. Even the entrenched apparatus of the largest union in the country, the Australian Workers Union (AWU), faced a serious challenge with an IWW supporter polling surprisingly well in the 1916 AWU elections against the union founder WG Spence. Then in May 1918, the radical Jock Garden, a delegate from the tiny Sailmakers Union, was elected secretary of the then most important peak union body – the NSW Labour Council. Garden, described by historian Stuart Macintyre as "[c]ourageous, generous, a born fixer and utterly shameless in his opportunism", grouped around himself a coterie of left-wing union officials – the Trades Hall reds – who went on to play a central role in the early CPA.[9]

Various syndicalist and socialist organisations were prominent in these upheavals and grew substantially. In Victoria a leading role in the anti-conscription movement was played by the left reformist Victorian Socialist Party (VSP) which grew to about 640 members in 1918. But the revolutionary syndicalists of the IWW were the most

---
8. Williams 1976, p. 69.
9. Macintyre 1998, p. 17.

flamboyant and well known, growing rapidly during the early years of the war from only 199 members at the end of 1913 to a peak of about 2,000 (1,500 of whom were in Sydney).[10] Yet the IWW was smashed by savage government repression which saw the core of its leadership and hundreds of members jailed and/or deported. Repression, however, could not put an end to the broader radicalisation, and under the inspiration of the successful socialist revolution in Russia, radicals began to rethink their politics and regroup.

The tentative first steps

The CPA's foundation is usually traced to a meeting of 26 leftists on Saturday 30 October 1920 in the Australian Socialist Party's hall in Liverpool Street, Sydney. But the reality was that under the impact of the Bolshevik triumph in Russia and the subsequent formation of the Communist International (Comintern), various currents on the left had been organising for some time to bring about the formation of a Communist party in Australia. An initial impetus came from radicals in the small but highly politicised Russian exile community associated with the paper *Knowledge and Unity*, many of whom had fled to Australia after the defeat of the 1905 Russian revolution. The Bolsheviks installed one of their leaders, Petr Simonov, as the Soviet consul for Australia. Simonov was supported by the two radical socialist MPs from the militant mining centre of Broken Hill, Mick Considine and Percy Brookfield.

In Melbourne Simonov linked up with left-wing VSP members, such as Bill Earsman, and the syndicalists Guido Baracchi and Percy Laidler, then leaders of the International Industrial Workers (IIW), one of the fragments that had regrouped some former members of the outlawed IWW. Baracchi and Laidler embraced the Russian revolution, proclaiming:

> The risen star of communist Russia is shining in the firmament, and not all the powers of darkness can dim its splendour. By its light we can see that the long vista of capitalism is nearly ended. Capitalism and Communism cannot continue to exist in the world

---

10. Burgmann 1995, p. 126.

together, and since Communism has come to stay, it is capitalism which must go.[11]

Baracchi and Laidler produced the *Proletarian Review*, which developed the clearest understanding of any Australian left-wing publication of the Bolsheviks' revolutionary Marxist politics. *Proletarian Review* played an important role in publicising the writings of Lenin and other Bolshevik leaders who had previously been completely unknown in Australia.

But in these years Sydney was the main game. It was where the workers' movement was strongest, where the mass radicalisation had most severely ruptured the ALP and where the Trades Hall reds controlled the most important labour council in the country. As well, the more left-wing socialist groups, like the Australian Socialist Party (ASP) and the De Leonite Socialist Labor Party (SLP), were led from Sydney.

Despite the smashing of the IWW, syndicalism in various forms easily remained the dominant current on the left. Syndicalism had developed a significant following among worker activists in the pre-war years, as industrial militancy slowly revived from the harsh defeats of the bitter class struggles of the 1890s and the long drawn out depression that followed. There was a wave of strikes between 1909 and 1912 that reached its high point in the Brisbane general strike of 1912 which brought the city to a virtual standstill. Syndicalism represented a healthy reaction against the failures of parliamentary reformism. Syndicalism, and above all the IWW version of it, was marked by a profound workerism, an irreverent defiance of the bosses and of all the institutions of capitalism and contempt for parliament and Labor politicians.[12]

Australia had the first social-democratic governments in the world. Before World War I Labor had already held office for prolonged periods federally and in most states (except Victoria) and had dismally failed to meet the expectations of militant activists. Syndicalism also grew as a reaction against the conservative bureaucratic approach of union officialdom and the sectional

---

11. Industrial Solidarity No 6, 22 November 1919.
12. See Armstrong 2006.

nature of the plethora of tiny craft-based unions. As early as 1909 the industrial unionist ideas of the US IWW were finding a resonance among militants in key sections of the workforce – coal miners, meat workers, shearers, railworkers and waterfront workers.

The IWW looked to organising all workers, whatever their trade, occupation, race, gender, religion or political allegiance, in industrial unions which would be linked up into the "One Big Union". They stood for unrelenting class struggle with militant direct action on the job to advance workers' immediate demands. They saw industrial unions as laying the basis of a new society of workers' power within the shell of the old world of capitalism. Capitalism would be overcome and socialism installed when workers were fully organised. For some syndicalists, once workers were organised in industrial unions they would simply have to fold their arms in a general strike to inherit the earth.

The war sharpened the appeal of syndicalism and hostility to middle-class politicians as it was a federal Labor government that was imposing sacrifices on workers to aid the imperial war effort. In the aftermath of the defeat of the 1917 Great Strike, support for the idea of the One Big Union (OBU) as a means to take on the bosses surged among unionised workers. Australia had the highest rate of unionisation in the world in this period – 46 percent of the workforce nationally in 1920 and 56 percent in NSW, the most important state.[13] A clear majority of these organised workers, even in right wing-led unions like the AWU, embraced the idea of the OBU.

There were, however, competing conceptions about how the OBU would be organised and heated debates among the various syndicalist currents. The most important debate was over whether the OBU would be built in a highly democratic way from the bottom up and based on strong shop floor organisation, as the more radical syndicalists organised in groups such as the Workers International Industrial Union (WIIU) and the One Big Union Propaganda League (OBUPL) advocated, or a more top-down approach advocated by left union officials.

The most powerful OBU-supporting current was headed by the

---

13. Markey 1994, p. 20.

Sydney Trades Hall reds – union officials and their coterie of supporters who were in alliance with the head of the powerful miners' union, AC Willis. The Trades Hall reds' OBU scheme, the Workers Industrial Union of Australia (WIUA), was endorsed by representatives of 150 NSW unions in August 1918 and a similar gathering of Queensland unions in the same month and subsequently by a national gathering of unions in Melbourne in January 1919.

These left officials basically had a top-down approach but couched it in ultra-maximalist rhetoric. Reflecting the radical mood among the rank and file, miners' leader Willis, who was in no sense the most left-wing of these officials, insisted at the national Trade Union Congress in June 1921 that it was impossible for workers to gain political power without resorting to violence: "[I]t is no good asking people to vote. Instead...we should be here discussing...the formation of a Red Army".[14]

There was a wildly utopian element to the OBU schema. Jock Garden in his Secretary's Report in December 1919 hailed the OBU:

> Organised Labour, I am conscious, will welcome the new order, and will march united to enter the promised land – the land of Freedom, the land of Liberty. He will exclaim, "Eureka! Eureka! I have found it. Emancipation! Emancipation!"[15]

Somehow the bosses and their state were going to surrender their wealth and power simply because workers had come together in one big industrial union. There was no practical plan for their overthrow; no strategy for challenging the capitalist state or the hegemony of reformist political forces over workers.

The Trades Hall reds' OBU scheme was initially backed by most socialist groups, including the ASP, VSP and even the arch-sectarian SLP. The overwhelming consensus of militant socialists at the end of the war was that the revolutionary tide sweeping Europe was unstoppable, that Australia too was on the brink of revolution and that the revolutionary force that would overthrow capitalism was the OBU. As VSP leader Bob Ross put it, the One Big Union was the

---

14. Penrose 1993.
15. Morrison 1977, p. 190.

"transition to revolution and the revolution itself".[16] But virtually no one on the left – be they socialists or syndicalists – had a clear idea of what the revolution would actually consist of. There was no conception of workers taking power via workers' councils or soviets, no clear understanding of the role of a revolutionary socialist party in a revolutionary upheaval, the strategic necessity of insurrection, and so on.

The actual program of the WIUA's version of the OBU was almost identical to that of the SLP which was affiliated to the De Leonite SLP in the US. The De Leonites combined abstract propagandism with a large dollop of both syndicalism and electoralism. They held to the "sword and shield" concept of working-class emancipation: industrial action would supposedly wrest control of industry from the capitalists, while parliamentary political action, by neutralising the state apparatus, would defend the industrial action. The SLP initially hailed the Russian Revolution as confirming their version of syndicalism:

> The Russian revolution has proved a thundering endorsement of the principles of Socialist Industrial Unionism... They [the Russian workers] are making realities of our theories.[17]

The SLP had no real understanding of the significance of what had been achieved in the Russian revolution or how it had been brought about.

An ill-planned split

The Trades Hall reds and their ALP supporters attempted to win the June 1919 NSW Labor conference to support their OBU schema for getting rid of capitalism and establishing socialism. They were only narrowly defeated. They immediately walked out and, in coalition with socialist groups already outside the ALP, tried to form a mass socialist party. This was a chaotic affair and not a well planned split. The left officials had not politically prepared the rank and file of the unions they led for the task of setting up a new socialist party to challenge the ALP.

---

16. Morrison 1977, p. 147.
17. Morrison 1977, p. 145.

The program of the Industrial Socialist Labor Party (ISLP) that eventually emerged was similar to that of the De Leonite SLP:

> Inasmuch as industrial action produces its political reflex, the ISLP recognises the use of revolutionary political action... as distinct from the palliative-mongering parliamentarianism of non-revolutionary parties, to be essential to the complete overthrow of the capitalist system.[18]

After some initial signs of promise the ISLP quickly collapsed.[19] It was unable to cohere a mass membership on a sustained basis. The exception was Broken Hill, where the socialist MP Percy Brookfield, supported by the syndicalist-led miners union, took out the bulk of the large local ALP membership. The difference was not simply that Broken Hill miners were exceptionally militant. A group of socialist and syndicalist leaders had emerged who had won widespread respect and support among workers because of their dynamic role in leading industrial and political struggles. These socialist leaders in turn had waged a prolonged and politically clarifying fight for some years against the reformist local Labor MPs and their craft union supporters who had not campaigned wholeheartedly against conscription.

There were clear lessons from the experience of the failed ISLP split. Very broad layers of workers had come to support the OBU as a means to fight to improve their immediate living standards. They also viewed favourably the idea of challenging capitalism and ushering in a socialist society. That didn't mean that they had developed a thorough critique of the ALP or saw Labor as totally unreformable, let alone a critique of reformism more generally. And it definitely did not mean that *overnight* they would abandon any lingering illusions in Labor merely on the say-so of their union officials, many of whom had long been active players in the ALP. There had to be a prolonged process of political and ideological clarification. The left officials could not simply summon a mass socialist party into existence by proclamation.

---

18. Morrison 1977, p. 136.
19. For the history of the ISLP see Adams 2013.

Turmoil on the left

In the period of profound ideological and organisational turmoil on the left between 1917 and 1921, numerous new socialist and syndicalist groups quickly blossomed and then disappeared seemingly overnight. Prominent activists might have passed through three or four different groups. Historian Ian Turner lists 13 different socialist and syndicalist groups in the period between July 1918 and 1920, and he undoubtedly overlooked a few.[20] Existing organisations underwent a process of splits and fusions. The Social Democratic League (SDL), for example, which split from the ASP in 1917 and joined the ALP, quickly grew to about 400 members in Sydney and 140 in Adelaide. By November 1918 the SDL was calling for socialist unity on the basis of Bolshevism, which it saw as superior to the outmoded syndicalist idea of the One Big Union. Some of its members then rejoined the ASP and by 1920 the SDL was defunct. The revolutionary syndicalists of the WIIU could sell 1,000 copies of their paper the *One Big Union Herald* every Saturday night in Melbourne's Bourke St – but were unable to build a stable organisation.[21]

In the immediate aftermath of the abortive ISLP split, the highly pragmatic and non-theoretical Jock Garden and some of his Trades Hall reds supporters briefly joined the most dogmatic and sectarian of all the socialist groups, the De Leonite SLP. This was a group which very much saw itself as the one true faith and adopted a sneering, superior tone towards all other socialist currents.

The SLP's key leader, Ernie Judd, was a prominent Trades Hall delegate and had played a leading role in the defence campaign for the IWW prisoners and in the OBU movement. Unbeknownst to Judd, however, the arch manoeuvrer Garden, while still formally an SLP member, began to work with the Soviet consul Simonov, various ex-Wobblies and other assorted syndicalists and radicals, including the grouping around Guido Baracchi and Percy Laidler in Melbourne, to form a secret underground Communist party. A major ideological force behind these developments appears to have been ex-VSP member and ex-syndicalist Bill Earsman, who had moved to Sydney

---
20. Turner 1965, p. 233.
21. Walker 1972, p. 162.

in December 1919 to develop a Labor College in close association with Trades Hall. Earsman, who quickly became a strong influence on Garden, was to become the first CPA secretary.

When Judd found out about these manoeuvrings in late 1920, he expelled Garden and his supporters. This did not prevent the SLP subsequently losing branches to the CPA once it had been openly declared. The SLP's sectarian aloofness made it incapable of holding the line among its own rank-and-file members against the enormous appeal for the founding of a Communist party that united all revolutionary socialists. The SLP lost most of its women members and its main bases in the NSW coal towns of West Wallsend, Corrimal, Lithgow and Cessnock, its most active branch.

Sussex St or Liverpool St?

By August or September 1920 word of the underground CP's existence was beginning to seep out. Specifically it came to the attention of the ASP, the largest of the small left-wing socialist groups, which had become more critical of the limitations of the OBU movement and was seeking to turn itself into a Communist party. Previously, in August 1919, the ASP had organised an abortive conference for socialist unity on the basis of support for Bolshevism, in which it had hoped to involve the SLP and other forces. Subsequently the ASP's December 1919 conference declared its support for the Communist International.[22] It was the ASP that took the initiative to call the unity conference on 20 October 1920 in an attempt to outflank its Trade Hall red rivals, whom the ASP viewed, not totally wrongly, as opportunist.

However the ASP turned out to be in a distinct minority among those who attended the 20 October 1920 conference, which included a heterogeneous collection of Trades Hall reds, syndicalists, ex-VSP members such as former militant British suffragette Adela Pankhurst, ex-SLP members and independent socialists. The ASP abandoned ship just weeks later, provoked by Earsman's and Garden's manoeuvrings. The ASP formed its own Communist Party, dubbed the Liverpool St CPA as opposed to the Trades Hall reds'

---

22. Australian Socialist Party 1919.

Sussex St CPA. Then for over 18 months there were two CPAs expending much of their energy in a highly sectarian battle on both sides for recognition from the Comintern, which consistently argued for them to unite.

So, a disastrous start. Members ebbed away, alienated by the sectarian infighting. Recruitment dried up. Momentum was lost and the opportunity to build on the enthusiasm for the Russian revolution wasted. The high point of working-class struggle and political radicalisation had passed by the end of 1922. The economy began to pick up and Australian capitalism temporarily stabilised.

The ASP had high hopes of winning out in the battle for Comintern recognition, in part because of its better connections in Moscow. Fedor Sergeev (Artem), a former ASP member, had been elected to the Bolshevik Central Committee. He and Paul Freeman, another former ASP supporter who had been briefly sent from Moscow as a Comintern agent to Australia, were active in Moscow pleading the ASP's case. Tragically both Sergeev and Freeman were killed in a train crash in July 1921. The ASP was also a more cohered force in 1921, with an established organisation in Sydney, though it had been somewhat weakened by earlier splits. It had lost its Adelaide and Melbourne branches, which continued to adhere to syndicalism after the ASP moved sharply away from it at its December 1918 conference. It was soon to lose more of its members outside Sydney, including its Brisbane and Newcastle branches, to the Sussex St party.

In June 1922 an increasingly exasperated Comintern Presidium wrote to the two Australian CPs demanding that they unite before 1 September 1922:

> Those who for any reason do anything to prevent unity...bear a heavy responsibility not only before the Communist International, to which they claim affiliation, but also before the mass of the working class.
>
> The existence of two small groups, *amidst a seething current of world shaking events*, engaged almost entirely in airing their petty differences, instead of unitedly plunging into the current and

mastering it, is not only a ridiculous and shameful spectacle, but also a crime committed against the working class.[23]

In a formal sense the ASP-aligned CPA had somewhat clearer revolutionary politics than the Sussex St party. For example it criticised Jock Garden's deals with the right-wing AWU to gain support for the OBU. Garden had gone as far as not opposing the AWU's racist exclusion clause banning Asians from membership. He had also offered to guarantee that the officials of unions that joined the OBU would still hold onto their full-time positions for three years. Add to all that Garden was manoeuvring to form a bloc with the AWU in order to obtain CPA affiliation to the ALP.

However the ASP's refusal to countenance unity on virtually any terms left it increasingly isolated. It began to suffer internal dissent and defections. Eventually the ASP leadership's rejection of a fair and democratic Comintern-backed proposal for unity led a majority of its Sydney rank-and-file members to split away and unite with the Sussex St CPA in July 1922. The "united" party then received formal recognition as the Australian section of the Communist International.

Fighting for clarity

The new party, however, remained extremely unclear politically. As previously stated, the main current on the Australian left at the time was syndicalism, which deprecated the need for a revolutionary party. The committed syndicalists were sincere working-class fighters with many great strengths compared to the opportunist Labor MPs and union bureaucrats. However the defeat of the 1917 Great Strike and the collapse of the IWW, when contrasted to the success of the Bolshevik revolution, sharply highlighted the need for a revolutionary party to lead workers to victory. Some syndicalist activists, such as those around Baracchi and Laidler in the IIW in Melbourne, had begun to draw some of these lessons by 1920. However, most of them still had little real understanding of the process of the Russian revolution, the role of soviets (workers' councils) or what a genuine revolutionary party would look like.

---
23. Lovell and Windle 2008, pp. 134-35.

Take the case of former IWW leader Tom Glynn, who on his release after nearly four years in prison, worked with the Trades Hall reds to form the CPA and briefly became the first editor of its paper, *Australian Communist*. In 1920 he wrote a foreword to the Australian edition of the pamphlet *To the IWW: A Special Message from the Communist International* by leading Bolshevik Zinoviev:

> [T]he Russian experience would indicate the necessity of something more than the industrial weapon for combatting the internal and external machinations of the capitalist class...but the view that the Industrial Union should ultimately be the unit of administration in the communist state remains unchallenged.[24]

Glynn's continuing adherence to the central role of industrial unions soon led him to fall out with the CPA. The differences were accentuated as the CPA came to an understanding that the One Big Union was not going to be an adequate vehicle for the overthrow of capitalism, and indeed that the movement for the OBU had by late 1921 clearly failed. Rejecting this, Glynn went on to form the Industrial Union Propaganda League with other ex-Wobblies, including JB King, Norman Rancie and George Washington, and left the CPA in November 1921. A brief rapprochement was patched together, but the final straw for Glynn and Co. came in March 1922 with the confirmation of the CPA's decision to give tactical but critical support to the ALP in the upcoming NSW elections.

The syndicalists had no serious strategy for winning over workers influenced by the ALP – other than virulent denunciations of the myriad betrayals of the Labor leaders. Indeed some syndicalists retreated even further into a sectarian "anti-political" standpoint. The Betsy Matthias-led Industrial Labor Party, which grouped around it a number of former IWW members, declared:

> The IWW in Australia was a non-political organization. The Industrial Labor Party is an anti-political organization. An aggressive fight is necessary against all misleading Labor fakirs... One of the misfortunes of the IWW in Australia and the tragic experience resulting and the new needs dictated by

---

24. Morrison 1977, p. 146.

new conditions, the ILP proceeds on more scientific lines in construction and propaganda.[25]

In a major step forward, the Comintern argued instead for a united front approach of working alongside reformist organisations in struggles around concrete demands to improve workers' lives. The breakthrough was understanding that winning masses of workers away from their reformist leaders would happen more easily in the heat of the struggle. The united front approach did not entail any political concessions to the reformist leaders. It was not a non-aggression pact. The revolutionaries needed to maintain their own independent organisations and not blunt their criticisms of the reformists. The approach was summed up in the slogan "March separately but strike together!" But in Australia in the early 1920s almost nobody on the left agreed with, understood or was capable of flexibly implementing a united front approach in a principled manner.[26]

Many syndicalists and sectarian socialists either refused to join or left the CPA in the 1920s as they decried the united front approach to social-democratic parties such as the ALP as a capitulation to reformism. Indeed, so wildly sectarian was the approach of some fragments from the old IWW that they were only attracted to the CPA at the height of the ultra-sectarian Third Period policy of the 1930s, when the party was denouncing the ALP as "social fascist" and left-wing ALP members as "left socialist fascists". The fact that the CPA was by then increasingly Stalinised and authoritarian did not deter the relatively strong Adelaide IWW group joining the CPA en bloc in February 1931.[27] IWW supporters also joined the CPA in Perth and other cities in this period, including former jailed Wobbly leader JB King. They were enamoured of Stalinist Russia precisely at the time that the few remaining gains of the revolution were being wiped out as Stalin unleashed a horrific wave of repression against workers and peasants. Tragically King, one of the Wobbly heroes, after rejoining the CPA in 1930, then went to

---

25. Burgmann 1995, p. 236.
26. For an outline of the united front strategy see Kuhn 2011.
27. Moss 1983, pp. 20-22.

Russia, where he spent years forcing workers to speed up production and do hours of unpaid overtime as part of Stalin's Stakhanovite operation.

Those who rightly rejected the sectarian dismissal of the ALP tried instead to permeate Labor to push it to the left or even to win it to socialism. That was the approach of numerous individual socialists and – with various fits and starts – of the Victorian Socialist Party. The CPA was initially much weaker in Victoria, where the VSP had long been the dominant force on the left. After appointing former British suffragette Adela Pankhurst as its paid organiser, the VSP put on a very militant face. In late 1917 Pankhurst led thousands of working-class women in cost of living protests which were marked by large scale rioting in the streets of Melbourne. Out of this activity the VSP recruited a substantial number of women and by 1918 women made up half of their membership, which was very unusual for any socialist organisation in this period.

The VSP, however, was increasingly divided over its attitude to Labor, with the left of the party in 1917 calling for running VSP candidates against Labor, while the mainstream leadership around Bob Ross maintained its attachment to Labor. The internal fight accelerated in the aftermath of the Russian revolution, which put wind in the sails of the radicals. The VSP left, which previously had a largely syndicalist outlook, now strongly identified with the Bolsheviks and called for the reorganisation of the VSP into a Communist Party and affiliation to the Comintern. The reformist leadership around Ross, who by 1919/1920 was moving further to the right, beat off the left challenge, but at great cost. Splits, resignations and expulsions reduced the VSP to only 85 members by 1921. It lost members both to its left and right with many simply dropping out of politics. The more revolutionary-inclined of its ex-members helped form the initially small Victorian CPA branch, while others on the more conservative wing retreated into the ALP. Why be active in a small reformist party when a much larger one existed? After 1922 the remaining rump of the VSP became a tiny and vitriolic anti-communist sect and by 1931 it had disbanded.

In Sydney the Garden-led Trades Hall reds adopted yet another mistaken third approach to the reformists. Desperate to regain influence in the ALP, they interpreted the united front in a thoroughly opportunist fashion. The Comintern leadership's lack of in-depth understanding of the Australian political situation did not help matters. At the Fourth Comintern Congress in November-December 1922 they were too easily taken in by Garden's bluster about how much influence the CPA had over the mass of workers, when in fact by then party membership had probably declined to no more than 250.[28] Garden's wild claims that the CPA had won the leadership over 400,000 workers and established Communist cells in virtually every union do not seem to have been challenged by the Comintern executive. Indeed, incredibly they even elected him to the executive! Meanwhile back in Australia an embarrassed CPA executive disowned Garden's report.[29]

The question of affiliation to the ALP

Lenin proposed that the small British CP attempt to affiliate to the newly formed British Labour Party. The idea was an extension of the united front approach; he hoped that it would give the Communists better access to Labour's mass working-class base and make it easier to win workers to revolutionary politics. Lenin was probably over optimistic. He seems to have underestimated the political weight and resilience of reformism in the West. Nonetheless Lenin was clear that the Communists still needed to maintain their own independent organisation and make no political concession to the reformist Labour leaders.

Whether the affiliation tactic was appropriate in Britain in the early 1920s is arguable. But there were dangers in transposing the tactic to the very different Australian circumstances. By the 1920s the ALP was a long established, deeply entrenched bureaucratic party with a vast cohort of duplicitous MPs. It had been in government at a state and federal level on numerous occasions and loyally served the interests of the capitalist class. Moreover by the early 1920s the ALP leadership was moving decisively back to the right. It had put behind it the more radical phase in which, under pressure from the anti-conscription movement and the mass industrial upsurge,

---

28. Macintyre 1998, p. 84.
29. The Communist, 16 February 1923.

the party had been forced to move left and adopt the Socialisation Objective.

In December 1922, immediately after the Fourth Comintern Congress, the Comintern Executive wrote to the CPA arguing: "We should rather fight within the Labor Party and capture it by waging the fight against the social traitors in the mass party".[30] However the idea that the small, politically confused CPA could have any hope of making substantial inroads into the ALP – let alone taking control – was a totally overblown orientation. As Ross Edmonds writes:

> While the CPA's short lived alliance with left wingers in the ALP succeeded in having numerous resolutions carried in favour of nationalisation of industry, little came of it. Many communists dropped their CPA membership preferring to stay in the ALP when faced with having to decide between the two. The policy also had the effect of submerging the identity of the CPA and lowering its public profile.[31]

The Comintern's approach unfortunately helped provide cover for Garden's wretched deal-making with the corrupt, right-wing AWU officials in order to gain CPA affiliation to the NSW ALP.

Opposition to affiliation to the ALP came from both the ASP Liverpool St CP and various members of Garden's own Sussex St CP. In mid-1921 the Sussex St party executive rejected Garden's proposal to join the ALP. At the Fourth Comintern Congress in 1922 CPA Secretary Bill Earsman argued vigorously against the Comintern's Anglo-American Bureau's decision to instruct the Australian party to immediately apply for ALP membership. Even the December 1922 conference of the united party formed between the Sussex St CP and the group of members who had broken away from the ASP CP voted that "as the policy of the Communist International was for party affiliation to and membership in the Labor party, the conference was bound to accept same and work for its realisation".[32] Not exactly a ringing endorsement!

Reflecting the CPA's lack of understanding of the nature

---

30. Lovell and Windle 2008, pp. 154-55.
31. Edmonds 1991, p. 10.
32. The Communist, 5 January 1923.

of reformist parties like the ALP, *The Communist*'s report of the conference declared: "The Labor Party is the Political expression of the working class".³³ But this is simply not the case at all. As I have argued elsewhere:

> [T]he Labor Party is a "capitalist workers' party". It defends the interests of capitalism (particularly when in government) but relies for support on the votes of workers. The leadership of the ALP is thoroughly committed to running capitalism in the interests of the bosses and if that means attacking workers' rights and living standards, so be it.³⁴

Far from expressing the interests of the working class, reformist parties like the ALP are the expression of the pro-capitalist interests of the parliamentarians, union officials and party apparatchiks that dominate and control them. The social interests of this labour bureaucracy are ultimately opposed to those of the working class. Indeed the labour bureaucrats act as the agents of the bourgeoisie within the working-class movement.

The Communist further argued:

> Politically the working class in Australia finds its fullest expression in the Labor Party. The aims, ideals, leadership of the Labor Party remain anti-revolutionary because the workers themselves lack class-consciousness, and, so far as large sections are concerned, are still dominated by middle class prejudices and ideology.³⁵

This approach wrongly blames the pro-capitalist politics of the ALP and its leaders on the working class. It reflects the classic elitist arguments of left-wing union bureaucrats who blame the "backwardness" of workers for their own opportunist sins. According to this mechanical logic, if the mass of workers became revolutionary the ALP and its leadership would follow. And flowing from this it would be possible to transform the ALP into a revolutionary party. But the MPs and union bureaucrats in control of the ALP were, and still are, totally committed to pro-capitalist reformist politics irrespective of

---

33. The Communist, 5 January 1923.
34. Armstrong and Bramble 2007, p. 2.
35. The Communist, 5 January 1923.

the opinions of the mass of workers. There was no way that they were going to abandon their loyalty to capitalism. They would use all the power and bureaucratic levers they possessed, including calling in the courts, the police and all the forces of the state, to ensure any rank-and-file insurgency was contained or crushed.

By 1923 Garden was clearly the dominant figure in the CPA. The party's continuing confusion about the nature of reformism was reflected at its December 1923 Congress, which after calling for "the intensification of the fight for affiliation to the ALP", declared that "[t]he attitude of the Communist Party to the Labor Party is identical with its attitude towards the trade unions".[36]

But there is a vital distinction between the union movement and the ALP. Unions are the basic defence organisation of the working class. To be effective they need to organise all the workers in any specific industry irrespective of their politics, whether they be reformists, conservatives, syndicalists or revolutionaries. In sharp distinction membership of the ALP involves a political selection – support for a parliamentary-oriented reformist party. Consequently there is much greater space for revolutionary activity in the unions than there is in a clear cut reformist party like the ALP.

At the June 1923 NSW Labor conference a motion agreeing in principle to CPA affiliation to the ALP was carried (after a tied vote of 122 for and 122 against) on the casting vote of the chair, Miners Union secretary AC Willis. Two Communists, Jock Garden and Jack Howie, present as union delegates, were elected to the ALP state executive. This galvanised the Labor right, who unleashed all their bureaucratic tricks to reverse the decision. In October 1923 the ALP executive purged Garden and Howie from the executive and expelled all known Communists. The ALP federal executive extended the ban nationally.

The CPA initiated a concerted campaign to reverse the expulsions, in the course of which it downplayed its differences with the ALP, claiming both parties desired socialism. However the Easter 1924 NSW ALP conference voted 159 to 110 to reject CPA affiliation – though the leading Stalinist historian EW Campbell claims it was

---

36. Workers Weekly, 11 January 1924.

a rigged vote and that "[t]he number of members represented by the supporters of the Executive was only 31,300, while the number represented by those in favour of unity was 113,000".[37] The affiliation campaign, however, did nothing to strengthen the CPA whose financial membership only averaged 75 in 1924.[38] Rank-and-file CPers were gradually being purged from the ALP, or worse still, giving up on the CPA and accommodating to the ALP.

In the immediate aftermath of the ALP ban on CPA membership, Garden argued that CPA comrades who were still in the ALP should keep their communist affiliations secret. He defended this approach at the December 1924 CPA congress. But by then Garden's influence was waning and the majority of the leadership opposed him as his approach flew in the face of the Comintern's insistence that the CPA maintain its own independent political existence and standpoint. Instead the leadership called on secret CPA members of the ALP to openly declare their party membership and defy the ALP bureaucrats to expel them. The leadership repeated this instruction a year later but found that many of the secret members refused to do so.[39] The shift in approach came way too late. The rot ran deep. A layer of rank-and-file members had been needlessly lost to reformism because of the opportunist approach championed by Garden and his supporters and left unchallenged by the Comintern.

Indeed in December 1924 Garden himself acknowledged the problem that he had done much to create via his incessant manoeuvring:

> In some cases the interpretation of the United Front has led to the subordination of the party – to the point of elimination. The Labor Party has been more to the party members than the party itself, many subordinating themselves completely to the tactics and ideology of the Labor Party... The tactics of the party must be to swing the workers into action, and at the same time to keep the identity of the Communist Party unimpaired.[40]

---

37. Campbell 1945, p. 117.
38. Macintyre 1998, p. 94.
39. Davidson 1969, pp. 33-34.
40. Workers Weekly, 19 December 1924.

By 1925 most of the union bureaucrats associated with the Trades Hall reds had decamped for the greener pastures of the ALP. Robert Heffron ended up NSW premier, Jack Beasley became a Curtin government cabinet minister, JJ Graves became NSW ALP secretary and Jack Kilburn became NSW ALP vice-president and a member of the executive of both the ACTU and federal Labor. Garden followed them in 1926. According to historian Irwin Young, in 1925 or 1926 Garden, desperate to be allowed back into the ALP, had quietly come to an arrangement with Labor's parliamentary leader Jack Lang. In return for Trades Hall backing Lang, who was under challenge from rivals in caucus, Garden would be allowed to rejoin the ALP.[41]

The departure of Garden and the coterie of left officials was no loss. They had made it impossible for the party to orient correctly on a range of fronts. The tragedy was that many good rank-and-file worker members, who had been the hope for the future of the party, had also been lost. As well, an enormous amount of party time and resources had been spent pursuing a fruitless campaign for ALP affiliation rather than pursuing other channels for building the party.

It could be argued by supporters of the affiliation tactic that Garden's unprincipled approach meant that it was never properly tested in the 1920s; that if a principled revolutionary approach had been adopted the CPA could have made substantial gains from entrism into the ALP. We can't rerun the film of history so we can never definitely know either way. However entrism by revolutionaries into a reformist party is never easy. There is an enormous pressure to accommodate and tone down your revolutionary politics to what is acceptable to the party mainstream and to avoid expulsion. The idea that the poorly cohered and ideologically weak CPA of the 1920s, even without the burden of Garden's opportunist presence, could have successfully withstood the pressure from an entrenched, rightward moving Labor apparatus and made substantial gains from entrism, seems to me highly fanciful.

---

41. Young 1971, p. 70.

A brief stabilisation before final Stalinisation

By 1925 the CPA was in utter disarray. Membership had shrunk substantially to a claimed 280, but with an activist core of just a few dozen, turnover was rapid, party education was weak and finances were in dire straits. One of the original party founders, Guido Baracchi, called for dissolving the party into the ALP. It took a concerted effort by the Irish Marxist Jack Kavanagh, who had been a leader of the Canadian CP, to turn things around. Quickly after arriving in Australia on May Day 1925, Kavanagh began to play a prominent role in the CPA and waged a spirited attack on Garden's opportunism in the union movement and the ALP. He did this through open democratic debate, not bureaucratic fiat. Kavanagh conducted a lengthy public debate with Garden in the party paper *Workers Weekly*, something that would have been unthinkable later in the authoritarian Stalinised CPA of the 1930s.

Though he still supported the tactic of voting for the ALP in elections Kavanagh declared: "In no circumstances can the ALP be converted into the party that can lead the workers into emancipation".[42] The December 1925 CPA National Conference, at which Kavanagh was elected party secretary, declared:

> The social composition of the ALP branches and the undemocratic method of the election of its officials makes it a ready weapon in the hands of middle class politicians. With the CP in a numerically weak state much valuable time was undoubtedly wasted which might have been profitably employed in building up a strong Communist Party.[43]

Kavanagh initiated a serious education program to raise the political level of the membership. He turned the party away from manoeuvrings at Trades Hall and in the ALP to a focus on building a base in the workplaces.[44] As Phil Griffiths put it, under Kavanagh's leadership,

> everything about the party became more serious and systematic.
> In this period, the Communist Party undertook a wide range

---

42. Workers Weekly, 24 September 1926.
43. Workers Weekly, 8 January 1926.
44. For the debate over the early CPA's trade union policy see Armstrong 2013.

of campaigns for women's rights – a level of activity that belies the party's small female membership. The party established the Militant Women's Group (MWG) in 1926, and then began to organise women's study circles and train speakers and organised Australia's first International Women's Day in 1928.[45]

Kavanagh faced objective difficulties in rebuilding the party, but it slowly revived in 1926 and 1927. By the end of 1928 the CPA under Kavanagh's leadership had grown to about 300 members. But the combination of its own small size and the less favourable objective situation meant the party was unable to sink deep roots in the working class outside a few restricted areas. Capitalism had temporarily stabilised before another great crash at the end of the 1920s. Yet there were still opportunities for Communist intervention and growth. Though living standards rose for some workers in the twenties, unemployment never fell below 8 percent. And while strike action declined markedly from the 1919/1920 high point, strikes were still much more prolific in the mid-twenties than they are today. There continued to be tumultuous events such as the 1923 police strike that provoked wide-scale rioting in Melbourne.[46]

The CPA threw itself into the industrial arena, playing an important role in the 1927 Queensland sugar workers' strike and the accompanying state-wide railway lockout. As spokesperson for the NSW Labour Council's Disputes Committee, Kavanagh also played a significant role in the nine-month timber workers' strike in 1929. By 1928 the CPA-initiated Militant Minority Movement had groups in the major mining centres. In 1929 its call for a total shutdown of the NSW coal industry won support among rank and file miners as the lockout in the Northern District dragged on.

Kavanagh was subsequently criticised as being overly propagandist, too conservative, soft on Trades Hall and not aggressive enough in seizing opportunities. However in 1927 Kavanagh was definitely on the left of the party. He continued to resist Comintern demands that the CPA campaign for ALP affiliation. In contrast Lance Sharkey, who later – following the Stalinised Comintern's orders – denounced

---

45. Griffiths 1998, p. 6.
46. Armstrong 2014.

the ALP as "social fascist", was in August 1927 on the right of the party, arguing for a stepped up campaign for ALP membership.

Unfortunately the space for further development of the CPA along revolutionary lines was soon closed off. The CPA had been less impacted by the Stalinist degeneration of the Comintern than many larger Communist parties because of Australia's geographical isolation and the CPA's relative insignificance. One reflection of this was the lack of any vociferous campaign in the pages of *Workers Weekly* in the mid- to late twenties against Leon Trotsky or the Left Opposition in the Russian CP. Indeed drawings of Lenin and Trotsky appeared together on the front page of *Workers Weekly's* Russian Revolution anniversary issue of 6 November 1925. As late as 26 November 1926 *Workers Weekly* ran a favourable article on Trotsky's book *Towards Socialism or Capitalism*. In 1927 and 1928 a few articles were run attacking Trotsky, but it is significant how few appear.

By the end of the 1920s Stalin was determined to mould all the far flung Communist parties into obedient servants of the interests of the Russian state rather than of the local working-class movements. From 1926 onwards the Comintern began to pay more attention to the CPA and there began to be a more regular flow of members to Moscow for training. They were subsequently to return, by and large, as hard-core Stalinists. The first task of these apparatchiks was to purge the communist movement of dedicated and honest revolutionaries like Kavanagh.

The Third Period "left" turn – proclaimed at the Sixth Comintern Congress in 1928 – ushered in a dramatic shift. Supporters of the new line in Australia, led by Lance Sharkey, Bert Moxon and JB Miles, began to demand the party aggressively oppose the ALP both in propaganda and electorally. Although Kavanagh was sympathetic to the Comintern's new perspective, he sought to moderate its application in view of local circumstances, for which he was attacked as adhering to "Australian exceptionalism".

The dispute came to a head in late 1929 when the Opposition appealed to the Comintern Executive for support. The Comintern obliged, sending a lengthy letter denouncing Kavanagh's leadership. It described the central executive's opposition to running CPA candidates at the October federal election as "a glaring example of right deviation deserving the severest condemnation".[47] Under pressure from both the Comintern and the internal opposition, Kavanagh and his supporters began to lose ground, and at the Ninth CPA Conference in December 1929, Sharkey, Moxon and Miles defeated Kavanagh and his allies. On the conclusion of the conference, the new leaders sent a telegram to Moscow reading: "Annual conference greets Comintern. Declares unswerving loyalty new line".[48]

The new leadership quickly sought to crush Kavanagh and his supporters who continued to dominate the Sydney district, the party's largest. In April 1930, Comintern emissary (later revealed as an FBI agent) Herbert Moore arrived from the US and took control, transforming the CPA leadership, program and constitution.[49] Moore initiated the "social fascist" line with gusto. Kavanagh was forced out of the party. He was readmitted in 1931 and then expelled again three years later for Trotskyist sympathies.[50] Moore then turned on Moxon. Moxon had suited Moscow's needs in deposing Kavanagh but, as someone with some independence of mind, the Comintern regarded him as unsuitable for their purposes. Stalin was not looking for leftists as such, only those who would unquestioningly do his bidding. By 1932 a hardened team of cynical bureaucrats had been installed who were to run the CPA for decades to come.

After the Tenth Party Congress in 1931, only two more were held in the rest of the decade; stage-managed exercises with no genuine debate allowed. In the name of "democratic centralism", the CPA established a new monolithism. Moore introduced the practice of "self-criticism", which required critics of the leadership to abase themselves in order to win the forgiveness of their comrades. This became standard practice for anyone who dared to dissent, chilling the space for critical thinking.[51] The result, Stuart Macintyre writes, was that "an organisation that had once allowed vigorous debate and open discussion of differences was reconstituted as a conventicle of

---

47. Lovell and Windle 2008, pp. 283-87.
48. Lovell and Windle 2008, p. 290.
49. Moore was also known as Harry Wicks. Curthoys 1993, pp. 23-36.
50. Kavanagh went on to join the tiny Trotskyist organisation, the Communist League of Australia, in the 1940s.
51. Penrose 1996, p. 102.

rigid conformity".[52] That was the end of the CPA as a revolutionary force in the workers' movement. A new party genuinely dedicated to the task of working-class liberation was going to have to be rebuilt.

Conclusion

The mass radicalisation that rocked Australia in the last years of World War I and its aftermath opened up tremendous opportunities for the revolutionary left. The problem was the disjuncture between the fighting spirit of the workers involved in these battles and the flawed politics of existing left organisations. Syndicalism, the dominant current on the left, failed to measure up to the challenge. Simply bringing workers together into the One Big Union could not overcome the hold of Laborite reformism, let alone defeat the power of the capitalist state. The other major current on the left – reflected in organisations such as the VSP – that sought to push the ALP to the left, proved an even worse dead end.

The revolutionary ideas of the Bolsheviks and the newly created Communist International offered a way out of this impasse. One of the great strengths of Bolshevism was that it overcame the dichotomy that plagued the Australian socialist movement – the separation between "industrial" and "political". A revolutionary party had to be built on similar lines to the Bolsheviks that organised the vanguard of the working class for a combined fight on both fronts. As well the Russian workers had created, as an alternative to redundant bourgeois parliaments, a new institution for democratic working class rule – the soviet or workers' council.

Because of Australia's isolation it was not until 1919 that some partial understanding of the Russian revolutionary experience began to seep through. But as Jeff Sparrow writes: "As local radicals became aware of the profound originality of Russian Marxism, the existing Left groups all slid into crisis".[53] The most advanced elements from a range of socialist and syndicalist currents had by 1920 embraced the idea of forming a Communist party.

By then, however, the peak of the radical wave had passed. A major opportunity to build a mass Communist party had been

---
52. Macintyre 1998, p. 175.
53. Sparrow 2007, p. 103.

missed. The task now for revolutionaries was to build up their forces to the extent that they could in the new situation and prepare for the next great period of class confrontation and capitalist crisis, which as it turned out was not very far away at all. The capitalist boom of the 1920s was short lived. By 1928 the Australian economy had already begun to slide into the Great Depression.

The young CPA was greatly impeded from making the most of the opportunities that did exist by its continuing lack of political clarity. Sectarian differences prevented Communists from uniting into one party for almost two years. It took time to make a full break with syndicalism and with Garden's blatant opportunism. The strategy of the united front was poorly understood and badly applied. Moreover it has to be said that some of the advice coming from the Comintern, even in its genuinely revolutionary years, was not particularly helpful, especially in relation to the ALP and the union bureaucracy.

Whatever its errors in the 1920s, the CPA had sought to build a base for socialist ideas in the working class and to take the class struggle forward. The tragedy was that the party was not given the opportunity to test itself as a revolutionary force in the new period opening up in the tumultuous 1930s. The Stalinisation of the party decisively ended any such prospect.

So the great hopes and aspirations of those revolutionaries who fought to found the CPA were crushed by the early 1930s. That does not mean that their efforts were simply wasted or that there are not important lessons that today's socialists can learn from their experience to help clarify our political approach to the challenges we continue to face.

The issue of how revolutionaries effectively combat reformist forces is just as much a live issue today on the international left as it was for the young CPA in the 1920s. Implementing a united front approach in a principled, yet flexible, manner is no straightforward task. But just as tailing behind the ALP in the early 1920s proved a disaster for the CPA, tailing behind the Sanders and Corbyns of this world has had an equally negative impact on much of today's socialist left. Revolutionaries have to be able to chart an independent course that enables them to work with and *against* reformist forces in an attempt to win away sections of their working-class supporters. There is nothing in the least sectarian about such an approach.

Similarly, a clear understanding of the nature and role of the union bureaucracy and of the limitations of syndicalism and narrow trade unionism is vital if revolutionaries are to build a base in the working class. Any revival of working-class struggle can well see the emergence of a new layer of militants fed up with the conservatism of union officials and hostile to Labor politicians but inclined to an anti-political militancy. But industrial militancy alone, as the experience of the syndicalists of the One Big Union movement graphically confirms, is never going to be sufficient to challenge the entrenched power of the capitalist state and break the hold of political reformism over large sections of the working class. A revolutionary political strategy is necessary. That in turn underlines the vital necessity of cohering and educating a layer of revolutionaries that can forge a party that can confidently confront the challenges posed by an increasingly crisis-torn world capitalist system.

References

Adams, Paul Robert 2013, "The Annihilation of the ILP: The Third Industrial Labor Party and the Sturt Vacancy", *Labour History*, 105, November.

Armstrong, Mick 2006, *The Industrial Workers of the World in Australia*, Socialist Alternative.

Armstrong, Mick and Tom Bramble, 2007, *The Labor Party: A Marxist analysis*, Socialist Alternative.

Armstrong, Mick 2013, "Socialist trade union strategy in the Bolshevik era", *Marxist Left Review*, 6, Winter. https://marxistleftreview.org/articles/socialist-trade-union-strategy-in-the-bolshevik-era/

Armstrong, Mick 2014, "Riotous behaviour in Australian history", *Red Flag*, 21 March. https://redflag.org.au/article/riotous-behaviour-australian-history

Armstrong, Mick 2015, "How World War I led to class war", *Marxist Left Review*, 9, Summer. https://marxistleftreview.org/articles/how-world-war-one-led-to-class-war/

Australian Socialist Party 1919, *Australia and the World Revolution Manifesto of the Australian Socialist party. A statement of Communist principles*, Marxian Printing Works.

Bollard, Robert 2013, *In the shadow of Gallipoli. The hidden history of Australia in World War I*, NewSouth.

Burgmann, Verity 1995, *Revolutionary Industrial Unionism. The Industrial Workers of the World in Australia*, Cambridge University Press.

Campbell, EW 1945, *History of the Australian labor movement. A Marxist interpretation*, Current Book Distributors.

Curthoys, Barbara 1993, "The Comintern, the CPA and the Impact of Harry Wicks", *The Australian Journal of Politics and History*, 39 (1).

Davidson, Alastair 1969, *The Communist Party of Australia. A short history*, Hoover Institution Press.

Edmonds, Ross 1991, *In Storm and Struggle. A History of the Communist Party in Newcastle, 1920-1940*, self published.

Griffiths, Phil 1998, *Women and the Communist Party of Australia 1920-1945*, https://www.google.com/search?client=firefox-b-d&q=Griffiths%2C+Phil+1998%2C+Women+and+the+Communist+Party+of+Australia+1920-1945

Kennedy, Brian 1978, *Silver, Sin, and Sixpenny Ale. A Social History of Broken Hill 1883-1921*, Melbourne University Press.

Kuhn, Rick 2011, "Revolutionary tactics, the united front and what we do today", *Marxist Left Review*, 3, Spring. https://marxistleftreview.org/articles/revolutionary-strategy-and-the-united-front/

Lovell, David W and Kevin Windle (eds) 2008, *Our unswerving loyalty. A documentary survey of relations between the Communist Party of Australia and Moscow, 1920-1940*, ANU press.

Macintyre, Stuart 1998, *The Reds*, Allen & Unwin.

Markey, Raymond 1994, *In case of oppression. The life and times of the Labor Council of New South Wales*, Pluto Press.

Morrison, Peter 1977, *The Communist Party of Australia and the Australian radical-socialist tradition, 1920-1939*, PhD thesis, University of Adelaide. https://digital.library.adelaide.edu.au/dspace/handle/2440/21071

Moss, Jim 1983, *Representatives of Discontent. History of the Communist Party in South Australia 1921-1981*, Communist and Labour Movement History Group.

O'Lincoln, Tom 1985, *Into the mainstream. The decline of Australian communism*, Stained Wattle Press.

Penrose, Beris 1993, *The Communist Party and trade union work in the Third Period 1928-1935*, PhD, University of Queensland.

Penrose, Beris 1996, "Herbert Moxon, a Victim of the 'Bolshevisation' of the Communist Party", *Labour History*, 70, May.

Sparrow, Jeff 2007, *Communism. A Love Story*, Melbourne University Press.

Turner, Ian 1965, *Industrial Labour and Politics. The Dynamics of the Labour Movement in Eastern Australia 1900-1921*, Australian National University.

Walker, Bertha 1972, *Solidarity Forever!*, The National Press.

Williams, Justina 1976, *The First Furrow*, Lone Hand Press.

Young, Irwin 1971, *Theodore, His Life & Times*, Alpha Books.

TESS LEE ACK

Reds at the blackboard: Militancy in the teacher unions

> Tess Lee Ack was a member of the teacher unions in Victoria (VSTA and AEU) and a union delegate for 40 years.

IN RECENT YEARS, teacher unions have not been noted for their militancy. Successive rounds of enterprise bargaining in many states have come and gone without any strikes, despite far from satisfactory outcomes. The Queensland Teachers Union, for example, has not held a statewide strike since 2009. In some states, one-day strikes have taken place but then any follow-up action has been called off. This is not because of any lack of issues confronting teachers – excessive workloads, poor pay, decrepit infrastructure and standardised testing to name a few. State leaderships have not wanted strikes beyond token stoppages and branch structures provide very limited opportunities for rank-and-file members to challenge them. The COVID crisis is just the latest example of the lack of a fighting lead in the union.

In the early days of the pandemic, state leaderships were slow to call for school closures, despite their members' concerns – expressed in motions and petitions from individual school union branches and social media platforms – for their own and their students' safety. In Melbourne, in response to the "second wave" of the virus that saw 87 schools forced to close after outbreaks, the Australian Principals'

Federation called for school closures on 28 July.[1] On the same day, the Victorian branch of the Australian Education Union (AEU) sent a statement to members noting that the government had "failed to genuinely support the health and safety of staff", and making other valid criticisms.[2] But – no doubt determined to maintain its cosy relationship with the Labor government – it still stopped short of calling for a full shutdown, instead just requesting "more flexibility" at the school level, and urging members to contact their state Labor MP to express their concerns.[3]

But teacher unions have not always lacked militancy. In this article I will revisit some of the high points of struggles by government school teachers to improve the public education system as well as their wages and conditions. In some cases these struggles were facilitated by left-wing union leaderships; in others, militants had to contend with hostility from the officials. But either way, teachers' campaigns owed much to the grass-roots leadership and organisational ability of rank-and-file union members, with socialists often playing a key role. A comprehensive history of militancy in the teacher unions is well beyond the scope of this article. Instead it will focus on a few highlights that illustrate what is possible when rank-and-file workers organise and fight.

Background

In 1856, the Education Commissioners of New South Wales wrote of teachers:

> His [sic] material reward is [a] state of poverty and misery; and his only distinction is to be a member of a profession despised by all around.[4]

This reflected teachers' perceived position in society and the nature of their work during the nineteenth century. On the one hand, teachers were seen as moral guardians who were supposed to set and enforce standards, and conform to middle-class notions of respectability

---
1. Carey 2020.
2. Peace 2020.
3. Stanton 2020.
4. Spaull 1977, page ix.

in dress and behaviour. Women were particularly constrained in this area. Teachers were expected to observe and instil respect for authority and the social hierarchy. On the other, they were mostly paid low wages and worked in substandard accommodation with minimal resources. And teachers were forbidden to express political opinions or engage in political activity.

In the late nineteenth century, teacher associations emerged around the country, and these evolved into unions in the early twentieth century. For example, in 1918 the Public School Teachers' Association of New South Wales, which had been operating since 1898, combined with several smaller sector associations to form the NSW Public School Teachers' Federation, which by 1920 covered 78 percent of teachers employed by the Department of Education. The State School Teachers Union of Victoria was formed in 1886 and quickly gained 50 percent membership in government schools; it was succeeded by the Victorian Teachers Union (VTU) in 1926. The formation of unions was crucial as teachers fought to transform the sector.

Teacher unions campaigned to raise standards of teacher training and education, to increase the often pitiful resources put into public education, and for a more progressive curriculum. They insisted that these issues were inextricably linked to the fight for higher wages, adequate staffing levels and decent working conditions. So teacher organisations have always had a dual character as both professional associations and trade unions.

This dual role often created tensions within teacher organisations. Conservative elements opposed industrial action of any kind as being "unprofessional"; they resisted identification with the wider trade union movement and argued that teacher organisations should confine themselves to educational matters and advancing the status of the profession. These attitudes often went hand in hand with terrible sectionalism, such as attempts to maintain divisions and pay differentials between men and women, primary and secondary teachers, and so on. In some cases, this sectionalism led to splits and the fragmentation of teacher unions into smaller sector organisations.

Early militancy

The first recorded teachers' strike took place in WA in 1920.[5] From its establishment in 1898 until 1912, the State School Teachers' Union of Western Australia (SSTUWA) saw itself largely as an advocate for improving the quality of education and developing an efficient educational system; it enjoyed a good relationship with the Education Department. But relations soured under the impact of worsening economic conditions, World War I and its aftermath and rising living costs. Teachers' wages were actually cut by 7.98 percent in 1915. In 1917, the SSTUWA joined with other public sector unions in a Grand Council of Affiliated Public Services to fight for their common interests. Continued government intransigence saw teachers vote overwhelmingly (892 to 30) to approve strike action to achieve higher wages and establish an independently chaired board to hear appeals on salaries, increments and grievances. In 1920, a mass meeting of teachers and members of the Civil Service Association issued an ultimatum demanding a 33.3 percent pay rise and the establishment of an appeals board. On 10 July, with the government having offered only minor concessions, teachers and public service workers went on strike. They stayed out for 18 days, only returning to work when all their demands had been met.

During the period after World War I, a minority of teachers, like other sections of the Australian working class, were drawn to progressive and radical ideas and influenced or inspired by the Industrial Workers of the World and the Russian Revolution.[6] The formation of the Communist Party of Australia (CPA) in October 1920 was a significant development, and by the 1930s it was building a powerful presence in the trade union movement. The party was by this time thoroughly Stalinised, and communist parties around the world had become tools of the USSR's foreign policy rather than organisations fighting for working-class emancipation.[7] Nonetheless, the CPA numbered many genuine militants in its ranks.

---

5. For a detailed account, see Horner, "The State School Teachers' Union of Western Australia", in Spaull (ed.) 1977, pp. 234-45.
6. Mitchell 1975, pp. 100-1.
7. For a summary of this process in the CPA, see Armstrong 2021.

During the Great Depression workers, including teachers, faced serious attacks. In an attempt to organise workers to resist the attacks, the CPA launched the Militant Minority Movement in the late 1920s.[8]

In Sydney in 1931 the CPA formed the Educational Workers' League (EWL) to help coordinate resistance when the NSW Teachers Federation leaders would not. The League openly stated its objective as "the abolition of Capitalism and the establishment...of a Workers' Socialist Commonwealth based on the ownership and control of the means of production by the organised working class".[9] Its members were also active in the anti-fascist and anti-war movements, and women played a leading role. Federation historian Bruce Mitchell describes the EWL as somewhat more moderate than the Militant Minority Movement – less ultra-left and more accommodating to "social fascists", in defiance of the party line.[10]

The EWL argued that improvements for teachers could only be won by an active rank and file, not through cosy negotiations with ministers and department heads. They deplored the presence of headmasters in the Federation, correctly believing that they dominated the organisation to the detriment of the majority of teachers.[11] They considered splitting from the Federation to form a more radical organisation, but according to Mitchell decided not to after reading Lenin's polemic against ultra-leftism, *Left-wing communism: an infantile disorder*.[12] This was also in line with CPA policy, which was generally opposed to the formation of "red unions". So the EWL remained with the Federation as a ginger group. Their numbers were small, in the dozens, though boosted by defections from the ALP when the Lang Labor government cut public sector wages. But despite their small size, they punched above their weight. They published a popular and influential journal, the *Educational Worker*, which had a circulation well beyond their own ranks. It was

---
8. See O'Lincoln 1986.
9. Mitchell 1975, p. 106.
10. Mitchell 1975, p. 174.
11. This remains a vexed question for many teachers, as the interests of teachers and principals are often counterposed; even more so in modern times, as principals have increasingly become more like CEOs than educational leaders.
12. Mitchell 1975, p. 109.

largely through the EWL that the CPA established long-term influence in and, at times, leadership of the Federation.

The EWL argued for rank-and-file militancy and cooperation with other public sector unions, and sought to include educational workers other than teachers, holding out "the hand of working-class unity to school cleaners and gardeners".[13] They also advocated radical educational philosophies. For example, they called for syllabus reform to "give due emphasis to the struggles and aspirations of the working class and the colonial masses", the abolition of exams that "sterilised knowledge and distorted education", as well as homework, weekly tests, religious education and corporal punishment. The *Educational Worker* included a column called "The Lies We Teach", covering issues such as European imperialism, the true character of national icons and ruling-class figures such as the Wentworths, etc.[14]

In the early 1930s, the EWL led a successful campaign in defence of Beatrice Taylor, a Sydney teacher who had been victimised for her political opinions and activity. Sponsored by the EWL, Taylor had been part of a Friends of the Soviet Union delegation that visited Russia in 1932. On her return, she wrote several articles about the experience in the *Educational Worker*, and spoke at over 70 meetings. In November, following a public meeting presided over by a Methodist clergyman, she received a letter from the Education Department demanding to know if she had addressed the meeting and was correctly described there as a delegate from the EWL to the Soviet Union. She wrote back, declining to answer these questions because they "concerned her private actions and infringed her rights as a citizen". She was then suspended from duty under the Public Service Act, guilty of "misconduct, wilful disobedience to a lawful order, and improper conduct".[15] A Public Service Board enquiry was set for 24 January 1933.

The EWL set up a Defence Committee, and in early January called a protest conference for the same date. It was a huge success; over 500 delegates from 278 organisations attended, including 50

---

13. Mitchell 1975, p. 107.
14. Mitchell 1975, pp. 173-74.
15. Mitchell 1975, p. 115.

trade unions, 111 Labor Party branches (but notably not the Labor Party executive), 17 Socialisation Units, 29 organisations of the unemployed and numerous other bodies. It made press headlines by calling on parents of children who attended Taylor's school in Paddington to keep their children at home on the first day of the school year. The hearing was postponed until 31 January, but this only provided another opportunity for the EWL to organise. They held a mass protest meeting in the Sydney Town Hall on 30 January, which opened with a talk by Taylor. The next day there were more headlines as several hundred protesters clashed with police at the Paddington school. The organisers of the school boycott calculated that about half the parents had kept their children at home.[16] It was undoubtedly these actions, rather than the eloquence of Taylor's counsel, that persuaded the board to drop the charges and immediately reinstate her. The education minister (David Drummond, a founding member of the Country Party and a rabid anti-communist) tried without success to pursue the case against Taylor, as well attempting to purge schools of any teachers associated with the CPA or the Socialisation Units.

The EWL rightly saw this victory as a vindication for the kind of tactics and activity they advocated for the union. They noted that the campaign had been supported by thousands of workers, and argued that the methods of organisation put forward by the EWL "will also achieve success, when properly applied, in opposition to attacks upon salaries and conditions".[17] Notably, the campaign had received no support from the official union leadership. The day after Taylor's reinstatement, the Federation council elected an executive on which radical views were barely represented.

After this triumph, things went backwards for teachers for a period. It was the height of the Depression and workers were under attack. Teachers' wages were cut with no effective resistance from the union, and membership declined to the lowest point since 1919, accounting for barely half of all teachers. In 1936, the EWL was disbanded as the CPA adopted the disastrous popular front strategy. But the CPA's decision to disband the EWL did not mean that the

---

16. Mitchell 1975, p. 116.
17. Mitchell 1975, p. 118.

party no longer played a role in the union. In the latter stages of World War II and its aftermath, there was a general shift to the left in the working class. As Mitchell explains:

> In the last three or four years of the war the mood of Australian political and social life was more sympathetic to socialist ideas than ever before: the Communist party enjoyed expanding membership, the Labor party won sweeping electoral victories, and there was much talk of reconstructing society when the war was over. The federation reflected all this in its policies and propaganda as well as in the composition of its executive.[18]

One symptom of this shift was that during World War II the Federation affiliated to the NSW Labour Council and the ACTU, signalling a growing consciousness that teachers were part of the broader workers' movement.

By the end of the war, union coverage had recovered to about 90 percent, and in 1945, Sam Lewis, a founder of the EWL and CPA member,[19] was elected as the Federation's president, a position he held until 1952. Former EWL members accounted for eight of the 17 positions on the executive, along with a few fellow-travellers. In 1946, now effectively led by the CPA, the union won a large pay rise, the biggest since 1920 and one that set the standard for other professional workers.

However, by now Lewis and the leadership group around him had pragmatically abandoned the radicalism of the EWL. The overriding issue for them was to maintain a single, united teachers' organisation, and this meant not alienating more conservative sections such as primary teachers and teachers in rural areas. The union leaders instead focused their energy on bread-and-butter industrial issues, such as wages and conditions.

This was at least partly attributable to the general rightward shift in the political climate as the Cold War ramped up and the Lewis leadership came under sustained attack from without and within. In late 1947, the former Labor premier Jack Lang repeatedly attacked

---

18. Mitchell 1975, p. 157.
19. However Mitchell says of Lewis that "his tactics did not often follow Communist party orthodoxy". Mitchell 1975, p. 174.

Lewis in the NSW parliament as "a notorious Communist [who] holds an important position in the inner Communist organisation in Australia",[20] receiving wide press coverage. Soon after, right-wing forces in the union formed the Teachers' Federation Anti-Communist League, an unlikely alliance of Catholics, Protestants, Liberal and Labor party supporters united only by their determination to oust the Lewis leadership.

In 1951 – the year of Menzies' anti-communist referendum and all the right-wing hysteria surrounding it – the Federation organised a successful student strike by trainee teachers over living allowances, which saw hundreds of students in NSW teachers' colleges boycott lectures and take to the streets. Historian Alan Barcan said of its political significance:

> It was the first open protest by trainee teachers. If seen as a strike, it was the first strike by (future) teachers in NSW. It was a step in the development of white-collar union militancy. It was a victory for the Lewis forces within the Teachers' Federation at a time when their strength was declining. It may have shaped the outlook of some future teachers.[21]

The following year, however, the right defeated the Lewis leadership, and for the next five years, the Federation was wracked by bitter factional disputes.

Transformation in the 1960s

Teachers generally thought of themselves as a "cut above" blue collar trade unionists. However, these conservative attitudes tended to dissipate as the sector evolved and proletarianised. The post-war boom created a demand for more highly skilled and educated workers, and this in turn led to a rapid and massive expansion of both secondary and tertiary education throughout the Western world. That meant training more teachers and building more schools. But in the mid-1960s, most state education systems in Australia were in crisis, suffering from long-term neglect and unable to keep pace with the expansion needed as a result of the post-war baby boom.

---

20. Mitchell 1975, p. 168.
21. Barcan 2002, p. 266.

Buildings were decrepit and there was a chronic shortage of qualified teachers.

In an effort to boost teacher numbers, governments offered teaching scholarships, and these provided a pathway for people from working-class backgrounds to access higher education in unprecedented numbers. There was a rapid influx of young teachers into the workforce, and many of them were influenced by the mass political radicalisation of the 1960s and '70s, and the upsurge of worker and union struggles of that time. Many activists with experience in the movement against the Vietnam War, or in campaigns against apartheid, for Indigenous rights, women's rights and so on, ended up as teachers.

This new generation brought with them a greater willingness to engage in union struggles, as well as an enthusiasm for radical pedagogy and a more democratic approach to education. They chafed against the authoritarianism that characterised relations within schools and between teachers and their employers. The dual character and role of teacher unions persisted, but now concern about "professional" issues tended to fuel a more militant stance. In her history of the Victorian Secondary Teachers Association (VSTA), Jan Bassett makes a point that is more widely applicable:

> The association's main policies during these years [1960s and early '70s]...were professional ones. But the methods it used to implement them, including stopworks and boycotts, were those of a union.[22]

Teachers now saw themselves as the vanguard for educational reform, and this was often linked to broader issues of social reform. Given this, it's not surprising that teacher unions have for the most part been on the left of the broader trade union movement. They have taken a stand and sometimes campaigned around such issues as war, racism and Indigenous rights, uranium mining and nuclear weapons testing. They have fought sexism and discrimination against lesbian and gay teachers and students. All of this underpinned the wave of teacher union militancy that took place in the

---

22. Bassett 1995, p. 204.

1960s and '70s. Teacher union historian Andrew Spaull noted that in the decade 1963-73, "teacher militancy emerged for the first time as a major and dominant feature of the Australian educational scene".[23] In the latter half of this article, I trace this process in the NSWTF and particularly in the VSTA, of which I was a member for some of the period discussed.

Radicalisation in the NSWTF

The anti-communist forces in the NSWTF which were dominant in the 1950s and early 1960s eventually declined, allowing the left to make a comeback, and Sam Lewis served another term as president from 1964-67. A left-wing union leadership, however, was no guarantee of industrial militancy. The Federation under Lewis "relied mostly on lobbying government ministers and appearances before the Teachers Tribunal".[24]

But things were starting to change. A long campaign over working conditions culminated in October 1968 with the first ever statewide strike by NSW teachers. It was a huge success: 80 percent of teachers walked off the job, and over 12,000 attended a mass meeting – the largest meeting of members of a single union in Australian history to that point. The strike bore immediate fruit: on the same day, the Cabinet voted to ask the Commonwealth for authority to borrow $5 million for school buildings, and within days announced an increase in education spending and the extension of teacher education from two to three years.

This was an enormous breakthrough: the strike was now seen as both a legitimate and effective weapon. There was no further statewide strike in NSW until 1973, although there were quite a few strikes in individual schools, reflecting a growing militancy among teachers.

One of the most inspiring of these was a strike at Warilla High School in Wollongong in 1976 that lasted for 28 days.[25] As well as being the longest teachers' strike in Australian history to that point, it provided a magnificent example of working-class community

---

23. Spaull, "Trends in teacher militancy", in Spaull (ed.) 1977, p. 302.
24. Bramble 2008, p. 21.
25. This account is largely based on Ashbolt 2006.

solidarity. Although it started in response to a specific local grievance, it was also part of a general struggle by the Federation for smaller class sizes and increased staffing for disadvantaged schools. The strike began on 10 February when the 75 striking teachers (all the staff except for the principal, deputy principal and two teachers who were not union members) marched on the local Education Office demanding a replacement science teacher. The strike was run democratically and with a focus on organising support and solidarity.

> Led by school-based activists, [the striking teachers] met every morning outside the school fence and voted on whether the dispute continued for another day. They would then disperse and go and speak to other schools to garner support and funds to sustain the strikers.[26]

This reaching out paid off: the first of many solidarity strikes occurred on 13 February, when teachers at Warrawong stopped work. This was more than a mere act of support; these workers took the opportunity to raise their own demands for more staff to provide remedial English classes for the 70 percent of Warrawong pupils who did not have an English-speaking background. Teachers in all Illawarra schools pledged $20 a fortnight to the strike fund, while the Federation planned regional and statewide rolling strikes.

On 17 February a meeting of 400 parents and students unanimously supported the Warilla teachers, and the school captain told the *Illawarra Mercury* that all the students supported the strike. Student sympathy strikes began at Warrawong and Berkeley High Schools.

On 23 February schools in Sydney began rolling stoppages, and students at Port Kembla High School staged a sympathy strike. Two days later 300 students marched down Crown Street, Wollongong, some carrying a banner reading "Two hour strike for better education".

South Coast Labour Council Secretary (and CPA member) Merv Nixon made it clear that all unions in the region supported the Warilla teachers, and this wasn't just talk. There were sympathy

---

26. Dixon 2018.

strikes by cleaners at Warilla, bread carters supplied free bread and barbers gave free haircuts. The Seamen's Union stopped work so that the Warilla teachers could address them, and the Port Kembla waterside workers passed a motion of support. The Ports Committee, representing eight maritime unions, started to talk about industrial action. Tugboat crews walked off the job in support of the teachers and tied up around 18 ships. Merv Nixon "famously took the regional director to his window overlooking the harbour and told him the harbour would not re-open until the Warilla staff's demands were met".[27]

Nixon described the strike as "the most principled dispute the South Coast TLC had been involved in. They were not seeking money or better conditions for themselves but better conditions for children in a working class area".[28]

There were casualties: not all of the 75 teachers who began the strike lasted the distance. After 26 days, 44 were still out, dropping to a final number of 40. Nonetheless, the strike ended in a total victory, and not just for the Warilla teachers. The school got an additional science teacher and mathematics teacher. But all disadvantaged schools in NSW eventually benefitted from a new staffing formula that was applied statewide. The "magnificent 40", as they were known, "met once again at the front gate of the school and as a group voted to return to work. They marched back into school as a unified group, victorious and unbowed".[29]

The Victorian Secondary Teachers Association

For a period in the 1960s and '70s, the Victorian Secondary Teachers Association (VSTA) was arguably one of the most radical and militant unions in Australia, certainly among white collar unions. "Between 1962 and 1974, the VSTA came down from the mountain and breathed fire among the people", wrote Andrew Spaull in 1975. He described it as "a pacesetter of Australian teacher unionism" and "one of the most important influences on both teachers' attitudes

---

27. Dixon 2018.
28. Quoted in Ashbolt 2006, p. 10.
29. Dixon 2018.

and the Victorian education system".[30] Bruce Mitchell noted the "more extensive and ambitious strikes of recent years in Victoria", as compared with NSW.[31]

Yet the VSTA's origins were far from auspicious. It began life as a right-wing breakaway from the Victorian Teachers' Union (VTU), formed in 1926. The VTU was then a left-wing union,[32] one of the few that advocated equal pay for women at the time. Like the NSWTF, it was influenced by the CPA, especially during World War II. From 1943, the VTU called for the abolition of secondary margins and the same rate of pay for all teachers.

In 1948 the secondary margin was reduced from 12 percent to 8 percent and this incensed a group of teachers at Melbourne High, an elite, selective-entry school within the state system. They called a protest meeting and out of this came the Victorian Secondary Masters' Professional Association (VSMPA), which excluded women and opposed equal pay for both women and primary teachers – a thoroughly reactionary and elitist outfit. But before long, there was agitation from below to admit women. On the ground, most male teachers could see that restricting membership undermined their potential strength and influence. Despite undemocratic resistance from the leadership, women were admitted in 1953 and the union's name changed. Three years later the VSTA also adopted a policy of equal pay for women.

Paradoxically, it was a series of affronts to their professional pride that drove the VSTA in the direction of militant unionism. Their first industrial campaign started in 1964, when the union called on members to stop signing the time-book. This was carried out despite threats of disciplinary action, and it wasn't long before the time-books disappeared.

30. Spaull 1975.
31. Mitchell 1977, p. 203.
32. In 1967, technical teachers also split from the VTU to form the Technical Teachers' Association (later Union) of Victoria (TTUV). Many of its members were former tradespeople and were more inclined to industrial militancy. It was the first of the Victorian teacher unions to affiliate to the Trades Hall Council, in 1974. The VSTA followed suit a year later. The VTU thus came to represent only primary teachers, and was considerably more conservative than either the VSTA or the TTUV.

In July 1965, VSTA members were the first teachers to take strike action since the WA strike of 1920, and this was the start of a sustained period of industrial militancy. Bill Hannan was a classroom teacher, held various positions in the VSTA leadership, edited the union magazine and was a leading contributor to progressive curriculum reform in Victoria. In his memoir, *The Best of Times*, he writes: "Between 1969 and 1971 the VSTA organised more strikes than perhaps any other teachers' union in world history". He estimates that there was an average of one strike per week in those years.[33]

Hannan gives a feel for the spirit of a time when Australian workers generally were experiencing a high level of class combativity:

> As in warfare so in industrial confrontations, engagements with the enemy can be stirring or demoralising. Stopworks especially are stirring events... [T]here is an element of release, purification even, when you walk off the job and join a lot of colleagues with the same purpose. You have defied the rules that are supposed to bind you. You have told your employer that there is something more important to you than the day's pay... You have shown the bosses that they have responsibilities beyond watching their backs and digging in. You have told the world that you are right and authority is wrong.[34]

Between 1965 and 1973, the VSTA waged simultaneous campaigns under the umbrella of "professional action": tribunal reform, curriculum and assessment reform, control of entry, inspection, working conditions and teachers' rights. This was an ambitious program for a small union whose membership in these years peaked at just over 7,000 members,[35] and by no means covered the entire secondary teaching workforce. It was not unusual for VSTA members to be on strike multiple times per year over different issues.

At the height of this period, VSTA members would simply walk out if an inspector appeared at a school, or when the limit the union imposed on teaching hours and class sizes was exceeded, or if a non-union-registered teacher was sent to the school. As well

---

33. Hannan 2009, p. 244.
34. Hannan 2009, p. 244.
35. Bassett 1995, p. 212.

as a large number of half-day, 24- and 48-hour statewide strikes, there were prolonged strikes at individual schools, with teachers supported by a central strike fund.

There were also strikes and protests in response to the stand-down, sacking or forced transfers of teachers. In most cases these victimisations arose out of the various industrial campaigns – for example teachers being sacked as "incompetent" if they refused to submit to inspection, or being issued with strike bans for taking industrial action. The arch-reactionary Liberal premier of the time, Henry Bolte, complained that "secondary school-teachers seemed to be on strike on 'matters of conscience' more than they were at work".[36]

The Teachers' Tribunal

The VSTA had long been unhappy with the Teachers' Tribunal, which determined salaries. In June 1965, when the tribunal brought down an award that saw some teachers receive no pay rise at all, while others received a miserable 3.5 percent, there was widespread anger. Over a thousand members attended an evening protest meeting and overwhelmingly supported an executive motion for a half-day strike on 2 July. This was the first of many actions for tribunal reform. The most spectacular – and controversial – was the indefinite strike by 41 of the 48 teachers at the elite Melbourne High School,[37] which lasted from 15 February to 12 March 1971. As was often to happen, the VSTA leadership called off the strike when the education minister offered to negotiate. And, as was usually the case when this happened, negotiations would drag out fruitlessly, and little headway was made. Eventually, the union changed its policy from reform of the tribunal to its abolition, calling instead for direct negotiations with the employer.[38]

---

36. Tom Prior, Bolte by Bolte, Craftsman, 1990, p. 153, cited in Bassett 1995.
37. The VSTA branch itself had volunteered to undertake this action; things had certainly changed since teachers there initiated the VSMPA!
38. Direct negotiations were eventually achieved after the election of a Labor government in April 1982. The Teachers' Tribunal was abolished in August of that year.

Inspection

By the early 1960s there was growing hostility to the demeaning system of classroom inspection, which was required for promotion, and the rigid classification system that accompanied it. At a meeting of the union's metropolitan group in 1962 it was argued that the inspection system "was unprofessional, had a stultifying effect on educational standards and practices, bred corruption of professional ideals, and was inefficient and unnecessary".[39] Members at a combined meeting of the Latrobe Valley and South Gippsland groups supported the abolition of inspection, but went even further, suggesting that promotion for positions other than those of principal should be automatic. The 1963 annual general meeting (AGM) passed a resolution from the Moreland High School branch, opposing in principle "all systems of obligatory assessment of teachers' efficiency by Inspectors or any representative of the employing authority".[40] Following fruitless negotiations, the 1969 AGM voted to take direct action against inspection, other than for probationary teachers. From the start of 1970, this would involve teachers walking out if an inspector entered their classroom for assessment purposes. Members responded enthusiastically, and in a remarkably short time won a major concession: in April the Committee of Secondary Classifiers agreed to accept references as evidence of aptitude for promotion, as an alternative to inspectors' reports. Building on this, the union stepped up its campaign the next year, calling on members to walk out if inspectors entered the school to assess anyone for promotion, and not to cooperate with the Department's "consultative panels". VSTA members continued to fight, and a number were victimised. In 1973, the director of secondary education, Bert Schruhm, issued a provocative memorandum which mandated that there would be no promotion without inspection. The VSTA responded with a one-day statewide strike, and a mass meeting voted for a further mass stopwork and indefinite strikes in selected schools if the memorandum wasn't withdrawn.

Statewide, regional and individual branch strikes continued

---
39. Bassett 1995, p. 53.
40. Bassett 1995, p. 53.

into 1974. A highlight of the campaign occurred in August 1974, when a long series of regional stopworks culminated in a march and the invasion of the Old Mint building in Melbourne (which housed the tribunal) by VSTA members. A trainee teacher at the time, I vividly remember the TV news footage of loud and angry teachers surrounding the car of a hapless bureaucrat. A further one-day statewide stopwork took place on 2 October, with an indefinite statewide strike scheduled to begin on 15 October. Once again, the union leadership called off the strike two days later, when the minister offered to negotiate. But local school action continued, and eventually, on 1 May 1975, the inspection of secondary teachers effectively ended, though skirmishes around the issue continued till the early 1980s.

Control of entry

The control of entry campaign was designed to stop the department plugging gaps in schools by employing untrained and/or unqualified people as temporary teachers as it struggled to keep up with the demand for more schools and more teachers. Like the recruitment of large numbers of teachers from the US and Britain, this was a cheaper option than actually providing suitable training. "The Department believed that putting bodies in front of classes was the supreme imperative. Qualifications...could wait on better times."[41] And "[t]he Department did not necessarily check the claims of temporary employees, since in effect there were no official standards anyway".[42] Bill Hannan recalls the incredulous response of people outside the sector:

> There must have been some qualifications required, they say. They couldn't just walk in off the street.
>
> They could and did. VSTA surveys...showed that about one third of teachers were temporary, few of them qualified, many of them with no higher qualifications than their students.[43]

---

41. Hannan 2009, p. 260.
42. Hannan 2009, p. 255.
43. Hannan 2009, p. 258. In 1962, Hannan was elected president of the newly formed Metropolitan Group, a discussion forum for union members in Melbourne. It took up the "in principle" support for control of entry from the 1962 AGM and

A union survey in April 1968 indicated that only about 39 percent of teachers held degrees.[44] The figure fell to 35.4 percent for teachers with both a degree and teacher training. "Fully qualified teachers... were 'a bare majority': 51 percent."[45]

The 1968 AGM resolved that the union would fight to control entry to secondary teaching under a plan to be implemented from 1 April 1969. This would involve the VSTA setting up its own registration system, requiring secondary teachers to have at least three years of tertiary education – a basic degree. Those who did not have this could be provisionally registered, and could continue teaching, but were required to upgrade their qualifications within seven years, with the union demanding full-time training on full pay to achieve this. Members would refuse to work alongside anyone not registered or provisionally registered with the union. A number of statewide strikes and mass meetings were held on this issue, but it was largely up to individual branches to enforce the policy. A teacher at Kew High School recalled "waiting at the front door of the school for an unqualified teacher to arrive. We had decided to tell her that we would take strike action if she were appointed".[46] This was a common experience.

On 3 October, 31 of 46 teachers at Northcote High School embarked on an indefinite strike to remove an unqualified teacher from teaching duties, and a statewide strike in their support took place on 31 October. But following unproductive negotiations, the VSTA leadership called off the strike and the Northcote teachers returned to work on 17 November. In 1970, despite some compromises on the part of the Department and the VSTA leadership, school-based action continued, with mixed results. A three-and-a-half-week strike at Murrumbeena High School ended in victory, with an unregistered teacher placed on non-teaching duties and a registered teacher employed. The longest control of entry strike took place in April the following year at Maribyrnong High School. Lasting 11 weeks, it was the longest teachers' strike in Australia to that time. It was unsuccessful

---

fleshed it out as a policy. Hannan 2009, p. 64.
44. Bassett 1995, p. 76.
45. Hannan 2009, p. 255.
46. Hannan 2009, p. 245.

in its immediate objective of removing unregistered teachers from the school, but the following year, few if any teachers were appointed without three years of VSTA-approved secondary teacher education.

Control of entry to some extent reflected the "professional" character of teacher unions, with undertones of a "craft union" defending its members' interests. An AGM resolution in 1962 demanded "strong and prompt action to safeguard and advance the professional status of secondary teachers".[47] But the policy, and particularly the industrial campaign to win it, also had elements of workers' control.[48] Moreover, many teachers saw control of entry as being in their students' interests and increasingly spoke of the policy in those terms. For example, striking teachers at Maribyrnong High in 1971 wrote in the *VSTA News*: "Teachers are prepared to stand firm, and for even longer periods, to improve the standard of education that children of this state are receiving".[49] And some of the strikers later told Hannan that:

> [T]hey were particularly resentful that unqualified teachers should be in a school where the students were mainly of working class background and many from a nearby migrant hostel. They did not see the VSTA as a conventional union, but one that was struggling, like them, to improve the system for the sake of the kids.[50]

On the eve of the control of entry campaign, Education Minister Lindsay Thompson had written to the VSTA, threatening that "the framing of these plans...could constitute a criminal conspiracy to effect a public mischief and that those framing the plans and those taking part in their implementation could be guilty of this offence against the State".[51] By 1972, control of entry was effectively won, with VSTA president Geoff Reid commenting that: "Three years

---

47. Hannan 2009, p. 63.
48. Unlike the modern Victorian Institute of Teaching (VIT), a bureaucratic "independent" statutory authority established by an act of parliament in 2002. Its Council is appointed on the recommendation of the minister for education.
49. Hannan 2009, p. 297.
50. Hannan 2009, p. 299.
51. Bassett 1995, pp. 76-77.

of public mischief produced remarkable improvements in teacher recruitment and training".[52]

An *Age* editorial at the time of the VSTA's first strike in July 1965 had praised the more conservative VTU's "shrewd restraint" (ie not striking) as opposed to the VSTA's "impetuous and unseemly behaviour".[53] But the evidence shows that it was the unseemly behaviour that got results.

Working conditions

In March 1971 the VSTA launched its "conditions case", which set limits on face-to-face teaching hours and class sizes. If implemented this would require the hiring of many more teachers, so it was also about needs-based staffing of schools. Members were to teach only until their union-approved allotments were reached, refuse to take more than one "extra" class per week and to inform their principals that they would not take classes larger than the union recommendation. Some principals sought to comply, for example by reducing the length of the school day. Others did not, and over the next few years, a number of teachers were reprimanded, fined or issued with "strike bans" as branches implemented the policy. Direct action often got results. For example, at the start of 1973 teachers at Huntingdale High School calculated that the school needed six more teachers to achieve union conditions. Seven strikes by an average of 34 teachers brought this number down to 0.5 by the beginning of second term.[54] Negotiations between the VSTA and the department over the related issues of staffing and conditions continued unproductively for some years, and the department's heavy-handed use of strike bans led to a two-day statewide strike in April 1979. An agreement over conditions and needs-based staffing was eventually reached as part of the log of claims thrashed out with the Labor government in 1982, though it didn't satisfy everyone.

---

52. Bassett 1995, p. 100.
53. Cited in Bassett 1995, p. 66.
54. Bassett 1995, p. 102.

Curriculum and assessment

The role of public education under capitalism is to produce suitably trained and socialised workers, conforming to workplace discipline and able to play a productive role in the economy – ie generate profits for employers. Most teachers, however, enter the profession believing that their role is to enrich their students' lives and help them to reach their full potential. This belief has often driven campaigns for reforms in the areas of curriculum and assessment, and the VSTA was a leader in this area. As Bassett notes:

> [T]here were increasing numbers of teachers in Victorian secondary schools, many of whom had been educated...during the "education explosion" of the 1950s and 1960s and at universities and colleges during the "protest years" of the late 1960s and early 1970s, who were keen to make education more egalitarian and less authoritarian.[55]

The most controversial of the VSTA's radical education policies was the "open entry" policy narrowly adopted at the AGM in 1973. The union position was that anyone who wanted to should be able to attend university, without passing exams in a system that inevitably disadvantaged working-class students. If there weren't enough places, then entry should be decided by a random ballot as the only selection method that put everyone on a level playing field. The 1974 AGM attempted to give the policy some teeth: in another narrow vote, members were called on to boycott the Higher School Certificate (HSC). This caused a huge furore inside and outside the union. An anti-ballot committee (ABC) was set up by right-wing members; it succeeded in calling a special general meeting in December 1974 which, again narrowly, overturned the policy. Open tertiary entry remained on the books as policy, but no further attempts were made to implement it. However, the union turned to developing alternative Year 12 courses and pathways to higher education, with some success.

---

55. Bassett 1995, p. 111.

Rank-and-file militancy

What is striking about the VSTA's campaigns in this period is the extent to which they depended on rank-and-file members in schools, which were the site of a lot of the action, whether it was spontaneous walk-outs or lengthy strikes. The inspection, conditions and control of entry campaigns in particular all relied on the initiative and organisation of individual branches, and members' willingness to stand up to principals and department bureaucrats, risking all kinds of victimisation, from fines to forced transfers to dismissal.

In his study of Australian unions in the post-war period, Tom Bramble writes: "Just as there were industrially militant unions with politically moderate union leaders, so there were industrially quiescent unions with left-wing leaders",[56] and he cites the NSW Teachers' Federation as an example of the latter. The VSTA was certainly an example of the former. Its radical policies and militant campaigns were for the most part led by a group of conservative officials who at times faced opposition from even more conservative elements, but also from the left.

Like all union officials, the VSTA leadership preferred negotiations to industrial action. So, as we have seen, they were all too ready to call off strikes if the department dangled the prospect of negotiations, which usually went nowhere. On numerous occasions they ignored or overturned resolutions from delegates' and mass stopwork meetings. This adversely affected the momentum of campaigns when more determined action could have brought better and speedier results. They were often prepared to make concessions that weren't acceptable to a lot of members, and they had a very poor record when it came to defending victimised teachers. They were opposed by small rank-and-file groups,[57] which argued for "militant, democratic and socially-conscious unionism", and regularly and often successfully intervened in union forums. At mass stopwork

---

56. Bramble 2008, p. 21.
57. Teacher Action and Links in the 1970s, Teacher Solidarity in the early 1980s; members of Socialist Alternative's precursor organisations, including myself, were involved in all of these groups.

meetings it was possible to win motions from the floor for indefinite strikes, in marked contrast to more recent times.

By the 1970s the VSTA Central Committee was increasingly split between the dominant right faction, the "Houndstooth and Tie Section", and the left-wing "Youth and Beards Section". These nicknames were coined by Joan Rosser, one of four teachers at Werribee High School victimised for striking in support of union policy and subsequently "betrayed", as Rosser put it, by the VSTA leadership.[58] For all their radicalism on education issues, the right were opposed to the union taking up broader social issues – "Vietnam with the lot" as one of the officials scathingly called it.[59] They opposed left initiatives such as the establishment of open subcommittees on women and homosexuality to address sexism and discrimination, opposition to uranium mining and affiliation to the Trades Hall Council, but they were rolled on these and other progressive policies at annual general meetings.

By late 1981, member dissatisfaction had reached the point where a reform group led by Brian Henderson was able to win the leadership under the slogan "Revitalise the VSTA". The following year, decades of Liberal government also came to an end, and under the new leadership and Labor government, a number of long-running issues were resolved, though not all of them satisfactorily. The "heroic phase" of the VSTA was over.

Conclusion

In the 1980s, union militancy entered a steep decline from which it is yet to recover. One of the most damaging outcomes of the Prices and Incomes Accord – sold to workers almost exclusively by the "left" unions – was the decline of rank-and-file organisation and increasing bureaucratisation and top-down union leadership. The state-based teacher unions were not immune from this, or from the general rightward shift in society. As Tom Bramble writes:

---

58. Bassett 1995, p. 112. As the nicknames indicate, they were mostly male. Although teaching was a female-dominated occupation, leadership positions at the time, both in schools and the teacher unions, were overwhelmingly male.
59. Bassett 1995, p. 107.

> In education departments across the country, union leaders became partners in the administration of the system and in many cases quit their posts to take up appointments in the public service or ministerial offices. These processes led to an increasing marginalisation of rank-and-file members in decision-making within the teacher unions.

He goes on to quote Graham Holt, a delegate of the technical teachers' union in Victoria:

> [D]ecisions that affected people in schools were being made by the Education Department after they had agreement from the central union. So the teachers wouldn't actually have much input. The decision would be announced that this had been negotiated with the teacher unions. So it would be decided at the top.[60]

Socialist and left-wing teachers today face a huge task in attempting to rebuild grass-roots union organisation in a situation where the rank-and-file members have largely been sidelined and at best used as a stage army. The memory of past struggles and victories should not only inspire us, but also provide valuable lessons for the struggles to come.

---

60. Bramble 2008, p. 130.

References

Armstrong, Mick 2021, "Between syndicalism and reformism: Founding the Communist Party of Australia", *Marxist Left Review*, 21, Summer. https://marxistleftreview.org/articles/between-syndicalism-and-reformism-founding-the-communist-party-of-australia/

Ashbolt, Anthony 2006, "The Warilla High School Strike: a veritable class struggle", *Illawarra Unity – Journal of the Illawarra Branch of the Australian Society for the Study of Labour History*, 6 (1), 2006, pp. 3-10. http://ro.uow.edu.au/unity/vol6/iss1/1

Barcan, Alan 2002, *Radical students: the old left at Sydney University*, Melbourne University Press.

Bassett, Jan 1995, *"Matters of Conscience". A History of the Victorian Secondary Teachers' Association*, (official history commissioned by the VSTA), PenFolk Publishing.

Bramble, Tom 2008, *Trade Unionism in Australia. A history from flood to ebb tide*, Cambridge University Press.

Carey, Adam 2020, "Principals demand end to face-to-face classes as school closures grow", *The Age*, 28 July. https://www.theage.com.au/national/victoria/principals-demand-end-to-face-to-face-classes-as-school-closures-grow-20200727-p55fy8.html

Dixon, John 2018, ""History Lesson: Local efforts at the core of union successes", NSW Teachers Federation website, 8 November. https://news.nswtf.org.au/blog/news/2018/11/history-lesson-local-efforts-core-union-successes

Hannan, Bill 2009, *The Best of Times. The story of the great secondary school expansion*, Lexis.

Mitchell, Bruce 1975, *Teachers, Education, and Politics. A History of Public School Teachers in New South Wales*, University of Queensland Press.

O'Lincoln, Tom 1986, "The Militant Minority. Organising rank and file workers in the thirties". https://sa.org.au/interventions/minority.htm

Peace, Meredith 2020, "COVID-19 update for schools members", AEU email to members, 28 July.

Spaull, Andrew 1975, "The Origins and Formation of the Victorian Secondary Teachers' Association 1948-1954", *Melbourne Studies in Education*, 17, 1, pp. 94-125.

Spaull, Andrew 1977, "Trends in teacher militancy", in Andrew Spaull (ed.), *Australian Teachers. From Colonial Schoolmasters to Militant Professionals*, Macmillan.

Stanton, Brendan 2020, "Victorian teachers speak out against reckless school policy", *Red Flag*, 29 July. https://redflag.org.au/node/7296

RICK KUHN

Economic crises are unavoidable under capitalism

Rick Kuhn has been active in numerous campaigns and his unions since the mid 1970s and was the convener of the anti-war coalition in Canberra opposing the invasion of Iraq.

His numerous writings include the Deutscher Prize-winning book *Henryk Grossman and the recovery of Marxism* and contributions to *Class and struggle in Australia*. He is the editor and one of the translators of the four volumes of *Henryk Grossman Works*, for each of which he has written an introduction.

RECURRENT ECONOMIC CRISES are unavoidable under capitalism. Marx's account of the mechanisms involved culminated in his discussion of the tendency for the rate of profit to fall in the third volume of *Capital*. Henryk Grossman, in his *The Law of Accumulation and Breakdown of the Capitalist System, Being also a Theory of Crises*,[1] was the first Marxist to highlight and develop Marx's account of the roots of economic crises. Grossman's and thus, often, Marx's arguments have been sharply criticised by writers identifying with both bourgeois and Marxist traditions.

Grossman was the most important Marxist economist of the twentieth century. The imminent publication of the first full translation of his book into English is an important event. Previously, aspects of his argument and his very important concluding chapter have not been accessible to an English-reading audience. The following discussion draws on the introduction to Jairus Banaji's and my translation of the work.[2]

Much of the criticism of Grossman's crisis theory has been based

---

1. First published as Grossmann (1929); abridged translation, Grossman 1992; quotations below, unless otherwise attributed, are from the full translation, Grossman 2021, forthcoming.
2. Grossman 2021.

on lazy or wilful misperceptions of it as an argument that capitalism will break down and be replaced without the need for working-class action. These travesties of his argument were often bolstered by the notion that the primary cause of economic crises lies outside the sphere of production, alien to Marx's conception.

Marx identified the tendency for capitalism to break down, due to the process of competitive capital accumulation lying at the heart of the system, the very mechanism which has led to repeated revolutionary increases in the productivity of human labour in the course of capitalist development. In his book, Grossman recovered Marx's account of this tendency and the way in which it is expressed in recurrent economic crises. While the book focused on economic questions, its purpose was also profoundly political: to identify circumstances under which revolutionary working-class struggles were most likely to arise and be successful.

The sections below assess the empirical and theoretical validity of substantive criticisms of the case he made. Brief outlines of Grossman's life and that case are necessary preliminaries.

Context

Born in 1881, Henryk Grossman became a socialist while a student at Kraków's academic high school.[3] Kraków, in the Austrian province of Galicia, was the cultural capital of partitioned Poland. When studying at the city's Jagiellonian University, he organised Yiddish-speaking Jewish workers, who had been neglected by the organisation to which he belonged, the Polish Social Democratic Party of Galicia (PPSD). On May Day 1905, when he was barely 24 years old, Grossman became the founding secretary and leading theoretician of the Jewish Social Democratic Party of Galicia (JPSD), which was modelled on the Bund (General Union of Jewish Workers) in the Russian Empire. This Marxist organisation, which split from the PPSD in order to express the interests of Jewish workers, soon had 2,000 members and a weekly newspaper.

The Russian revolution of 1905-7 had a major impact over the border in Austria-Hungary where this was also a period of heightened

---

3. Information about Grossman's life is from Kuhn 2007.

class struggle. The JSDP's secretary was a revolutionary, declaring at the Party's 1906 Congress that

> ...the use of power takes different forms. There were times when the proletariat fought with weapons on the barricades. Then weapons gave way to voting slips. Now we are preparing for a mass strike which is again the prelude to active revolutionary struggle. That is the dialectic of history: after a period of active revolution there is a period of legal struggle that again gives way to revolutionary struggle. We can therefore say that legal struggle prepares for illegal struggle. That is, a period of *accumulating* forces prepares the way for the moment when a revolutionary outbreak opens a period when rights are extended.[4]

As the level of class struggle subsided, Grossman devoted more attention to his university studies and, in late 1908, moved to Vienna where he undertook research under Carl Grünberg, the first Marxist professor at a German-speaking university. His project was to study aspects of the initial phase of the transition from feudalism to capitalism in eighteenth-century Galicia. It gave rise to several publications, including a book, which was eventually recognised as his higher doctoral thesis (*Habilitation*).[5]

During World War I Grossman served in the Austro-Hungarian army, at the front and in research posts. Deemed ineligible for citizenship by the racist policies of the post-war, rump Austrian state's first government, led by social democrats, Grossman was unable to take up the offer of a senior post in its Central Statistical Commission. Then he was appointed to a senior position in the Polish Central Statistical Office in Warsaw and charged with the organisation of the new Republic's first census. He also joined the Communist Workers Party of Poland (KPRP), the success of the Russian revolution and the policies of the Soviet state having persuaded him to abandon an aspect of the Bund's and JSDP's politics: support for national cultural autonomy for eastern European Jews.

Unwilling to fudge the results of the census in favour of ethnic Poles, Grossman left the Statistical Office for a full professorial post in

---

4. Grossman 2020b; also see Grossman 2020c.
5. Grossmann 1914.

economic policy at the non-governmental Free University of Poland (WWP) in 1922. For his political views and activities, Grossman was subjected to police repression, including five arrests between 1922 and 1925, and, although he was never convicted, periods of "investigative custody", the longest for eight months in Warsaw's infamous Pawiak Prison.

In 1925 Grossman went into qualified exile in Germany. Grünberg, now the Director of the Institute for Social Research, which was associated with the university in Frankfurt, had arranged for him to become one of his assistants. His political situation along with the comfortable income and time for research afforded by this post insulated Grossman from two pressures: from the discipline of the German Communist Party, with which he sympathised, as it succumbed to the effects of the Russian revolution's degeneration; and from some of the pressures associated with employment by a publicly financed university. After being granted a higher doctorate in 1927, he began to teach courses related to his research at the university.

This was Grossman's most productive period, during which he wrote *The Law of Accumulation and Breakdown of the Capitalist System, Being also a Theory of Crises*, published in 1929, and several related essays.

The Institute and most of its members went into exile early in 1933, after the Nazis were handed power in Germany and soon re-established itself in New York. But Grossman went to Paris, where he associated with exiled members of the Socialist Workers Party of Germany, a split from the Social Democratic Party led by prominent former members of the Communist Party of Germany. Disillusioned with Stalinism while there, he recommended Trotsky's analysis of the German catastrophe to a correspondent, the council communist Paul Mattick.

After a period in London, Grossman moved to rejoin the rest of the Institute in New York in 1937. But there was a rupture between him and the Institute in the early 1940s, although he remained on the payroll. Influenced by what he regarded as the Communist International's support for the Spanish revolution during the civil war, his faith in the Stalinist leadership of the International and Russia revived. But he never abjured his subjective commitment to working-class self-emancipation or his own work in Marxist economics, which had already been anathematised in the Communist movement in 1929. Meanwhile Max Horkheimer, at the head of the Institute, had moved away from Marxism and embraced a liberal critique of Stalinism. Pay cuts for most Institute employees, to sustain Horkheimer's comfortable lifestyle in sunny Los Angeles, were also an issue.

In 1949, Grossman left the United States of America to take up a professorial chair at Leipzig University, in Communist East Germany. This was part of a short-lived effort to re-establish the University's prestige, by recruiting prominent academics who had been in exile in the west. Despite his efforts to arrange the republication of some of his writings, that never happened in what became the Democratic Republic of Germany, where he died in 1950.

Grossman's argument

The following outline focuses on the main steps in Grossman's argument in *The Law of Accumulation*. The introduction included a description of Marx's method, which structures *Capital*, as a process of successive approximation (*Annäherungsverfahren*). Marx made a series of assumptions that bracketed out less fundamental aspects of capitalism's economic mechanism, in order to study the system's essential logic. In subsequent steps, these assumptions were lifted and the consequences examined, bringing the analysis progressively closer to the features and movements of capitalism which can be observed empirically. This approach also structured Grossman's book.

While Marx's labour theory of value entailed a theory of breakdown, it was rejected by both "revisionists", like Eduard Bernstein and Mikhail Ivanovich Tugan-Baranovsky, and apparently orthodox Marxists, like Karl Kautsky and Rudolf Hilferding. But "[i]t was Rosa Luxemburg's great historical contribution that she – in conscious opposition to and protest against the distortions of the neo-harmonists – held fast to the fundamental insight of *Capital* and sought to support it by proving that there is an *absolute economic limit* to the further development of the capitalist mode of production". Her explanation of that limit, based on the progressive disappearance of non-capitalist markets, was, however, mistaken. Quoting Lenin, Grossman stressed that, for capitalism, *"There is no such thing as an absolutely hopeless situation"*.[6] Having recovered Marx's theory, in whose elucidation the reproduction schemas of *Capital*'s second volume played a crucial role, rather than being faulty as Luxemburg argued, he returned to the relationship between capitalism's tendency to break down and working-class struggle in his book's conclusion.

Otto Bauer had elaborated a useful model of capital accumulation in a reproduction schema which he used to refute Luxemburg's contention that capitalism's survival depended on the realisation of surplus value in non-capitalist domains. Realistically, Bauer assumed with Marx that the rate of accumulation of constant capital was more rapid than that of variable capital, ie that the organic composition of capital rises. The organic composition of capital is the ratio of the value of machinery, equipment, buildings and raw materials compared to the wages bill, "in so far as it is determined by" the ratio of the physical quantity of machinery compared to the number of workers.[7]

By extending Bauer's own schema beyond the four years of his exposition, Grossman proved that accumulation cannot be sustained forever and breaks down. Given the model's assumptions, the absolute amount of surplus value set aside for the capitalist class's consumption would eventually have to decline, if the assumed rates of accumulation of constant and variable capital were to be sustained. Subsequently, even further inroads into and then the elimination of the capitalists' pleasures and subsistence would not suffice to maintain the assumed rates of accumulation. As the model assumed a constant rate of population growth, further accumulation would then also result in rising unemployment. If accumulation nevertheless continued, a point would be reached at which there was no scope for investment in further variable capital and additional outlays on constant capital would not, therefore, yield an increase in the mass of surplus value.

A crisis would already set in, however, once the incentive for

---

6. Lenin 1966, pp. 226-7.
7. Marx 1981, p. 958.

capitalists to invest disappeared, ie when their consumption fund began to decline. Even before that point, capitalists would pursue counter-measures: wage reductions or a reduction in the rate of accumulation of constant capital.

The operation of countertendencies, which Marx had identified and Grossman explored in greater detail, means that in the real world the breakdown tendency is interrupted and transformed into periods of growth punctuated by crises. Contrary to other theories of economic crises, Grossman argued that crises would recur even when prices remained constant, there was no credit squeeze, no miscalculation by capitalists, and there was proportional growth between the two departments of production, which create producer goods (department I) and consumer goods (department II).

Given the effect of countertendencies, Grossman again invoked Lenin on the absence of "hopeless situations" for capitalism. He then provided a formula for the time at which Otto Bauer's schema broke down. That point would change if the assumptions of the schema were modified by countertendencies.

The breakdown tendency expresses the way in which capitalist relations of production constitute a fetter on the development of the forces of production. The tendency for the rate of profit to fall, as the foundation for Marx's theory of breakdown and crisis, is itself an expression of the contradiction between the relations and forces of production. The output of the *labour process* creating use values knows no limits, as productivity grows. But, under capitalism, this labour process is subordinated to the *valorisation process* (the process of value creation) in the pursuit of profits. New technology is not applied wherever it can save the expenditure of labour but only where expenditure on it is outweighed by savings on wages. Moreover, as the amount of accumulated capital increases and hence the rate of profit falls, the incentive to invest in new, more expensive technology declines. The unemployment not only of machinery and equipment but also the most fundamental force of production, human labour power, as a feature of economic crises is another expression of the way capitalism fetters society's productive forces.

Grossman's concluding chapter returned to his concern with the significance of Marx's theory of breakdown and crisis for the class struggle, by discussing the logic of movements in wages and criticising the predominant social democratic contention that a non-revolutionary transition from "organised capitalism" to socialism was already under way.

Hilferding had argued that planned production could eliminate crises under capitalism and the transition to socialism could be consummated by subordinating a "general cartel", which embraced the whole of society's production, to democratic, parliamentary control.[8] But, Grossman pointed out, greater regulation of the economy by cartels does not resolve the underlying problem, which derives from the accumulation of capital in pursuit of profits, which is a fundamental feature of capitalism. The elimination of competition by monopolies and cartels on domestic markets only stimulates greater competition on international markets: the system's inherent tendency to breakdown cannot be avoided. Quoting from Marx's discussion of the commodity fetishism, Grossman contrasted Hilferding's internally inconsistent, reformist utopia with socialism:

> The *veil* [of value, concealing "the practical relations of everyday life between man and man, and man and nature"] *is not removed* from the countenance of the social life-process, ie the process of material production, until it becomes production by freely associated men, and stands under their conscious and planned control.[9]

Criticisms and responses

A plethora of objections has been raised against Grossman's arguments. Here only the most widespread and substantive ones are considered.

---

8. Hilferding 1981, p. 297; Hilferding 2017, pp. 569, 571-2.
9. Marx 1976, p. 173. Grossman's emphasis. My interpolation, which includes part of Marx's previous sentence.

A mechanical theory of automatic breakdown?

Marx has long been portrayed as a crude determinist, on the basis of trivial readings and/or ignorance of his works.[10] The argument that any materialist analysis is mechanical or determinist goes back a long way. Moses Mendelssohn made this unwarranted criticism of Baruch Spinoza's materialist understanding of the world in the late 18th century.[11]

Otto Bauer, in a similar vein, accused Luxemburg of making the economic argument that "Capitalism will...founder on the mechanical impossibility of realising surplus-value", an assessment which Bukharin repeated.[12] And Grossman went along with this, arguing that "[i]t could also suggest that capitalism could break down automatically, without the need for working class struggle". Hardly an accurate or fair charge, given Luxemburg's own political activity, her important published interventions, notably *Social Reform or Revolution* and *The Mass Strike*, and her explicit statements about the relationship among Marxist theory, capitalism's breakdown and class struggles.[13]

The same accusation was made against Grossman himself, in the strongest form: that his theory of capitalism's tendency to break down was not only mechanical but also led to the conclusion that the class struggle was irrelevant. Critics of his book on a left spectrum from council communism, through to Stalinism and social democracy, asserted that he had a mechanical theory of capitalism's breakdown.[14] It is absolutely clear, on the basis of his personal

---

10. Barth 1967, particularly p. 61, was an early example. Ferdinand Tönnies, the bourgeois sociologist, already identified how incorrect this characterisation was, Tönnies 1894, pp. 502-12. See Berlin 2013, particularly, pp. 121 and 129, and Popper 1947, particularly, pp. 97 and 127 for a more recent version of the argument about determinism.
11. Spinoza 2002, eg pp. 324-5, 447-8. Mendelssohn 2011, p. 78. On the parallels between the treatment of Spinoza and Marx see Greene and Fluss 2020.
12. Otto Bauer 2012, p. 273. Bukharin 1972, p. 149.
13. For example, Luxemburg 2008; Luxemburg 2015, pp. 362, 375.
14. Just a few examples follow. Council communist: Pannekoek 1977, pp. 77-8. Stalinist: Varga 1930, pp. 62, 95; Behrens 1952, pp. 27, 46. Social democratic: Braunthal 1929, p. 304; Helene Bauer 1929, p. 280. Also Sweezy 1962, pp. 11-20; Foster and McChesney 2010, pp. 53-4; Milios et al 2002, pp. 149.

political commitments and engagement from his youth through to his old age that this was not how he formulated or understood his own arguments. At two points in *The Law of Accumulation*, as we have seen, he was also quite explicit that capitalism will not face a "hopeless situation" in the absence of successful revolutionary class struggles. The book's conclusion affirmed that:

> The final goal which the working class struggles for is not, therefore, some ideal that is brought into the workers' movement "from the outside", in a speculative manner, whose realisation is reserved for the distant future, quite independently of the struggles that occur in the present. It is, on the contrary, as the law of breakdown developed here suggests, a result that flows from immediate day to day class struggles and whose realisation is accelerated by these struggles.

Grossman's account, like Marx's, identified how the system's tendency to break down did not result in monotonic decline but in cyclical economic crises. These, he maintained, were the circumstances in which revolutionary working-class action had the greatest likelihood of arising and of success. Hence his statements, not only in letters and manuscripts, and *The Law of Accumulation* itself, but also in publications before and after the appearance of the book. For example, before:

> "The totality of all these objective changes is called a revolutionary situation." It is not merely revolutionary consciousness (which, incidentally, cannot be produced outside a revolutionary situation, merely by hammering the final goal into heads) that only figures in addition as a further condition with a subjective character. It is rather something entirely different: *"the ability of the revolutionary class to take revolutionary mass action"*, which presupposes an *organisation* of the coherent will of the masses and *extensive experience in the class struggles* of everyday life.[15]

And after:

> The point of breakdown theory is that the revolutionary action of

---

15. Grossman 2019c, p. 143, quoting Lenin 1964, pp. 213-4, Grossman's emphasis.

the proletariat only receives its most powerful impetus *from the objective convulsion* of the established system and, at the same time, only this creates the circumstances necessary to successfully wrestle down the ruling class's resistance.[16]

But were the arguments in his book so sloppily formulated that they invited the conclusion that he advanced a theory of capitalism's automatic breakdown? This can only be asserted if unqualified statements by Grossman, such as "a relative decline in the mass of profit necessarily results in the capitalist system's breakdown", are plucked from the context of their repeated qualification in discussions of countervailing factors to the *tendency* to breakdown. For Grossman, the law of capitalism's breakdown is, undoubtedly, a corollary of Marx's law of the tendency for the rate of profit to fall.

> Even though the breakdown tendency is periodically interrupted and weakened, more and more the mechanism as a whole necessarily approaches its end, with the progress of capital accumulation, because the valorisation of this expanded capital becomes progressively more difficult as the accumulation of capital grows absolutely. If these countertendencies are themselves weakened or brought to a halt...the breakdown tendency gains the upper hand and is realised in the *absolute* form of the "last crisis".

The "last crisis" is contingent. Increases in the rate of surplus value, as a consequence of ruling-class victories in the class struggle, constitute a significant countertendency. Given that capitalism knows no "hopeless situations", the "last crisis" is best understood as class struggle which results in a successful working-class revolution. Many commentators, including critics of Grossman's work, have had no difficulty in recognising that he was not arguing that capitalism would collapse without conscious working-class intervention.[17] The evidence that he argued capitalism's downfall would occur independently of working-class struggle is as thin as that for

---

16. Grossman 2019g, p. 385. Also see Grossman 2019i, pp. 596-7.
17. Mattick 1934, pp. 19-20; Marramao 1975, p. 63; Krahl 2008, pp. 88-9, 213; Shaikh 1978, p. 236; Tula 1979, ppxxx, xxxvi-xxxvii; Glaser 1981, p. 237; Howard and King 1989, pp. 329, 331-2.

attributing the same view to Marx and Engels on the basis of rhetorical flourishes, such as the assertion in the *Communist Manifesto* that the bourgeoisie's "fall and the victory of the proletariat are equally inevitable".[18] On this issue, Grossman's position, expressed with particular clarity in a publication which appeared after *The Law of Accumulation*, was the same as Marx's: "regularly recurring catastrophes lead to their repetition on a higher scale, and finally to its [capital's] violent overthrow".[19]

Countertendencies

Before Grossman, Marxists had noted Marx's "law of the tendential fall in the rate of profit" but failed to attribute significance to it in the explanation of crises and capitalism's tendency to break down. Criticisms of Grossman's discussion of the law opened the way to the same criticisms being directly targeted against Marx *by Marxists*. The criticisms raised early by the social democratic Marxist Helene Bauer have often been repeated. They focus on two factors which countervail to the tendency for the rate of profit to fall: the way improved technology increases the productivity of labour and therefore reduces the value of both means of consumption and means for production.[20] Sweezy explicitly argued against Marx that the balance between rises in the organic composition of capital and increases in the rate of surplus value was indeterminate and that the tendency for the rate of profit to fall could only be maintained on the basis of a falling rate of surplus value.[21]

Hans Neisser, a mainstream economist and social democrat, was a pioneer in explicitly extending criticisms of Grossman to Marx, within a social democratic framework. While Ladislaus von Bortkiewicz in 1907 had maintained that new technology would *never* reduce the rate of profit, Neisser in 1931 argued that the introduction

---

18. Marx and Engels 1976, p. 496.
19. Marx 1987, p. 134. Grossman's interpolation. My emphasis.
20. Helene Bauer 1929, p. 274. The conservative Muhs 1931, pp. 14-5, asserted that increases in relative surplus value "at least" offset rises in the organic composition of capital. Much earlier, Tugan-Baranowsky 1901, pp. 211-5, had attempted to refute the law of the tendency for the rate of profit to fall in terms of a rising rate of surplus value as a consequence of the introduction of new technology.
21. Sweezy 1962, pp. 100-6.

of new technology does *not necessarily* result in a higher organic composition of capital and hence a lower rate of profit, because it increases the productivity of labour and hence cheapens the value of commodities, including means of production.[22] Bortkiewicz's categorical argument was repeated against Grossman and Marx by the conservative Marxologist Karl Muhs[23] and, more recently via the mathematical demonstration of Nobuo Okishio, by leftists and Marxists.[24]

Marx and Grossman included a higher rate of surplus value and cheapening of constant capital in their discussion of countervailing factors. The scope for increasing absolute surplus value (making workers labour longer for the same pay) is limited by the fact that there are only 24 hours in a day; and for increasing relative surplus value (by increasing the proportion of the day workers labour to create the value appropriated by capitalists, as opposed to the value of their wages, that is the value of what they consume) by the length of the working day. Both must be under 100 percent. The value composition of capital, understood as the relationship between dead and living labour in the production process, on the other hand, can rise indefinitely, overwhelming increases in the rate of surplus value.[25]

The notion that not only the technical but also the organic composition of capital, simply expressed as that the ratio of investment in constant capital to outlays on wages, has not risen in the long run under capitalism is simply fanciful. If improvements in productivity due to improved technology are similar in the departments producing means of production and means of consumption, then

---

22. Bortkiewicz 1952, pp. 58-74; Neisser 1931, pp. 79-80. The bourgeois economist Miksch 1930 made the same point against Marx and Grossman.
23. "There is no doubt that a higher organic composition only becomes a reality, even it can be achieved technically, if it yields higher profits. A falling rate of profit and rising organic composition are therefore in fundamental contradiction with each other". Muhs 1931, p. 17.
24. Okishio 1961. Accepting the Okishio theorem were, for example, Parijs 1980; and, citing Parijs in support, Harvey 1982, p. 185; Heinrich 2014, pp. 339-40; and, citing Heinrich in support, Milios et al 2002, pp. 150-7.
25. Argued and mathematically demonstrated in Yaffe 1973, pp 201-2; Cogoy 1987, pp. 61-4; Shaikh 1987. Also see Harman 1999, p. 28; and the classic defence of Marx's account of the tendency for the rate of profit to fall, Rosdolsky 1977, pp. 376-82.

changes in the organic composition of capital will parallel changes in the technical composition of capital.[26] Moreover Grossman, in an unpublished manuscript, later pointed out that:

> [T]he question of whether devaluation is of the same extent as the growth in the mass of the MP [means of production] and thus the growth in mass is paralysed by the decline in value, or rather whether devaluation is not as great and consequently that despite the devaluation of the MP, *its value in relation to L [labour] grows*, cannot be abstractly, deductively decided and has to be decided through *empirical observation. Experience*, indeed experience of more than one hundred years, teaches that the value of constant capital, thus also of the total capital, in relation to variable capital *grows more quickly* than variable...[27]

The refutation of the Bortkiewicz/Okishio contention that technological change cannot reduce the rate of profit is relatively straightforward. Technological innovation can raise the rate of profit for the first capitalists to invest in it, because they can sell their products at prices determined by the average costs of production in the industry, above their lower costs of production, ie above their values. In order to stay in business, competitors have to adopt the new technology too. But once the bulk of the industry is using that technology, the average costs of production and hence prices will be close to that experienced by the innovators. The extra profit will evaporate and, other things being equal, the average rate of profit will fall. This temporal process cannot be captured by mainstream economics with its assumption of instantaneous adjustments.[28]

A different countertendency to those discussed by Grossman's critics was particularly important during the 1950s and 1960s. Massive, competitive arms spending helped sustain the long post-World War II boom. Unlike the products of departments

---

26. Shaikh 1978, p. 251.
27. Grossman 2019d, p. 212. My interpolations.
28. For an extensive and mathematical refutation of the "Okishio theorem" and outline of its history see Kliman 2007, especially pp. 44-5, 113-38. Carchedi and Roberts 2013 provided a systematic defence of Marx's theory of the tendency for the rate of profit to fall against the Okishio and other criticisms.

producing means of production and means of consumption, the output of the arms industry cannot return to the circuit of capital. The expansion of the arms industry therefore slowed down accumulation and the tendency for the rate of profit to fall, by diverting surplus value which could otherwise have been invested and thus raised the organic composition of capital.[29]

A permanently falling rate of profit

Neisser and Anton Pannekoek argued that accumulation of both constant and variable capital could grow forever in Grossman's schema, but at lower rates. The schema only gave rise to idle machinery, equipment and buildings with insufficient workers to set them in motion because Grossman had made the arbitrary assumption that constant capital would be prioritised over variable capital in the allocation of surplus value for investment.[30] This objection ignored the point of Grossman's argument. Where Otto Bauer's reproduction schema, with its equally arbitrary assumptions, was intended to show that capital accumulation could continue forever, Grossman's schema, based on Bauer's, effectively demonstrated that accumulation cannot be maintained indefinitely at any given rate of additional investment. The allocation of additional investment was not, furthermore, arbitrary in Grossman's schema. Taking use values into account, the production of means of consumption in it became insufficient to sustain accumulation of variable capital first, before production of means of production had a chance to become insufficient to sustain accumulation of constant capital.

A rational *collective* response to a falling average rate of profit

---

29. Harman 2009, pp. 129-32, 166-8. Harman had previously explained the effect of military spending on the rate of profit, in part, by invoking Bortkiewicz's neo-Ricardian solution of the "transformation problem", which meant that a high organic composition of capital in industries producing commodities which are not means of production or of consumption did not undermine the rate of profit in other sectors (for example, Harman 1999, pp. 81, 167). Schmiede and Yaffe 1972, p. 8, criticised this argument. In his 2009 book, Harman tacitly abandoned that approach and simply argued that unproductive expenditure on arms slowed the rise in the organic composition of capital, referencing Grossman as well as Marx.
30. Neisser 1931, pp. 83-4; Pannekoek 1977, pp. 69-70. Also see the suggestion that the personal consumption fund for capitalists can be maintained at the expense of unemployment (and hence the rate of accumulation) in Trottmann 1956, pp. 26-8.

would be for the whole of the capitalist class to lower the rate of accumulation in concert. But, as both Grossman himself, earlier, and Harman pointed out, competition among capitals means that the rational response of *individual* capitals may be to maintain or even raise their rate of investment, in order to keep up with or undercut their rivals by reducing the price of their output below the average price for the industry, thus maintaining or improving their share of total surplus value.[31]

The lumpiness of constant capital as use values, Grossman later observed, is also a factor which can disrupt accumulation as the rate of profit falls.[32] Particularly at very low rates of profit, the amount of surplus value created in a single year may not be sufficient to purchase the minimum unit increments of constant capital, embodied in a large productive complex, which can generate new commodities and maintain the circuit of capital.

Impoverishment

The social democrats Alfred Braunthal and Helene Bauer both joked that Grossman had derived the breakdown of capitalism from the impoverishment of the capitalists rather than of the proletariat.[33] Another of Grossman's unpublished manuscripts included the response that:

> Nowhere did I say that capitalism will go under due to the impoverishment of the capitalists. I showed, rather, that an increasingly large part of surplus value (a_c) is, under the assumptions of Bauer's schema, devoted to accumulation. The remainder available for the consumption of the capitalists and workers does not suffice. As a consequence an increasingly sharp struggle between workers and entrepreneurs over the level of wages necessarily flares up. *If* workers continue to receive the same wage, then nothing *remains* for the entrepreneurs. If, however, the latter maintain and, where possible, even increase their living standard then they force down the level of wages, ie

---

31. Grossman 2019b, p. 47; Harman 2009, p. 78.
32. Grossman 2019h, p. 532.
33. Braunthal 1929, p. 294; Helene Bauer 1929, p. 275. Similarly Muhs 1931, p. 23.

from this point on the *impoverishment of the workers* necessarily sets in. That, however, drives the workers to revolution and, as a result of this impoverishment of the workers, and [sic] capitalism will go under.[34]

Method

There have been debates over Grossman's account, in *The Law of Accumulation* and his essay on "Change in the Original Plan for Marx's *Capital*", of Marx's method and the structure of *Capital*. That debate and evidence supporting Grossman's assessment have been discussed at some length elsewhere.[35] Overall, his explanation of the structure of *Capital*, in terms of Marx's method of successive approximation, along with the logic of the change in Marx's plan for *Capital*, if not its timing, have withstood criticism.[36]

One-sidedness

According to Arkadij Gurland and Roman Rosdolsky, Grossman's analysis was one-sided, because it ignored capitalism's realisation problems.[37] This is true and it could be added that he also ignored, for example, capitalism's transient problems in maintaining proportional outputs among industries, economic disruption caused by war and difficulties that arise in the credit system (not to mention the economic impact of a deadly global epidemic), all of which can give rise to difficulties in the process of accumulation and can trigger crises. But this was deliberate. Grossman's purpose in *The Law of Accumulation* was to carefully identify *fundamental* contradictions of capitalism which emerge from its core in the *process of production* itself. Varga's (erroneous) complaint that the book had not

---

34. Grossman 2019d, pp. 216-7. My interpolation.
35. Kuhn 2013.
36. On Marx's method in Capital, see Callinicos 2014, particularly p. 130.
37. Gurland 1930, p. 80; Rosdolsky 1957, p. 355. For similar criticisms, which regard additional factors as of equal importance to Marx's account of the tendency for the rate of profit to fall in the explanation of crises, see Clarke 1994; and Harvey 2016. For a response to the condemnation of "monocausal explanations" see Carchedi 2010, p. 124.

mentioned the Bolshevik revolution or the circumstances in which it occurred,[38] was likewise beside the point.

Relevance of the value-price transformation

Neisser argued that Grossman's analysis did not take into account the transformation of commodities' values into prices of production, through the equalisation of profit rates across industries. (According to Marx, market prices fluctuate around prices of production.) Basing his argument on Tugan-Baranovsky's and Bortkiewicz's criticisms of the way Marx handled this transformation, Neisser asserted that the prices-of-production rate of profit could vary from the value rate of profit and that it was therefore "in no way certain that giving up this assumption [that commodities exchange at their values] must not alone finally lead to the profound modifications of Grossman's theory".[39] In response, Grossman asserted that his analysis was an aggregate one of general crises embracing all spheres of production, which would not be affected by changes in relative prices because total values equal total prices. Elements of his analysis did, however, include the allocation of surplus value between the departments of production. In a counter-attack, Grossman also noted that the neoharmonists' contention that capital accumulation could continue smoothly, ie proportionately, was made on the basis of the reproduction schemes of the second volume of *Capital*. But this conclusion was not justified before the transformation of values into prices of production and further modifications, which result from the introduction of commercial profit, interest and ground rent, are taken into account.[40]

The "transformation problem" has subsequently, moreover, been satisfactorily resolved in a way which, contrary to Bortkiewicz, maintains the equivalence of the value and prices-of-production rates of profit.[41]

---

38. Varga 1930, p. 62. Bukharin 1972 is criticised in The Law of Accumulation for neglecting to systematically examine the economic causes of the breakdown which contributed to the Bolshevik revolution and overgeneralising from the Russian case.
39. Neisser 1931, pp. 74. Grossman's interpolation.
40. Grossman 2019f, pp. 311-14.
41. See Kliman 2007 and Moseley 2016.

Inconsistencies

The arguments in *The Law of Accumulation* were not flawless. There were inconsistencies and errors. In places, Grossman sloppily wrote that the mass of surplus value/profit declined in his schema, for example:

> In the final phase of the business cycle, the mass of profit (s), and therefore also its accumulated constant (a_c) and variable (a_v) parts, contract so sharply that it no longer suffices to sustain accumulation on the previous assumptions, that is, in accord with the annual increase in population.

But the mass of employed variable capital never fell during the 36 years of the schema Grossman presented and, as the rate of surplus value was constant, the mass of surplus value/profit did not fall either. Grossman conflated an accurate account of what happens during empirical business cycles with an accurate description of his reproduction schema. "In the final stages of the business cycle", but not in Grossman's schema, the mass of profit does contract sharply. The mass of profit does become insufficient to sustain the assumed rate of accumulation in Grossman's schema but it, as opposed to the size of the capitalists' personal consumption fund k, does *not* decline.

Likewise, rather than writing "a decline in the mass of profit", in the following passage, Grossman should have referred to "too great a *relative* decline in the mass of profit".

> [F]rom the law of accumulation it follows...that at any *given* population [growth rate] capital accumulation encounters an insuperable barrier beyond which any further accumulation is pointless, because it will be accompanied by a decline in the mass of profit and therefore also with the emergence of a reserve army.

And the use of a quotation from Marx to justify Grossman's identification of the pivotal role of capitalists' personal consumption was questionable: "The fall in the rate of profit would be accompanied *this time by an absolute decline in the mass of profit*... And the reduced mass of profit would have to be calculated on an enlarged total capital".[42] Marx's observation was made in the course of a discussion which was not entirely clear and included the possibility of a fall in the rate of surplus value as wages were bid up.

Elsewhere Grossman was more careful, specifying that "a relative decline [or fall] in the mass of profit" was the trigger for breakdown.[43]

There was also inconsistency in Grossman's use of the terms "absolute overaccumulation",[44] "overaccumulation", and "overproduction". They were used to designate both the point in his schema beyond which the capitalists' consumption fund began to decline and the point beyond which, in reality and following Marx, further accumulation produces no additional surplus value. Grossman also conflated the latter with the point in his schema at which the capitalists' consumption fund disappeared and it broke down because its assumed rate of accumulation of constant and variable capital cannot be sustained.[45] This terminological confusion does not invalidate his schema, which demonstrates that capitalism tends to break down, given any specific rate of accumulation, nor his account of capitalism's inevitable experience of economic crises and his claim to have derived these from Marx's analysis, if more creatively than he implied.

Credit

Grossman's attempt to encompass credit in a reproduction schema failed. He portrayed the source of credit as a fund made up of deductions from new investment, slowing it over several years, which is subsequently drawn down to sustain investment in later years. This would disrupt the circuit of capital because surplus value, in concrete form, would lie idle for years until it was redeployed back

---

42. Marx 1981, p. 360. Grossman's emphasis.
43. My interpolations. Grossman later asserted that "I do not claim that surplus value becomes smaller. It can become larger. And still it is insufficient...", Grossman 2019e, p. 229. This was true of the claims embodied in his numerical examples but not consistently in his textual argument.
44. As pointed out by Trottmann 1956, pp. 9-10.
45. In Grossman's discussion of the formation of a reserve army of labour both the points at which the capitalists' consumption funds starts to decline and at which it disappears seem to be equated with Marx's account of overproduction.

into production.⁴⁶ In a different context, after the publication of *The Law of Accumulation*, Grossman himself warned against the introduction of credit into Marx's schemas:

> After all, it is one of the many simplifying assumptions of Marx's reproduction schema that it *abstracts from credit*. The very purpose of the schema is to show the exchange relations between its two departments and to investigate whether *complete sale* is possible. It is not permissible to change the initial assumptions after the fact, once one has encountered difficulties in solving the problem.⁴⁷

Empirical verification

Since 1957, there have been studies which have attempted to test Marx's law of the tendency for the rate of profit to fall against statistical evidence, especially of trends in the economy of the United States.⁴⁸ But the translation of the categories of bourgeois economics and statistical collections into aggregates which match Marxist concepts remains a challenge. From the 1980s, statistical studies became more frequent and, in some cases, more sophisticated. Differences in results have often arisen from different approaches to the translation. That there have not been any attempts to operationalise Grossman's account of the role of capitalists' private consumption statistically is understandable, given that it was an heuristic device to highlight the role of class struggle in patterns of economic growth, the course and the onset of crises.

A collection, edited by Guglielmo Carchedi and Michael Roberts, in which Grossman's insights were invoked at several points, offered extensive evidence for Marx's account of the tendency for the rate of profit to fall in the long run, due to a rising organic composition of capital, at the level of several national economies and globally. Contributors also related fluctuations in the rate of profit to periods of economic contraction and growth and also provided

---

46. See Trottman 1956, pp. 45-7; Howard and King 1989, p. 331.
47. Grossman 2019f, p. 326.
48. See the pioneering work of Gillman 1957 and Mage 1963.

extensive references to the previous, very substantial empirical literature.[49]

In summary

Grossman's fundamental arguments about capitalism's tendency to break down because of the law of the tendency for the rate of profit to fall, and the way this takes the form of recurrent economic crises, withstands the criticisms made of it. There are, in *The Law of Accumulation*, some exaggerated statements, some mis-specifications and an inadequate attempt to incorporate credit into Marx's reproduction schemas. But, far more importantly, it grounds Marx's and Engels's proposition that bourgeoisie "is unfit to rule because it is incompetent to assure an existence to its slave within his slavery"[50] in a powerful analysis of economic crises as arising from the very essence of the capitalist process of production. That analysis also reinforces their conclusion that capitalism can only be superseded through its revolutionary overthrow by the working class.

---

49. Carchedi and Roberts 2018. Also see Jones 2014.
50. Marx and Engels 1976, p. 495.

References

Barth, Paul 1967 [1890], *Die Geschichtsphilosophie Hegels und der Hegelianer bis auf Marx and Hartmann*, Wissenschaftliche Buchgesellschaft.

Bauer, Helene 1929, "Ein neuer Zusammenbruchstheoretiker", *Der Kampf*, 22, 6, June, pp. 270-80.

Bauer, Otto 2012 [1913], "The Accumulation of Capital", in *Discovering Imperialism: Social Democracy to World War I*, translated, edited and introduced by Richard B Day and Daniel Gaido, Brill, pp. 719-43.

Behrens, Fritz 1952, *Zur Methode der polischen Ökonomie: Ein Beitrag zur Geschichte der politischen Ökonomie*, Akademie.

Berlin, Isaiah 2013 [1939], *Karl Marx*, Princeton University Press.

Bortkiewicz, Ladislaus von 1952 [1907], "Value and Price in the Marxian System", translated by J Kahane. http://classiques,uqac,ca/classiques/Bortkiewicz_ladislaus_von/value_and_price_marxian_system/value_price_marxian_system.pdf

Braunthal, Alfred 1929, "Der Zusammenbruch der Zusammenbruchstheorie", *Die Gesellschaft*, 6, 10, pp. 289-304.

Bukharin Nikolai 1972 [1925], *Imperialism and the Accumulation of Capital*, with Rosa Luxemburg, *The Accumulation of Capital: An Anti-Critique*, edited by Kenneth Tarbuck, translated by Rudolf Wichmann, Monthly Review Press.

Callinicos, Alex 2104, *Deciphering Capital: Marx's Capital and Its Destiny*, Bookmarks.

Carchedi, Guglielmo 2010, "Zombie Capitalism and the origin of crises", *International Socialism*, 125, Winter, pp. 113-26. https://isj.org.uk/zombie-capitalism-and-the-origin-of-crises/

Carchedi, Guglielmo and Michael Roberts 2013, "Marx's Law of Profitability: Answering Old and New Misconceptions", *Critique*, 41, 4, pp. 571-97.

Carchedi, Guglielmo and Michael Roberts (eds) 2018, *World in Crisis: A Global Analysis of Marx's Law of Profitability*, Haymarket.

Clarke, Simon 1994, *Marx's Theory of Crisis*, Macmillan.

Cogoy, Mario 1987 [1973], "The Falling Rate of Profit and the Theory of Accumulation", *International Journal of Political Economy*, 17, 2, Summer, pp. 54-74.

Foster, John Bellamy and Robert W McChesney 2010, "Listen Keynesians, it's the system! Response to Palley", *Monthly Review*, 61, 11, April, pp. 44-56.

Gillman, Joseph Moses 1957, *The Falling Rate of Profit, Marx's Law and Its Significance to Twentieth-Century Capitalism*, Dobson.

Glaser, Ernst 1981, *Im Umfeld des Austromarxismus: Ein Beitrag zur Geschichte des österreichischen Sozialismus*, Europa Verlag.

Greene, Doug Enaa and Harrison Fluss 2020, "Enlightenment Betrayed: Part I", *Left Voice*, July 14. https://www.leftvoice.org/enlightenment-betrayed-jonathan-israel-marxism-and-the-enlightenment-legacy.

Grossmann, Henryk 1914, "Österreichs Handelspolitik mit Bezug auf Galizien in der Reformperiode 1772-1790", in series *Studien zur Soziale-, Wirtschafts- und Verwaltungsgeschichte*, herausgegeben von Carl Grünberg, 10. Heft, Konegen.

Grossman, Henryk 1929, *Das Akkumulations- und Zusammenbruchsgesetz des kapitalistischen Systems (zugleich eine Krisentheorie)*, Hirschfeld.

Grossman, Henryk 1992 [1929], *The Law of Accumulation and Breakdown of the Capitalist System: Being also a Theory of Crises*, abridged and translated by Jairus Banaji, Pluto Press.

Grossman, Henryk 2019a, *Henryk Grossman Works, Volume 1: Essays and Letters on Economic Theory*, translated by Domenika Balwin et al, edited and introduced by Rick Kuhn, Brill.

Grossman, Henryk 2019b [1922, paper presented 1919], "The Theory of Economic Crisis" in *Henryk Grossman Works, Volume 1: Essays and Letters on Economic Theory*, edited and introduced by Rick Kuhn, Brill, pp. 44-9.

Grossman, Henryk 2019c [1928], "A New Theory of Imperialism and the Social Revolution", translated by Geoffrey McCormack and Julian Germann, in *Henryk Grossman Works, Volume 1: Essays and Letters on Economic Theory*, edited and introduced by Rick Kuhn, Brill, pp. 120-76.

Grossman, Henryk 2019d [circa 1929-32], "Notes for 'Response to Criticisms of the Principle Work'", translated by Rick Kuhn, in *Henryk Grossman Works, Volume 1: Essays and Letters on Economic Theory*, edited and introduced by Rick Kuhn, Brill, pp. 210-25.

Grossman, Henryk 2019e [1931-7], "Letters to Frieda and Paul Mattick", translated by Ben Fowkes, Tom O'Lincoln and Rick Kuhn, in *Henryk Grossman Works, Volume 1: Essays and Letters on Economic Theory*, edited and introduced by Rick Kuhn, Brill, pp. 226-75.

Grossman, Henryk 2019f [1931], "The Value-Price Transformation in Marx and the Problem of Crisis", translated by David Meienreis, in *Henryk Grossman Works, Volume 1: Essays and Letters on Economic Theory*, edited and introduced by Rick Kuhn, Brill, pp. 304-31.

Grossman, Henryk 2019g [1932/1933], "Fifty Years of Struggle over Marxism 1883-1932", translated by Rick Kuhn and Einde O'Callaghan, in *Henryk Grossman Works, Volume 1: Essays and Letters on Economic Theory*, edited and introduced by Rick Kuhn, Brill, pp. 332-89.

Grossman, Henryk 2019h [1941], "Marx, Classical Political Economy and the Problem of Dynamics", translated by Rick Kuhn, in *Henryk Grossman Works, Volume 1: Essays and Letters on Economic Theory*, edited and introduced by Rick Kuhn, Brill, pp. 469-533.

Grossman, Henryk 2019i [1943], "The Evolutionist Revolt against Classical Economics", in *Henryk Grossman Works, Volume 1: Essays and Letters on Economic Theory*, edited and introduced by Rick Kuhn, Brill, pp. 556-99.

Grossman, Henryk 2020a, *Henryk Grossman Works, Volume 2: Political Writings*, translated by Dominika Balwin et al, edited and introduced by Rick Kuhn, Brill.

Grossman, Henryk 2020b [1906], "Our Position on Electoral Reform", translated by Rick Kuhn, in *Henryk Grossman Works, Volume 2: Political Writings*, edited and introduced by Rick Kuhn, Brill, pp. 136-46.

Grossman, Henryk 2020c [1907], "Bundism in Galicia", translated by Floris Kalman and Rick Kuhn, in *Henryk Grossman Works, Volume 2: Political Writings*, edited and introduced by Rick Kuhn, Brill, pp. 161-90.

Grossman, Henryk 2021 forthcoming [1929], *Henryk Grossman Works, Volume 3: The Law of Accumulation and Breakdown of the Capitalist System, Being also a Theory of Crises*, translated by Jairus Banaji and Rick Kuhn, edited and introduced by Rick Kuhn, Brill.

Gurland, Arkadij 1930, "Absatz und Verwertung im Kapitalismus: Zur neueren Diskussion des Zusammenbruchsproblems", *Klassenkampf*, 4, 3, pp. 75-83.

Harman, Chris 1999 [1984], *Explaining the Crisis: A Marxist Reappraisal*, Bookmarks. https://www.marxists.org/archive/harman/1984/explain/index.html

Harman, Chris 2009, *Zombie Capitalism: Global Crisis and the Relevance of Marx*, Bookmarks. https://www.marxists.org/archive/harman/2009/zombiecap/index.html

Harvey, David 1982, *The Limits to Capital*, Blackwell.

Harvey, David 2016, "Crisis theory and the Falling Rate Of Profit", in *The Great Financial Meltdown: Systemic, Conjunctural or Policy Created?*, edited by Turan Subasat, Elgar, pp. 37-54.

Heinrich, Michael 2014 [1991], *Die Wissenschaft vom Wert: Die Marxsche Kritik der politischen Ökonomie zwischen Wissenschaftlicher Revolution und klassischer Tradition*, Westfälisches Dampfboot.

Hilferding, Rudolf 1981 [1910], *Finance Capital: A Study of the Latest Phase of Capitalist Development*, translated by Morris Watnick and Sam Gordon, Routledge & Kegan Paul.

Hilferding, Rudolf 2017 [1927], "The Tasks of Social Democracy in the Republic", in *Austro-Marxism: The Ideology of Unity, Volume II: Changing the World: The Politics of Austro-Marxism*, edited by Mark E Blum and William Smaldone, Brill, pp. 568-90.

Howard, Michael Charles and John Edward King 1989, *A History of Marxian Economics, Volume I: 1883-1929*, Princeton University Press.

Jones, Peter 2014, "The Falling Rate of Profit and the Great Recession", PhD thesis, Australian National University.

Kliman, Andrew 2007, *Reclaiming Marx's "Capital": A Refutation of the Myth of Inconsistency*, Lexington. http://ecopol.sociales.uba.ar/wp-content/uploads/sites/202/2013/09/Kliman_Reclaiming-Marxs-Capital.pdf

Krahl, Hans Jürgen 2008 [1971, written 1966-7], "Bemerkungen zur Akkumulation und Krisentendenz des Kapitals", in Hans-Jürgen Krahl, *Konstitution und Klassenkampf Zur historischen Dialektik von bürgerlichen Emanzipation und proletarischer Revolution: Schriften, Reden und Entwürfe aus den Jahren 1966-1970*, Neue Kritik, pp. 84-99.

Kuhn, Rick 2007, *Henryk Grossman and the Recovery of Marxism*, University of Illinois Press.

Kuhn, Rick 2013, "Introduction to 'The Change in the Original Plan for Marx's *Capital* and Its Causes'", *Historical Materialism*, 21, 3, pp. 117-37.

Lenin, Vladimir Ilyich 1964 [1915], "The Collapse of the Second International", in Vladimir Ilych Lenin, *Collected Works, Volume 21*, Progress, pp. 205-59. https://www.marxists.org/archive/lenin/works/1915/csi/

Lenin, Vladimir Ilyich 1966 [1920], "Report on the international situation and the fundamental tasks of the Communist International", in Vladimir Ilyich Lenin, *Collected Works, Volume 31*, Progress, pp. 215-34. https://www.marxists.org/archive/lenin/works/1920/jul/x03.htm

Luxemburg, Rosa 2008 [1899, 1908], *The Essential Rosa Luxemburg: "Reform or Revolution" and "The Mass Strike"*, Haymarket.

Luxemburg, Rosa 2015 [1921, written 1915], *The Accumulation of Capital, Or, What the Epigones Have Made out of Marx's Theory – An Anti-critique*, in Rosa Luxemburg, *The Complete Works of Rosa Luxemburg: Volume II, Economic Writings 2*, translated by George Shriver, edited by Peter Hudis and Paul Le Blanc, Verso, pp. 345-449.

Mage, Shane 1963, "The "Law of the Falling Tendency of the Rate of Profit': Its Place in the Marxian Theoretical System and Relevance to the U.S. Economy", PhD thesis, Columbia University.

Marramao, Giacomo 1975 [1973], "Political Economy and Critical Theory", translated by Ray Morrow, *Telos*, 24, Summer, pp. 56-80.

Marx, Karl 1976 [1867], *Capital: A Critique of Political Economy, Volume 1*, translated by Ben Fowkes, Penguin. https://www.marxists.org/archive/marx/works/1867-c1/

Marx, Karl 1981, [1894], *Capital: A Critique of Political Economy, Volume 3*, translated by David Fernbach, Harmondsworth: Penguin. https://www.marxists.org/archive/marx/works/download/pdf/Capital-Volume-III.pdf

Marx, Karl 1987 [written 1857-8], "Outlines of the Critique of Political Economy (Rough Draft of 1857-58) [Second Instalment]", in Karl Marx and Frederick Engels, *Collected Works, Volume 29*, International Publishers, pp. 5-251.

Marx, Karl and Frederick Engels 1976 [1848], *Manifesto of the Communist Party*, in Karl Marx and Frederick Engels, *Collected Works, Volume 6*, International Publishers, pp. 477-519. https://www.marxists.org/archive/marx/works/1848/communist-manifesto/

Mattick, Paul 1934, "The Permanent Crisis: Henryk Grossmann's Interpretation of Marx's Theory of Capitalist Accumulation", *International Council Correspondence*, 1, 2, November, pp. 1-20.

Mendelssohn, Moses 2011 [1785], *Morning Hours: Lectures on God's Existence*, translated by Daniel O Dahlstrom and Corey Dyck, Springer.

Miksch, Leonhard 1930, "Zusammenbruch des kapitalistischen Systems?" *Frankfurter Zeitung*, 75 (610), Sunday 17 August, second morning edition, p. 7.

Milios, John, Dimitri Dimoulis and George Economakis 2002, *Karl Marx and the Classics: An Essay on Value, Crises and the Capitalist Mode of Production*, Ashgate.

Moseley, Fred 2016, *Money and Totality: A Macro-Monetary Interpretation of Marx's Logic in* Capital *and the End of the "Transformation Problem"*, Brill.

Muhs, Karl 1931, "Das Gesetz der fallenden Profitrate und die Zusammenbruchstendenz des Kapitalismus", *Jahrbuch für Nationalökonomie und Statistik*, 135, 1, July, pp. 1-29.

Neisser, Hans 1931, "Das Gesetz der fallenden Profitrate als Krisen- und Zusammenbruchsgesetz", *Die Gesellschaft*, 8, 1, pp. 72-85.

Okishio, Nobuo 1961, "Technical Change and the Rate of Profit", *Kobe University Economic Review*, 7, pp. 85-99.

Pannekoek, Anton 1977 [1934], "The theory of the collapse of capitalism", translated by Adam Buick, *Capital and Class*, 1, pp. 59-81.

Parijs, Philippe Van 1980, "The Falling-Rate-of Profit Theory of Crisis: A Rational Reconstruction by Way of Obituary", *Review of Radical Political Economics*, 12, 1, Spring, pp. 1-16.

Popper, Karl Raimund 1947, *The Open Society and Its Enemies, Volume II: The High Tide of Prophecy Hegel, Marx, and the Aftermath*, Routledge.

Rosdolsky, Roman 1957, review of Martin Trottmann, *Zur Interpretation und Kritik der Zusammenbruchstheorie von Henryk Grossmann*, Kyklos, 10, 3, pp. 353-5.

Rosdolsky, Roman 1977 [1968], *The Making of Marx's "Capital"*, Pluto.

Schmiede, Rudi and David Yaffe 1972 [written 1971], *State Expenditure and the Marxian Theory of Crisis*, London.

Shaikh, Anwar 1978, "An Introduction to the History of Crisis Theories", in *U.S. Capitalism in Crisis*, edited by Bruce Steinberg et al, Union for Radical Political Economics, pp. 219-41.

Shaikh, Anwar 1987, "Organic Composition of Capital", in *Marxian Economics*, edited by John Eatwell, Murray Milgate and Peter Newman, Palgrave Macmillan, pp. 304-9.

Spinoza, Benedict de 2004 [1662-77], *Spinoza: Complete Works*, translated by Samuel Shirley, Hackett.

Sweezy, Paul 1962 [1942], *The Theory of Capitalist Development*, Dobson.

Tönnies, Ferdinand, 1894, "Neuere Philosophie der Geschichte: Hegel, Marx, Comte", *Archiv für Geschichte der Philosophie*, 7, pp. 486-515.

Trottmann, Martin 1956, *Zur Interpretation und Kritik der Zusammenbruchstheorie von Henryk Grossmann*, Polygraphischer Verlag.

Tugan-Baranowsky, Mikhail Ivanovich 1901 [1894], *Studien zur Theorie und Geschichte der Handelskrisen in England*, translation of second Russian edition, Fischer.

Tula, Jorge, 1979, "Prefacio" in Henryk Grossmann, *La ley de la acumulación y del derrumbe del sistema capitalista: una teoría de la crisis*, Siglo Veintiuno, ppix-xxxvii.

Varga, Eugen 1930, "Akkumulation und Zusammenbruch des Kapitalismus", *Unter dem Banner des Marxismus*, 4, 1, pp. 60-95.

Yaffe David 1973 [1972], "The Marxian Theory of Crisis, Capital and the State", *Economy and Society*, 2, 2, pp. 186-232.

TERRY IRVING

From the rising tide to Govett's Leap: The socialist life of Gordon Childe

Terry Irving (https://www.terryirving.net/) is a radical educationist and historian whose ASIO file begins in 1953.

He helped found the Free University in Sydney, and was a prominent New Left figure in the labour history movement. With Rowan Cahill he runs the blog Radical Sydney/Radical History (http://radicalsydney.blogspot.com.au/). He is an Honorary Professorial Fellow at the University of Wollongong.

Delivered on 14 November 2020 to the Blackheath History Forum, its 9th annual "VG Childe Lecture".

IT IS HARD to think about Vere Gordon Childe, the Australian socialist and pioneering Marxist archaeologist, without thinking about his death. As a man, as a scholar, as a socialist, he is rarely presented as if his death was inconsequential, something natural – because it wasn't. He jumped off a cliff at Blackheath in the NSW Blue Mountains. And as we struggle to understand that wilful ending of life in the spring of 1957, to replace a fading full stop with an incandescent question mark, we can take two paths.

Taking the first path, one gathers arguments about Childe's experiences in the last few months of his life, because, on this path, suicide is regarded as such a denial of life's worth that something must have happened near its end to upend it; some existential crisis must have occurred. For example: he must have been suffering from depression because he was old, ill and without family. Or, he was politically disillusioned by the events of 1956 because Khrushchev's secret speech about Stalin's crimes, and the Soviet invasion of Hungary, had killed his communist faith. Or, he was experiencing an "epistemological crisis" because younger scholars were undermining the foundations of his contribution to archaeology. Or, more mundanely, that he was suffering intellectual burn-out, having completed his life's work, and as there was nothing else in his life, he might as well end it. You will notice that each of these explanations assumes that Childe's suicide was the result of private issues. The focus is on Childe as an individual in 1957.

The difficulty with this path is that the biographer can find evidence in Childe's final months that contradicts, or at least weakens, the assumptions of these arguments. The alternative path is to try to understand his death in relation to his whole life – as a man, as a scholar and as a socialist. In tonight's lecture I will talk about his socialism. This is not, however, as limiting as it may seem, for my book, *The Fatal Lure of Politics: The Life and Thought of Vere Gordon Childe*, clarifies, for the first time, that Childe was a revolutionary socialist before he was an archaeologist, and that his socialism influenced his archaeology.

I think that there is a direct line between his early political life and his final – and fatal – political act at Blackheath. And Childe thought so too, writing calmly and rationally a suicide note that is not just about himself but about a social problem.

1. Discovering the rising tide of socialism in Sydney

When did Childe become a socialist? There were some early shaping moments. He grew up in the rectory of St Thomas's Church of England in North Sydney. The rector, his English-born father, leant towards the Oxford Tractarians in Church politics; his colonial-born mother was from a family, the Gordons, who were important members of the colony's Anglican establishment. They supported the opposing Evangelical tendency. So, there was, possibly, a culture of theological argument in the rectory that may have sparked a young boy's interest in ideas. As far as we can tell there were no political arguments; Childe grew up in a conservative family in a conservative suburb.

It may have been religion that began Childe's radicalisation. His mother died when he was in his last year at the Sydney Church of England Grammar School (known as "Shore"). A few months later he translated from Greek an elegy by Xenöphanes of Colophon, a religious sceptic who lived in the sixth century BCE. Childe's translation put the emphasis on the immorality of religion when it upheld the power of the state. Appearing in the school magazine, it was his first publication. A few years later, as an undergraduate at Sydney University he was the secretary of the Social Service Department of the Men's Christian Union. His religion, it seems, was drawing him away from state-worship and into a critique of social arrangements.

The year before Childe enrolled at Sydney University, the first majority Labor governments in the world were elected in New South Wales and in the Commonwealth. His years as a student – 1911 to 1913 – coincided with the failure of the New South Wales government to implement those elements of party policy most desired by working-class militants, and, in response, there was an explosion of unofficial strikes that revealed the depth of working-class disaffection. When Labor politicians and union officials condemned the strikes, many workers turned away from parliamentary politics altogether, embracing syndicalism; some of them set up industrial labour parties to compete with Labor. Here we see the roots of the 1916 split in the labour movement.

From *How Labour Governs* – the first of his 21 books, published in 1923 – we know that Childe followed these developments closely, and that, at least by the time of the book, his sympathies were with the workers, not the politicians. He wrote scathingly in that book about the state's Labor Premier, James McGowen, who called for scabs to break the gas strike of 1913.

Childe's best friend on campus was Bert Evatt, the future leader of the ALP. By 1913, Childe and Evatt were campus characters, known for their careless dress and socialist principles. His future wife, Mary Alice, also a Sydney student, would later recall that she was warned off both Gordon and Bert because they were "visionary dreamers", and would come to nothing. While they were students, a university socialist club – Australia's first – was active, and it was through this club that Childe met one of its invited speakers, Harald Jensen.

Childe read his book, *The Rising Tide: An Exposition of Australian Socialism*. The exposition was Darwinian; the socialism was evolutionary. Childe rose on the tide. At a debate in the Men's Union he led the case for the nationalising of medical services (but the proposition was defeated); he campaigned for Labor at the State elections; and he became a foundation member of the Workers' Educational Association of New South Wales. By the end of 1913, there were clear signs that Childe had committed to a socialism that was Christian, meliorist, and evolutionary.

2. Becoming a revolutionary in Oxford

In Oxford, where Childe arrived in September 1914, his political education continued, and very quickly, too, because in 1915 he declared to the authorities in his College – Queen's – that he had become "thoroughly unorthodox". By the time he returned to Australia in August 1917 he had an MI5 file, in which he was described as "thoroughly perverted and probably a very dangerous person". Between these two dates he had been part of a secret group in the Oxford University Socialist Society studying revolutionary politics. He had become an activist, lobbying on behalf of conscientious objectors to the 1914-18 war. He had been a delegate to the "Great Labour, Socialist, and Democratic Convention" in Leeds that voted to set up Soviets in Britain. Among his comrades in the Socialist Society and the Oxford Union of Democratic Control – in each of which he held the position of secretary – he was known for his leadership and outspokenness. Despite his "manifold activities" – a phrase used about him by one of his friends – he left Oxford with a First in Greats (Literae Humaniores).

The socialist orthodoxy that Childe brought with him to Oxford was that the state should be the locus of working-class politics. Laborists wanted to govern through the state; Fabians wanted to permeate it; Marxists wanted to smash it. In Oxford, however, he discovered a group of rebels within the Fabian Society who pointed out that the combination of capitalist ownership and an elected socialist government would actually lead to less power for the workers, to a "servile state". They advocated that the socialist movement should turn away from state-centred "collectivism" in order to encourage the spirit of self-government in the working class through the trade unions. This would allow the emergence of a "Newer Unionism" that would agitate for workers' control of industry. If economic resources were vested in co-operatively run, industry-based occupational groups, an ideal society would emerge characterised by devolved self-government, civil society pluralism, and a state representing consumers rather than dominant capitalists and subordinate workers. The name for this vision of pluralist democracy was Guild Socialism.

The leader of the Fabian rebels was GDH Cole, an Oxford don (at Balliol). A few months after Childe joined the Oxford University Fabian Society, Cole persuaded it to commit to political and industrial democracy through class-conscious unionism. As this was a clear rejection of the strategy of permeating the state, a break with the central Fabian Society was inevitable. In 1915, Childe followed Cole into a new organisation, the Oxford University Socialist Society. Cole was also the theoretician of Guild Socialism, and here too, Childe became a follower. Childe's journalism in Australia is full of phrases and ideas from Cole's 1913 book, *The World of Labour*. Through Cole, Childe was able to connect to the fashion in British political philosophy for pluralist thinking about diminishing the power of the state, and about popular sovereignty. In particular, Childe learned to base his approach to democracy on Rousseau's radical concept of the general will rather than the liberal concept of representation.

A second intellectual influence on Childe was Hegelian Marxism, to which he was exposed through his friendship with Rajani Palme Dutt. They had much in common: both highly intelligent; both opposed to colonialism and war; and both kind of foreign. Dutt's Indian father was a medical doctor in Cambridge, while his mother was Swedish. For his part, Childe never forgot that in Britain he was regarded as a colonial. After meeting in the Socialist Society, they became close friends. Almost every day they walked, organised and socialised together. As Dutt recorded in his diary for Thursday 9 November 1916: "Out with Childe in afternoon and much pleasant philosophy". When Dutt was conscripted and then jailed for refusing to serve, Childe ran a campaign to obtain his release from the army. He was released, because the governments feared that making Dutt a martyr would arouse nationalist disaffection among the Indian troops.

In 1917, Childe and Dutt shared digs in Oxford. According to Dutt: "There in the somewhat cramped surroundings of a tiny common working and sitting room we pursued our arguments on Hegel and Marx far into the night". For his diary he summed up their shared experiences: "Living with Childe's pleasant and constant companionship" made it "without question the best term I have ever had… it went off perfectly…[and] we did not tire of each other's company". For Childe, it was also significant. It was his closest relationship as an adult; it was certainly the only one involving a domestic arrangement. They remained friends, continuing to spar about Hegel and Marx into the 1940s.

Out of these discussions Childe developed an attitude to Marx that would place him, today, in the Western – ie non-Soviet – tradition of Marxism. He was very explicit about his kind of Marxism, describing himself as a follower of the Italian neo-Hegelian philosopher, Benedetto Croce. Childe said that Croce engaged critically with Marxism, bringing together its insights into cultural practices with its historical theory of changing economic structures – that is, changes in the mode and relations of production. In particular, Childe was impressed by the way Croce removed the concept of the supernatural, the idea that there were transcendental laws of history, from Hegel's "grand conception" of the dialectical movement of history. In its neo-Hegelian iteration, Marxism remained a theory of economic domination and subordination but with an emphasis on the resistance to domination by the subordinate class. Marxism was thus on the way to becoming a theory of agency as well as structures.

3. Vacillating in Sydney and Brisbane

Arriving back in Sydney with a theoretical suspicion of the state, Childe soon discovered its actual power. It was not just a dead-end for socialist strategies, but a force to punish those who acted against its interests. Childe was punished five times, over a period of eighteen months. He was forced to resign from the post of senior resident tutor at St. Andrew's College in the University of Sydney; he was vetoed by the Senate of the University for a position as tutor in Ancient History; he was forced to resign after a month from the post of Classics master at Maryborough Boys' Grammar School in Queensland; the offer of a teaching position at Newington College in Sydney was mysteriously withdrawn at the last moment by the headmaster; and he was passed over for a lectureship in Classics at University of Queensland because, according to the professor, having no military experience, "his fitness for dealing with university classes was open to grave doubt". Apparently, in Queensland you had to know how to use a rifle in order to take a University class.

Meanwhile, Childe continued to involve himself in "manifold activities", performing a range of tasks for labour and left movements. He lectured to the Labor Party, to the Australian Peace Alliance and to the Queensland Socialists. He carried out secretarial duties for the Sydney branch of the peace movement. He published letters in the labour press in Sydney and Brisbane on various topics. He ran classes for the Workers' Educational Association on Labor's philosophy (in Sydney) and Marx's *Capital* (in Brisbane, in this case, as he said with tongue in cheek, he was "applying Croce's idea with brilliant results"). He led a delegation on behalf of the NSW State ALP Executive to the Minister for Justice in order to seek prison indulgences for socialist trade union leader, Vance Marshall, and he advised the left unions in the Sydney Labor Council, helping them pass a resolution committing the Council to support calls for a negotiated peace and an end to military recruitment. In 1919 he successfully lobbied the Labor leadership in Queensland to persuade them that the One Big Union idea was compatible with party policy. It was a topic that he also promoted in a series of articles about the benefits of industrial democracy, published in Sydney and Brisbane. Clearly, Childe was not a socialist dilettante, paddling on the edge of the wave of working-class militancy, but an eager surfer.

Vance Marshall has left us a picture of Childe in action in those years. At meetings where "the fiery spirits" were gathering,

> he would rise in ungainly fashion to his feet... His speech...was slow, measured, scholastic – no vigour, no fire, but insistent, relentless, hammer-like. Like others who, though not born of the working class, come to the working class knowing that therein lies the pulsating heart of humanity's progress, he out-Heroded Herod in the espousal of its ideals. One theme alone marked the tenor of his logic – "No compromise! No compromise! No compromise!"

After a year in Sydney, followed by a year in Brisbane, Childe returned to Sydney to work as the private secretary of the New South Wales Labor leader, John Storey. When Storey became premier in 1920 he inserted Childe into the premier's department to provide research dedicated to the needs of a Labor government. The public service mandarins were horrified.

It's not hard to imagine why he took the job, having been blocked so many times from earning a steady middle-class income. The more interesting question is: did it help him develop his understanding of Australia's path to socialism? Was he able to help Labor take a few steps down that path? Or was it an unexpected moment of compromise?

Did he compromise? Oh, yes. The militant workers, whom he had championed in Brisbane, were calling for revolution in Sydney: "invade the food stores". Childe found himself advising a government that did not have the parliamentary numbers nor the required solidarity to respond. He was moreover complicit in the government's failure to fulfil its pre-election promises, unable to stop it cutting wages and increasing the state debt. Childe was shocked that under a Labor government unemployment continued to increase. He admitted all this later, in London. He knew that he was on the wrong side.

Was he able to insert a little socialist consciousness into the workings of this Labor government? No. He tried hard to promote the state enterprises, especially their economic and social contributions to the state, but to no avail.

Did he learn something about the impediments to a parliamentary transition to socialism? Yes, he did. He discovered that the public service establishment would not tolerate a radical socialist in its midst.

But what kind of socialist was Childe at this moment? The question at the root of Childe's thinking in Australia was: how could a socialist movement, with its strength in the working class, develop and come to power in this country? You may be surprised to learn that this was not an unusual question at that time, and that *How Labour Governs* (1923) was not his last word on it.

In fact, he moved through three separate but related positions on this question. When he arrived back in Australia in 1917, he was more interested in the power of the unions than Labor's parliamentary strategy. His friends even detected that he leant towards "direct action". By early 1919 he could see syndicalism's limitations, and having moved to Queensland, he could see what a progressive Labor government could do, especially when key workers, organised on "industrial union" lines, were prepared to act militantly, thus pushing the party to the left. He started to campaign to get the Labor Party to support the One Big Union movement and workers' control in the state enterprises.

This, his second or "politicalist" moment, was when he began to write *How Labour Governs*. He continued to write it while he was a political minder and researcher for the Labor premier in New South Wales, John Storey. At the end of 1921 the Labor government sent him to London to keep it up to date on "advanced democratic legislation".

By the time he got to England, he was thoroughly disillusioned with politicalism. So, the mood at the front of the book is positive, but by the end it is negative. He begins by describing how an Australian "proletarian democracy" set out to form a political party that would represent the working class in a bourgeois parliament. Then he shows how the mechanisms that it used – pledge, conference and caucus – were unable to achieve that form of "class" representation. He went on to show in the second half of the book that the revolt of the "industrialists" in the movement against the politicians also failed, leading not to the OBU but to union bossism.

The analysis in *How Labour Governs* was a major advance in our understanding of the impediments to parliamentary socialism. It was, however, lacking in one major respect: it did not provide the analysis of the class relations between capital and labour that would show the futility of parliamentary socialism.

In 1922, Childe published an article titled, "When Labour Ruled – in Australia – by an Ex-Ruler". In it, he went far beyond the analysis in *How Labour Governs*, in order to refute the basic assumptions of Labor-Socialism. Capitalists, he wrote, can always circumvent Labor's pro-worker legislation (by inflation; capital-strikes, etc); secondly, the state will always use violence against militant workers; thirdly, capitalist financial power will strangle the socialist enterprises of progressive Labor governments. Socialism will never be achieved through "duly compensated expropriation" enshrined in legislation. Childe had finally arrived at his third position: a class analysis of labourism. He published it in London in the *Labour Monthly*.

4. Consorting with Communism in Britain

When Childe returned to London, he joined the Labour Research Department and hooked up with his friends, the former young Fabian rebels, many of whom were now members of the Communist Party, including Rajani Palme Dutt, the founding editor of the *Labour Monthly*.

In London, Childe was open to a new kind of political dynamic among socialists. In Sydney, that dynamic was skewed by the fatal attraction of parliamentarism; a revolution of the Leninist kind was barely on the horizon. In Britain, however, a large section of militant workers and many radical intellectuals were captivated by the Bolshevik revolution. Historian Kevin Morgan has coined the term "non-party communism" to describe this left culture, which survived into the mid-1920s. Through the Labour Research Department, which would publish *How Labour Governs*, Childe was soon immersed in this "non-party" culture of communism.

Childe remained a "non-party communist" for the rest of his life, happy to associate himself with Communist organisations and campaigns. Here's a quick résumé of those associations. He renewed his friendship with Jack Lindsay, whom he had met in Brisbane. In the 1930s and '40s, Lindsay was a leading figure in the British Party's cultural activities. In the Association of Scientific Workers, Childe rubbed shoulders with famous Communist scientists including JD Bernal and Hyman Levy. He was part of the Communist Historians Group that established *Past and Present*, and subscribed to the *Daily Worker*, leaving his copy conspicuously on his office desk. He accepted the Communist Party's invitation in 1937 to become a founding editor of its intellectual journal, *The Modern Quarterly*, and he remained on its board until 1951. And during the 1940s and '50s, he was an open supporter of international Communist-led peace movements.

In the mid-1920s Childe published a series of works in

archaeology, and in 1927 he was appointed to the position of Abercromby Professor of Archaeology at the University of Edinburgh where he worked until 1946. As a professor whose scholarship was recognised by awards and distinctions, Childe was able to lend his high status to Communist and left organisations simply by associating with them, but he did more, taking on "honorary" official roles. Two such connections of long standing were with the Society for Cultural Relations with the USSR, and the Association of Scientific Workers, but he was also an office-bearer in the Left Book Club, the India League, the Marx Memorial Library, the Britain-China Friendship Society and the National Council for Civil Liberties.

Fundamental to Childe's willingness to associate with the Communist Party was his support for the idea of revolutionary change. He called the Bolshevik revolution "a grand and hopeful experiment". He supported Communist efforts in the 1930s to protect the state that emerged from this revolution, the Soviet Union, through an international movement against war and fascism. In 1942, at a critical moment in the war, he supported the Communist call for the opening of a "second front" in Europe to take the pressure off the Soviet forces. At this fraught moment for the survival of the Soviet Union he concluded *What Happened in History* with these words:

> Progress is real if discontinuous. The upward curve resolves itself into a series of troughs and crests. But in those domains that archaeology as well as written history can survey, no trough ever declines to the low of the preceding one, each crest out-tops its last precursor.

For Childe, progress was not a metaphysical idea but an aspect of historical change. It was discoverable by the science of history in the material traces of human activity, in the knowledge created by that activity, and in the obstacles that it had to overcome. Hence the need for revolutionary transformations. His materialism in short was dialectical as well as historical. One of the great themes of both *Man Makes Himself* and *What Happened in History* is the stagnation of civilisation after the urban revolution, its collapse into war, slavery and oppression. He explained that the emergence of a ruling class and a totalitarian form of the state created this collapse.

Considering his own times Childe warned that the conduct of the war should not be left to politicians; instead "every citizen had to be a politician". And after World War II, he supported the world peace movement, because the alternative – a Cold War – threatened the free exchange of scientific knowledge and the political rights of citizens.

So, why did he *not* join the Communist Party? In fact, during these years he was often critical of it. In the 1920s, he was disappointed by its failure to insert itself more widely into working-class life and politics. This he thought was due to its bureaucratic ethos and anti-democratic style of leadership. In the 1930s, he disagreed with its "Third Period" line that seemed to equate social democrats and fascists. In 1939, he was aghast when the British party endorsed the Nazi-Soviet Pact and delayed its support for the war against fascism until Germany attacked the Soviet Union.

In short, there were two main reasons why he kept his distance from the party: one, because he was a democrat, but the CP was not, and Stalinism, as he said, was a form of totalitarianism; and two, because he was a Marxist and could not stomach the party's mechanistic and formulaic rendition of Marxism. We will get to that in the next section.

In 1946, Childe moved to London and became Professor of Prehistoric Archaeology and Director of the Institute of Archaeology. London was also the centre of British Communism's intellectual activity, and Childe was quickly assuming national roles in organisations where the Party had influence, in particular the Association of Scientific Workers and the Society for Cultural Relations with the USSR. He was even invited to attend discussions organised by the Party's Cultural Committee.

He moved into a tiny flat in the Isokon Building in Hampstead – a building which incidentally had been Soviet spy-central in the 1930s. Designed by Wells Coates, it was one of London's earliest examples of domestic modern architecture, "a machine for living", with built-in cupboards, cooking and washing facilities. It was also an experiment in communal living. There were gardens and other common spaces and a club-room-cum-restaurant, where Childe loved to entertain. The first meetings of the *Past and Present* editorial board were held in his Lawn Road flat.

5. Revolutionising prehistory

In 1938, Childe and Dutt had a falling out. The Communist Party, wanting to make Childe's sympathy with communism into a more public connection, asked Dutt to persuade him to join the faculty of Marx House, the Party's educational arm. Childe reacted angrily: "The only practical effect would be to tie a label around my neck, and I don't like labels". Worse, this label would be misleading because he and the Party disagreed about Marxism: "To the average communist and anti-communist alike...Marxism means a set of dogmas – the words of the master from which one must deduce truths". Then Childe clearly stated his own understanding: "To me Marxism means effectively a way of approach to and a methodological device for the interpretation of historical and archaeological material and I accept it because and insofar as it works". And he underlined "works". He was, he said, a scientist who used experiment and observation to get at the truth.

Yet, concerning the materialist conception of history, Childe was as evangelical as the Communist Party – but his understanding of it was different. He wanted to give the Marxist conception of history a scientific basis, drawing on the discoveries of archaeology, and then he wanted to spread his understanding as widely as possible – to introduce it to "wider democratic circles" – a phrase that he used in 1942. And so, he discussed his ideas about prehistory in many of the non-academic periodicals read by the left: *The Plebs, The Rationalist Annual, The Anglo-Soviet Journal, Scientific Worker, Labour Monthly, The Daily Worker* and *The Modern Quarterly* – the last three published by the Communist Party.

He was also careful to avoid the jargon of Marxism-Leninism, telling Rajani Dutt in 1938:

> I want to get good Marxist ideas across to my colleagues and students, and in that I have had some success, but they would not listen if I began as a Marxist (in *Man Makes Himself* the class

struggle is disclosed as a deduction from an imposing looking array of facts).

He called this "white-anting" (an Australian labour movement term) or "sugaring". Predictably, Dutt, who was by this time a defender of Communist loyalty and Marxist orthodoxy, treated the idea with contempt.

Man Makes Himself, published in 1936, and *What Happened in History*, in 1942, are often mistakenly labelled as popularisations, but they are also works in which he begins an exploration of historical reasoning. They form part of a series of works including *The Story of Tools* (1944), "Rational Order in History" (1945), *History* (1947), *Social Worlds of Knowledge* (1949), and *Society and Knowledge* (1956) which draw on archaeology to provide a more robust, scientific basis for historical materialism.

In terms of Childe's career, this project of connecting archaeology and historical materialism and of introducing the result into "wider democratic circles" lasted from 1936 to 1956, or two-thirds of his academic life. Among archaeologists, Childe is mainly known for works that he wrote before 1936, but as Timothy Champion has recently pointed out, these later works are "still relevant to current debates about archaeology".

Archaeologists often assume that the explanation for this series of works is that Childe discovered Marxism in the mid-1930s. But, as we have seen, Childe was actually a labour intellectual who took his already well-established theory of revolutionary change into the study of archaeology. Even in the book that launched his reputation, *The Dawn of European Civilisation* (1925), he can be seen thinking structurally about "the several stages of the transformation of the world of food-gatherers" during the Bronze Age. By the time he published *New Light on the Most Ancient East* in 1934 he is referring to the "two great revolutions in human culture". The first is named as the Neolithic Revolution in his 1935 presidential address to the Prehistoric Society. And then in *Man Makes Himself* the familiar terms Neolithic Revolution and Urban Revolution appear as chapter headings.

6. Being rational at Govett's Leap

Childe arrived in Sydney on his 65th birthday in April 1957 and was soon as busy writing, travelling and lecturing as he always had been. He finished the manuscript of his last book, *The Prehistory of European Society*, and wrote articles for *Past and Present* and *Antiquity*. He also wrote an autobiographical essay and a valediction to archaeology, setting out his ideas about the "main tasks confronting archaeology in Britain", which was a very communist thing to do. He criss-crossed the country, writing in trains and in hotels for he was hardly in one place for more than a few days. He reconnected with family in Sydney and the Darling Downs. He visited archaeologists (notably John Mulvaney in Melbourne and James Stewart in Bathurst), and leftists (including the Evatts in Sydney, Russell Ward in Armidale, Bob Gollan in Canberra and Brian Fitzpatrick in Melbourne). He lectured to history societies in Sydney and Adelaide, and to undergraduates in Canberra and Melbourne. He lunched with Percy Stephensen in Sydney before going to a performance of *Hamlet*. He delivered a "guest of honour" talk on ABC radio, and accepted an honorary doctorate from the University of Sydney.

He was interviewed by the *Daily Telegraph* in Sydney and the *Age* in Melbourne. He hiked in Tasmania and looked for lyrebirds in the Dandenongs. And, in between, he spent several short breaks at Katoomba, staying at the Carrington, from where he travelled to Jenolan Caves, the Southern Highlands, and his childhood family retreat overlooking Wentworth Falls – Chalet Fontenelle.

Then in October 1957 his body was found at the bottom of a cliff near Govett's Leap in the Blue Mountains west of Sydney.

Surely his death was an accident. A few weeks later a coronial inquiry considered the manner of his death. Witnesses showed that Childe was in good spirits, that he was contemplating new intellectual projects and that he had money in the bank. There was no suicide note, and on the cliff, his hat, spectacles and compass were near the edge, suggesting that he slipped and fell while taking a compass reading of Pulpit Rock on the other side of the Grose Valley. The coroner's finding confirmed the expected and comforting view that Childe's death was accidental.

But then, in 1980, *Antiquity* published a short essay that Childe had written a few days before his death. He had sent it to a colleague at the Institute of Archaeology in London with a covering letter asking that it not be published until 1968. It was in effect a suicide note.

When it became clear that Childe had deliberately chosen to die by jumping off that cliff, the search for explanations began. The underlying assumptions of this search were that we should concentrate on the period just before his death, and that we would be looking for signs of instability.

My approach to understanding his death is different. We should place it in the context of his whole life, and we should focus on his political thought and submit his suicide note to intellectual analysis.

In fact, he had contemplated suicide on several occasions during his life. In 1939, watching the advance of the Nazi armies across Europe, and believing that he was on a "Nazi death list" because of his public attack on the Nazi minister of the interior, he determined that he would take his own life rather than let the Nazis execute him. He had calculated his chances of survival in a dire political situation. He made sure his best friends knew about his decision. He was contemplating suicide as a political act.

He made another calculation as he thought about retirement in 1956. He began to worry about the effects of ageing on his health. Suicide once again offered a solution. As he wound up his affairs in London, he told two colleagues separately that he would jump off a cliff in Australia. Next year, back home in Australia, he startled a dinner party of left-wing academics by stating, when asked about his plans, "I think I'll go over a cliff at Katoomba". When news of his death was reported in the English press, his friend OGS Crawford assumed immediately that it was a suicide.

Looking at his whole life also helps us to take a more balanced view of Childe's reaction to the double-whammy of 1956, the year when socialists were forced to face up to the crimes of Stalin and the reality of Soviet imperialism. About Childe's reaction to Khrushchev's secret speech, we have no direct knowledge. Perhaps he wasn't surprised at its revelations, as he had characterised Stalin as a dictator in 1939. We also know that he reconfirmed this assessment on a trip to Russia in 1956 when he discovered how Stalinism had damaged the personal lives of his Russian colleagues in archaeology.

As for Hungary, in a letter to his cousin Alexander in Sydney, he wrote about his deep disgust at the Russian invasion. And at the end of the year he wrote a damning letter about the appalling deficiencies of Soviet archaeology, a private letter that he copied and distributed to a handful of the leading Russian scholars in his field. So, for a long part of his life, Childe had lived with the knowledge that while revolutions might release creativity in working people, in Russia's case the revolution had produced a totalitarian regime.

So much for being flayed by the revelations of 1956: Childe was protected by the calluses formed by long exposure to the failures of the left. What about 1957? Did his contact with the Australian left suck him into a whirlpool of despair? In September, he delivered a lecture in Melbourne to the Australasian Book Society, a left-wing group of writers and intellectuals formed by the Communist Party. His opening words were: "Australia today is far from a socialist society". He went on to explain that, although workers had "got what they wanted" – the material benefits of a better standard of living and the power to influence government through a strong labour movement, Australia was not a socialist society. There had been no proletarian revolution, and the alternative that the labour movement *had* created, a wage-earners' welfare state, existed only because the ruling class permitted it. Moreover, if a labour leader threatened this uneasy compact, he would be savagely attacked. This was Childe's take on the vicious campaign in the press against his friend, the parliamentary leader of the Labor Party, Bert Evatt (then fighting to prevent the party being captured by a secret anti-communist organisation). So, Childe was disappointed that Australia had not fulfilled the revolutionary socialist potential that he had written about in the 1920s. He realised now that he had been too idealistic. But it is clear from this lecture that he was still committed to Marxist class analysis, and therefore to the possibility of socialist revolution.

When he went to dinner with Percy Stephensen, he made sure to tell him that he was "a near Commy". So, it does not seem that he was losing his political faith. But maybe he was mourning the failure of Marxism to accommodate new directions in archaeology? Well, no. He wrote, just before he died, a long review of archaeology as he had observed it over forty years, reaffirming his materialist vision for it: "what Marxists call the relations of production" must be a central inference for archaeologists.

Finally let us turn to the suicide note itself. Hardly a "note", for it is over 1,000 words, and hardly about Childe, for he appears only in the last two paragraphs. In it he adopts a radical humanist position. He writes not about himself but about society. How should society deal with the aged, "the horde of parasites" created by advances in medical science?

Why are they parasites? Because: the aged can't look after themselves, they get in the way of younger people and they have nothing new to say. The solution?

> I have always considered that a sane society would disembarrass itself by offering euthanasia as a crowning glory, or even imposing it in bad cases...

He writes next about his own situation. He is forgetting things, his savings are disappearing, every cold turns into bronchitis. What will be the outcome? That he will become a burden on the community? He refuses: "I have always intended to cease living before that happens". Then he signals how he will carry out his intention: "An accident may easily and naturally befall me on a mountain cliff". Followed by the intellectual justification:

> The British prejudice against suicide is utterly irrational. To end his life deliberately is in fact something that distinguishes *Homo sapiens* from other animals even better than ceremonial burial of the dead.

This is certainly a suicide note with a difference. It is positive, not despairing. Childe says he is actually quite well at the moment. He invokes our common humanity by reminding us that our lives will end with many desires unrealised. In Childe's case, he sees no prospect of solving problems in prehistory that interest him most, and he lacks the willpower to face the discomforts and anxieties of travel in the USSR and China. Why did he mention Soviet Russia and Communist China? As a gesture of socialist solidarity, but also as a reminder of the revolutionary processes that we should be desiring.

Then he expresses his love of his native land. He has returned to the Blue Mountains:

> Now I have seen the Australian spring; I have smelt the boronia, watched snakes and lizards, listened to the locusts. There is nothing more I want to do here; nothing I feel I ought and could do. I hate the prospects of the summer, but I hate still more the fogs and snows of a British winter.

He had already explained that he did not want the manner of his death to hurt his friends. Hence that careful arrangement of artefacts on the edge of the cliff and the embargo placed on the suicide note. Now he concludes with words that cannot be twisted to suit an argument about either existential despair or mental instability: "Life ends best when one is happy and strong".

As his suicide note shows, at the end of his life Childe was not just happy, he was strong in his life-long commitment to reason and humanity, qualities that for him were the foundational values of socialism.

LIZ ROSS

Review: Gordon Childe and the fatal lure of politics

Liz Ross has been active in socialist politics since the early 1970s. She has written extensively on a range of issues including women's and gay liberation, the environment and the Australian union movement. Her most recent book is *Stuff the Accord! Pay Up! Workers' resistance to the ALP-ACTU Accord* (2020).

Terry Irving, *The fatal lure of politics: the life and thought of Vere Gordon Childe*, Monash University Press, 2020.

VERE GORDON CHILDE was born into a time of world-shattering events, arguably one of the most politically challenging periods of world history and, like so many, was radicalised by it. Mass strike waves, revolutions and defeats, the first successful workers' revolution in Russia, alongside wars, Depression, the rise of fascism, the Cold War and McCarthyism and capitalism's biggest boom period. He was an Australian left-wing Labor Party activist and then scathing critic of its reformism. A committed socialist, he was a follower of Marx and supporter of the Russian Revolution, though not the Bolsheviks. He followed his early political period with a stellar career as a prehistorian, revolutionising the interpretation of past societies through Marxist methodology.

All this has been captured by Terry Irving in this absorbing political biography of Childe. In the first section Irving recovers Childe's political contribution to Australian politics, primarily within the ALP, followed by his critique, *How Labour Governs: A study of workers' representation in Australia* in 1923, his last major intervention in party politics. Irving then shows Childe's continuity of socialist or historical materialist thought and method from his early political experiences, through his anti-war and later anti-fascist activities, to his many years as a revolutionising prehistorian and social theorist.

Irving begins with a detailed description of the formative years of Australian Labor, the organisational and theoretical ferment that swept through the party from its beginning. Arising from the major working-class defeats of the 1890s, including the maritime strike, had come the call for a party to represent workers in parliament, where workers would take power from the ruling class and run society themselves.

It was a politics which would attract many young activists such as Childe. By the 1910s Labor had won both federal and state government, accompanied by a rise in working-class combativity, which both encouraged support for Labor, but also threw up more left-wing alternatives. A number of the more militant unions and ALP members looked to stand their own candidates, form new social democratic parties, or join the Industrial Workers of the World (IWW). Ideas of One Big Union, socialism and challenges to accepted ideologies were swirling round in the mix, not just in Australia but around the world, with uprisings and strikes in cities across seven major countries in Europe and the Americas between 1911 and 1912.

The campuses, though still elite institutions, saw the stirrings of radicalism, with Sydney University forming a Socialist Society. Childe was radicalising too and even as he continued to support Labor, he was becoming increasingly disillusioned with the party in government. Labor, he wrote later, "instead of standing up boldly in defence of the one class that put them in power", attacked workers and in the case of NSW Premier Jim McGowan, called on the public to assist the scabs against a gasworkers' strike.[1]

These years were an important political prelude, preparing Childe for the major upheavals – war and revolution – that were about to explode on the world scene. In 1914 he headed to England, to a country at war, full of military propaganda, but also a growing anti-war movement. It was at Oxford that he was to embark on his

---
1. Childe 1923.

first studies of archaeology that were to shape his future career in a discipline he played a significant role in revolutionising.

Arriving at the university he soon met left-wing activists, including guild socialist GDH Cole and soon to be close friend Ranjani Palme Dutt, a future leader of the British Communist Party. Here he deepened his left-wing politics, as Irving describes, with "the idea of the class war...firmly lodged in his mind" (pp. 76-77). He became involved in anti-war campaigns, opposing the increased censorship, conscription and other war-time controls, which led to a life-long surveillance by both British and Australian spy agencies.

Childe returned to Australia in October 1917 and launched into his second phase of involvement with the ALP, including as private secretary to NSW Labor Premier John Storey. He formulated an idea of a "genuine Labor government" which would enact progressive policies, "relying on organised militant unionism [through a] One Big Union for electoral and financial support, and in return protecting and extending worker control of production" (p. 173). This ideal, however, could never have been realised given the nature of a social-democratic party such as the ALP, which as Tom Bramble and Rick Kuhn note, adapted its program to what is acceptable to the capitalists and their state.[2] While Childe's *How Labour Governs* pointed out the failures of Labor, how the party "offers [workers] no escape from capitalism" (p. 265), because of his political limitations, he had no solutions to reformism, no insight into the revolutionary role of the working class.[3]

As the political situation changed Childe's political positions changed, ranging from supporting the IWW, through business cooperation with Labor, to worker control of state enterprises. Marxist historian Neil Faulkner provides the clearest framework for understanding Childe's centrist political position. Centrists he explains, move "from reformism to revolutionary socialism in periods of radicalisation, retaining elements of both in their outlook and activity". Childe "did not capitulate, but he was trapped in a political impasse by the contradictions of centrism".[4] Though privately

---

2. Bramble and Kuhn 2011, p. 10.
3. Faulkner 2007.
4. Faulkner 2007.

critical of Stalin from the 1930s, he did not lose faith in the Soviet Union as "a grand and hopeful experiment" until Khrushchev's shock revelations and the invasion of Hungary in 1956 (p. 300).

Irving makes an extensive contribution to our understanding of early twentieth century Labor history and Childe's continuity of a left-wing analysis throughout his life of opposition to imperialism, fascism, oppression and injustice, and his contribution to a historical materialist understanding of societies past. Childe, he shows, represents the hope of those early revolutionary years of the twentieth century, but also represents the many who could not break through the bounds of Stalinism and who were, ultimately, betrayed by it.

References

Bramble, Tom and Rick Kuhn 2011, *Labor's conflict: Big business, workers and the politics of class*, Cambridge University Press.

Childe, Vere Gordon 1923, *How Labour Governs: A study of workers' representation in Australia*. https://www.marxists.org/archive/childe/how-labor-governs/index.htm.

Faulkner, Neil 2007, "Gordon Childe and Marxist archaeology". *International Socialism*, 116, Autumn. http://isj.org.uk/gordon-childe-and-marxist-archaeology/

RYAN STANTON

Review: The real history of World War I

Ryan Stanton is a socialist and trade union activist working in construction.

Alan Woods, *The First World War: A Marxist Analysis of the Great Slaughter*, Well Red Books, 2019.

HAS ANY EVENT in history had more written about it, while being less well understood, than the First World War? Woods' detailed and engrossing book directly challenges many commonly held myths, refuting the nationalist propaganda that too often substitutes for genuine historical analysis. He shows how the world was led to catastrophe by the imperial brinksmanship of ruling elites bent on power and economic expansion. The book also tells stories of rank-and-file soldiers: their pain, fear, misery and suffering, as well as their changing conceptions of the war and capitalist society more broadly. This political awakening would lead to workers' revolutions across Europe and Asia – ending the war and shaking capitalism to its very foundations.

The War

It is true that the immediate origins of the war flowed from the decisions taken by statesmen and generals following the assassination of the Archduke Franz Ferdinand by Gavrilo

Princip. But the real causes of the war are to be found, not in the haphazard realm of historical accidents, but in the solid ground of historical necessity, which, as Hegel teaches us, can be expressed in accidents of all kinds. (p. 7)

The war was sparked by the assassination of Archduke Franz Ferdinand, heir to the Austro-Hungarian throne, by a Serbian separatist during a parade in Sarajevo. Over the following weeks the great powers of Europe declared war on each other across two broad alliances: the Allied powers (Britain, France and Russia, eventually joined by Italy and the United States, among others) and the Central powers (Germany and Austro-Hungary, soon to be joined by the Ottoman Empire and Bulgaria). One is reminded of falling dominoes or a collapsing house of cards, not in the sense that any random event will automatically lead to catastrophe, but in the sense that the conditions for catastrophe were meticulously prepared beforehand by the contending powers.

Franz Ferdinand's public visit to a country in the throes of a violent separatist movement seems like sheer stupidity, and his poorly executed assassination bordered on the accidental. However, the stupidity of the Archduke was an expression of the brazen arrogance of an empire that strove to subject the Balkans to its interests. The accident of his assassination was only the spark that lit a huge powder keg which had already been filled by powerful historical forces. It could have been detonated in many other ways.

Likewise, German expansionism cannot be explained by the fetishisation of German exceptionalism or Prussian militarism, or, as some historians do, by speculating about whether the Kaiser's insecurity about his disfigured left arm may have given him a hyper-aggressive personality. By 1914 Germany had risen to become the preeminent industrial power of Europe, but its access to global markets and resources was blocked by the established colonial empires of Britain and France. Ultimately, it could only break this deadlock by smashing through it.

On the other side, the French wanted to contain and, if possible, dismember the German Empire in order to re-establish itself as the dominant power on the continent. Russia strove to control the

Balkans, as well as the Black and Aegean Seas. Britain, for its part, is often portrayed as being unable to make up its mind about just who to support, only to stumble blindly into the war. It was continually engrossed in double-dealing alliances between France, Germany and Russia, to the point that Germany was not sure what exactly Britain might do right up to the eve of war.

However, the outward ambiguity of Britain's intentions was actually a mask for its predatory cunning. Britain hoped to remain aloof from a land war on the continent, while its competitors (not only Germany, but France and Russia as well) bled each other dry. This tried and true strategy had historically allowed Britain to retain a commanding position over the affairs of Europe, but this time the strength of Germany forced Britain to play its hand. The United States, on the other hand, played Britain's game much more successfully. Its corporations piled up vast fortunes as they funded and armed both sides of the war, only to swoop in during the final 19 months as the new masters of global finance and industry.

In truth the First World War cannot be explained by historical accidents, or the ideas and proclivities of world leaders. That method is akin to studying the formation of hurricanes, not by understanding the way vast quantities of energy flow dynamically throughout the Atlantic Ocean, but by analysing the way a butterfly flaps its wings in Africa. World War I was the climax of years of competition and military build-up. Germany overtook France and Britain economically and demanded a restructuring of the global order in its own interests. The Allies, in turn, could only defend their dominance against Germany's surging power by utilising military alliances and trade barriers. This contradiction drove a great arms race and finally erupted in the most violent and destructive war the world had ever seen. In other words, the war was the ultimate expression of the competition for the accumulation that lies at the heart of capitalism itself.

This analysis exposes the sheer hypocrisy of the Allied powers as they claimed to fight for democracy and self-determination, even while they jealously protected their right to plunder vast colonial empires in Asia and Africa. Likewise, victorious France and Britain paid no mind to the desires of Arabs or Kurds when they carved up

The soldiers

> Beautiful? Oh, hell! It's just as if an ox were to say, "What a fine sight it must be, all those droves of cattle driven forward to the slaughter-house!" (p. 155)

It is difficult to adequately describe the trauma of the First World War. It was unlike anything the world had ever seen. Upwards of 65 million military personnel were mobilised, 18 million people were killed and tens of millions more were physically and psychologically shattered. All of the productive power of early twentieth century capitalism was directed toward murder and destruction on a truly industrial scale. During the Battle of the Somme, which lasted 141 days, over a million soldiers were killed – nearly 70 thousand British troops died on the first day alone. Despite the mountains of dead, the front line hardly shifted at all for four gruelling, blood-soaked years.

For all of the nationalistic pomp and ceremony that usually accompany commemorations of the war, relatively little attention is paid to the bestial suffering endured by the soldiers that were sent to the front. Woods proves that, contrary to what we are told by nationalist warmongers, those who oppose imperialist wars in principle are best placed to solidarise with the people who are made to fight in them. He captures the experience of the rank-and-file soldiers, who were overwhelmingly drawn from the working class, mostly by using excerpts from the novels and poetry of the era.

Woods commits a chapter to *Le Feu: journal d'une escouade* (*Under Fire: The Story of a Squad*), a visceral novel by Henri Barbusse. There is no fighting at all until the end of the *Le Feu*. The soldiers spend their days in tedious boredom, languishing in trenches full of mud, parasites and excrement.

> We are waiting. Weary of sitting, we get up, our joints creaking like warping wood or old hinges. Damp rusts men as it rusts rifles;

more slowly, but deeper. And we begin again, but not in the same way, to wait. In a state of war, one is always waiting. We have become waiting-machines. (p. 155)

The waiting is ended abruptly as the novel falls into a hell reminiscent of Dante's *Inferno*. When the dreaded whistles blow, soldiers scale the trench walls into "no man's land", sprinting headlong into a wall of machine-gun fire, desperately scrambling over barbed wire, mud-filled craters and unrecognisably mutilated corpses. At least they are assumed to be corpses – it becomes impossible to tell who is alive and who is dead in the muck. Anyone lucky enough to survive this crucible is rewarded with the privilege of bayonetting, or being bayonetted by, the young boys cowering in fear in the enemy trenches.

Woods' use of literature doesn't just paint a poignant picture of the horror that soldiers endured; he also illuminates their changing consciousness under the impact of the war. The book recounts several nightmarish poems by Wilfred Owen, the great English poet-soldier. Owen arrived at the front "full of boyish high spirits and patriotic fervour" (p. 83), but is soon transformed by his experiences. Owen's *The Dead-Beat* describes a catatonic soldier who is mocked as a faker by his own doctor even as he dies of shell-shock (now known as PTSD) (p. 87). The following excerpt from another poem, *Anthem for a Doomed Youth*, portrays Owen's bitter disillusionment with the war:

> *What passing-bells for these who die as cattle?*
> *Only the monstrous anger of the guns.*
> *Only the stuttering rifles' rapid rattle*
> *Can patter out their hasty orisons.*
> *No mockeries now for them, no prayers nor bells;*
> *Nor any voice of mourning save the choirs, –*
> *The shrill demented choirs of wailing shells;*
> *And bugles calling for them from sad shires.* (p. 89)

Tragically, Owen survived two years on the front line, only to be killed a week before the signing of the armistice that ended the war on 11 November, 1918. On the day that church bells rang out all over

Europe, heralding the end of the war, his mother received the letter informing her of her son's death (p. 91).

Resistance

> Popular disillusionment and war-weariness was manifested in growing labour unrest and food riots, which were becoming increasingly common. Conversations on the street corner, in the marketplace, and in the factories turned to the injustice, not just of the war, but of an economic system that put all the burdens on the shoulders of the poor and the working class while the rich got ever richer. Talk of everybody making sacrifice sounded hollow to a woman standing in the bread queue while the rich drank champagne and went to parties. (p. 169)

The ruling classes of both sides endlessly predicted that victory was just around the corner; that "one more push" would be enough to tip the scales in their favour. However, the scale of death and carnage only increased with each new battle, without ever achieving a decisive advantage for either side. Meanwhile, all of society's resources were thrown into the war effort. The masses of Europe were subjected to ever-worsening hunger and destitution, even as the rich filled their pockets with the gains of war profiteering. To whom could the workers look for aid? They were abandoned by most of their traditional representatives. Almost all of the socialist and labour parties of the time, and the leadership of the trade unions along with them, offered up their own membership for the slaughter.

Nonetheless, an isolated but important minority opposed the war from very early on. The first seeds of opposition were planted in Germany by Karl Liebknecht, the revolutionary socialist MP, who famously stood alone as he voted against funding the war soon after it began in 1914. Small groups of revolutionaries, led by Liebknecht and Rosa Luxembourg, began rebuilding left opposition to the war in Germany. Another important step was taken in 1915, when a small conference of the anti-war left from across Europe met covertly in Zimmerwald, Switzerland. Among the attendees was Vladimir Lenin, the leader of the Bolsheviks in Russia.

The book also highlights Eugene Debs, the icon of American

socialism, who never backed down from opposition to the war, even as the United States became fully engaged in it. "A bayonet", said Debs, "was a weapon with a worker at each end" (p. 133). His principled defiance earned him a mass following among US workers, which culminated in his winning a million votes for president from a prison cell in 1920. One of the most inspiring examples given by Woods is the Christmas Day truce in 1914, when as many as 100,000 British and German soldiers ignored their own officers to fraternise across no man's land, exchange pleasantries, sing Christmas carols and play football (p. 83). As the war took an ever greater toll on workers and soldiers, opposition to the war increased and became more radical. In 1916, the Irish rose up against conscription to the British army during the Easter Rebellion in Dublin.

> For the soldiers, the war was a seemly unending nightmare; for the civilians on the home front, especially the women, hardly less so. In the end, large tracts of Europe lay wasted, millions were dead or wounded. The great majority of casualties were from the working class. Survivors lived on with severe mental trauma. The streets of every European city were full of limbless veterans. Nations were bankrupt – not just the losers, but also the victors... By 1917, in all the belligerent states, the discontent of the masses was growing. (p. 195)

Revolution

> This bloody conflict was brought to an end by revolution – a fact that has been buried under a mountain of myths, pacifist sentimentality, and lying patriotic propaganda. (p. 195)

The war inflicted more suffering on Russia than any other country. Russian workers, peasants and soldiers had endured more than two years of uninterrupted military defeat, more casualties than any other country, brutal oppression, mass hunger and deepening economic crisis. By February 1917, they'd had enough. They rose up in one of history's great popular revolutions, overthrew the centuries-old tsarist dynasty, and set up democratic councils (known as soviets) in their factories, farms and barracks. The principled opposition of

Lenin and the Bolsheviks to the war from its very beginning, along with their tireless agitation for bread for the workers and land for the peasants, eventually placed them at the head of the revolution. The masses of Russia, led by the Bolsheviks, overthrew capitalist power in October 1917, set up a new workers' state and finally ended Russia's involvement in the war.

The workers of the world took tremendous inspiration from the Russian Revolution, and tried to emulate it. Networks of radicalising shop stewards initiated and led mass strikes of hundreds of thousands of German workers in 1916. They led even larger strikes in early 1918, this time setting up workers' councils similar to the Russian soviets. Meanwhile, mass strikes, demonstrations and mutinies drove Austro-Hungary to the brink of collapse (p. 177). Disastrous defeats at the Somme led to waves of mutinies in the French army, affecting nearly half of the French frontline forces (p. 175). These mutinies held the French back from any other major offensives in 1917, probably saving hundreds of thousands of lives.

By the end of 1918, the German high command knew that victory was impossible. They hoped, however, to increase their bargaining position in negotiations with the Allies by launching a final, desperate naval assault on the British Royal Navy. The sailors stationed at Kiel, however, were somewhat less enthusiastic about this proposal. They mutinied, and their rebellion quickly spread throughout the German military and into the working class. It became a mass revolution along the lines of the February revolution in Russia – overthrowing the German Kaiser and finally ending the Great War.

The end

> The war had an enormous economic, political, and human cost... It dislocated economic life, destroying the means of production on a massive scale and condemning millions to hunger and privation. It resulted in the dissolution of the Austrian, Ottoman, German, and Russian empires, and culminated in a wave of revolutions between 1917 and 1920. Sailors and soldiers mutinied, while massive strikes broke out everywhere: from Berlin to Vienna, from

Paris to Brussels to Glasgow, and stretching across the Atlantic to Chicago, San Francisco, and Canada. (p. 199)

The war was over, but this was not the end of things. The next five years would bring Europe to a boil. Germany, the Balkans, Eastern Europe, Italy and France were rocked by mass rebellion. This mighty revolutionary wave had the potential to do much more than just end the war. Millions of workers rose up in the hope of eliminating the economic system that created the war in the first place; and all the poverty, inequality and oppression that came along with it. For the workers of Europe, who had endured unspeakable violence and hardship during the war years, capitalism's legitimacy was shattered. They took hope and inspiration from the Russian Revolution. They wanted a new type of society that would be governed by the democratic interests of the mass of humanity, rather than the bloodthirsty impulses of capital.

Hope and inspiration, however, were not enough. The waves of post-war revolutions had no other organisations that were, like the Bolsheviks, willing and able to lead them. They would be gradually smothered under the weight of mass reformist parties, which proved to be infinitely more hostile to revolution than to capitalism. Russia, isolated and economically ruined, eventually succumbed to its own counter-revolution, led by Stalin. Humanity has paid a very high price for the defeat of the post-war revolutions. In the coming years capitalism would plummet into the worst economic crisis in its history. Fascism and Stalinism would subject the world to hitherto unimaginable dimensions of barbarity. The Treaty of Versailles, aptly described by Woods as the "peace to end all peace", would only prepare the ground for a second, far more violent and destructive world war (p. 207).

Many lessons can be drawn from Alan Woods' book. Imperialist war is as inseparable from capitalism as the accumulation of wealth. This is as vitally important today as it was a century ago. The imperialist competition for global resources and markets is, if anything, stronger now. The growing rivalry between the US and China is only one example, although it is particularly terrifying.

The ruling classes of Europe and North America, along with their lackeys in the reformist political parties and trade union bureaucracies, fought each other to the last drop of workers' blood. However, they all put their differences aside when faced with revolutions that threatened their power. The natural allies of the working class weren't found in the parliaments or boardrooms of either side of the front; they were in the factories and trenches on both sides. Indeed, if we are to oppose imperialism entirely, we must also oppose the capitalist order that gives birth to it in the first place.

Woods takes care to highlight the final chapter of *Le Feu*, the book by Henri Barbusse mentioned above, titled "Dawn". In it the characters are inspired by Karl Liebknecht as they begin to look to an alternative idea of what the world might be. They begin to see the struggle against war as linked to the struggle between classes. Barbusse would go on to become a communist. Despite the fact that it was born from the blood and dirt of war, Barbusse described the Russian Revolution as "the greatest and most beautiful phenomenon in world history" (p. 166). Woods' history of the First World War demonstrates that resistance and rebellion flow from the contradictions of the capitalist system, just as inevitably as war and imperialism do.

DIANE FIELDES

Review: Radical Australian trade unionism

> **Diane Fieldes** has been active since the early 1970s in many campaigns including those for Indigenous and refugee rights. She has written about a range of working class struggles such as the struggle for equal pay.

Sam Oldham, *Without Bosses: Radical Australian Trade Unionism in the 1970s*, Interventions, 2020.

SAM OLDHAM HAS produced a book that will benefit anyone wanting to learn something of the class struggle in Australia during the last major radicalisation, that of the late 1960s to the early 1970s. *Without Bosses* covers a broad range of actions – from job control and conflicts over hiring and firing, to challenges to the rights of managers and bosses to manage industry at all, including where workers "dismissed" their managers and worked without bosses. The book also gives an overview of the context of more general radicalisation in which these actions took place.

There was a new mood of rebellion and defiance in society. The Vietnam war had a direct impact, with anti-war activism becoming in some places a feature of workplace strikes and work bans from the waterfront to the metal industry. Resistance to conscription – which saw 20-year-old men sent off to fight in Vietnam – helped fuel dissent and disdain for authority. This was part of a broader youth revolt, added to by the electrifying effect of the student and workers' struggles in France in May 1968. Social movements such as women's liberation, the Aboriginal land rights movement and gay liberation involved strike action – by those directly affected, but also solidarity actions by male, non-Aboriginal and straight workers on a significant scale. In chapter 7, "Radical unions beyond the workplace", Oldham describes "political strikes, bans and similar actions as a kind of workers' control beyond the workplace" (p. 113).

But the key focus, and the strength of the book, is the rank-and-file union action in the workplace with which it abounds. Successful strikes over issues of pay and conditions were often the catalyst for struggles which further encroached on what management like to call their prerogatives. So struggles about union hire, the closed shop where only unionists will be employed, about blacklisting scabs from employment, fill the pages of the union journals and left-wing newspapers in this period – and the pages of this book. A few examples will whet potential readers' appetites.

Some significant resistance to the sacred right of bosses to hire and fire was embodied in the tactic of the "work-in". This was the method by which the New South Wales branch of the Builders Labourers Federation (BLF) forced bosses to employ women on site for the first time. Women workers would turn up and start work with the men. The bosses quickly learnt that if they didn't accept them the job would soon stop. More often, however, work-ins were a response to closures of workplaces. Workers would take over the job for weeks – or occasionally months – rather than accept the sack. While these did not save jobs in the longer term, they were deeply disturbing to the bosses, whose role was shown to be irrelevant, and inspiring to the workers, on the job and off, whose mastery of all aspects of production was irrefutable.

The elation with which workers greeted the experience is clearly indicated in one of the successful work-ins, that at the Sydney Opera House in April-May 1972. Significantly, in this case the job was not being shut down. Instead management attempted to use sackings to discipline an unruly workforce. Refusing to leave the site, the 45 workers, members of the Amalgamated Metalworkers' Union (AMWU) and the BLF, smashed open the padlocked equipment boxes. As BLF observers said at the time, enthusiasm was unbelievable and work proceeded at a rate unknown on the job... It was like being released from prison after years of hard labour. Boredom and the hatred of oppression were gone, leaving an exhilarating feeling of release (p. 87).

After six weeks all the Opera House workers were reinstated, paid in full for the period without managers, allowed to elect their own supervisors, and granted a 35-hour working week.

Indicative of the bosses' qualms about all this was the *Courier Mail* report on a strike at Evans Deakin shipyards in 1969: "The real trouble is rank and file control... The campaign is being run by a bunch of stirrers... Every time the Metal Trades Federation [of unions] makes a decision, the rank and file knock it over" (p. 29).

This raises an issue which Oldham never really clarifies: the role that trade union officials play. So his outline that "What occurred during this decade was a surge in democratic trade union power, a tendency among some trade unionists to challenge the traditional authority of bosses, managers, and even governments" (p. 6) omits a vital element. Despite this omission, the degree to which the interests of workers and the full-time trade union bureaucracy differed appears in examples throughout the book.

A 1970 strike over conditions at the General Motors-Holden car factory in Elizabeth in Adelaide's northern suburbs saw Vehicle Builders Employees' Federation (VBEF) officials who told workers to go back to work "physically chased out of the plant and anything movable was thrown at them" (p. 75). The workers won the right to extended breaks and a degree of control over the speed of the production line. This was similar to the better-known case of workers at Ford Broadmeadows in 1973 attacking and chasing out their officials (including left-wing officials such as Laurie Carmichael of the AMWU and Communist Party) after a very unwelcome suggestion to end their strike.

The flowering of rank-and-file organisation was a key precondition for workers to assert themselves against the different class interests of their officials. NSW electricity workers formed the Electricity Commission Combined Union Delegates' Organisation (ECCUDO) in the course of a successful major strike over the 35-hour week in 1973.

It was an exclusively rank-and-file organisation of elected delegates from the shopfloor across all unions.

As the 1973 ECCUDO strike and the work-in at the Opera House showed, defying the bosses won some real reforms. But as recession and the bosses' offensive were to prove, capitalism was more than capable of wresting them back. When the long post-war boom ended, the bosses hardened their stance.

The limits of "workers' control", which Oldham does not draw out nearly enough, were exposed. It is true, as he notes at the end of the book, that "workers' control was vulnerable to co-option by employers from the start" (p. 151). In the new situation, as well as attacks on strikes, large employers and their associations began to promote "employee participation" schemes as an alternative to unions.

It could not have been otherwise. While inspiring, none of the examples moved in a more revolutionary direction towards the overthrow of the capitalist state and the creation of a new one based on workers' power. Syndicalist politics – the idea that Oldham expresses as "revolutionary trade unions have been organisations by which working people have sought to seize control of their workplaces and industries to build a socialist society from the bottom up" (pp. 7-9) – proved inadequate to the task. The reformist politics of the Communist Party union officials referred to above were even less useful.

That said, the book has much to recommend it. This was an important period of Australian radicalism in which the working class played a key role. Many thousands of workers defied the bosses, the courts, the governments and often their own union officials. It gave a glimpse of what the world could be: as one miner recalled after a work-in at the South Clifton New South Wales coal mine in 1972, "It gives you a bit of an idea of how it would be to work under socialism without bosses" (p. 5).

Oldham wants "those struggling and fighting in Australia today to find inspiration and renewed courage" (p. 14) from his account. He succeeds.

EMMA NORTON

Review: The making of Australia's security state

Emma Norton is a train driver and activist in the Rail, Tram and Bus Union.

Brian Toohey, *Secret: The Making of Australia's Security State*, Melbourne University Publishing Limited, 2019.

BRIAN TOOHEY'S *SECRET* reveals a sordid history of over 70 years of Australian secrecy, spying and surveillance, from the Australian Security Intelligence Organisation (ASIO)'s Cold War hunt for "communist sympathisers", to Liberal Prime Minister Scott Morrison's world-first legislation allowing authorities to "add, copy, delete or alter" data forcibly taken from our devices.[1] Toohey details a plethora of terrible crimes carried out by the Australian state under the cover of secrecy and concerns for national security. He argues that Australian politicians' undying commitment to secrecy has not made the public safer, as is often claimed. It has only drawn a veil over the government's more sinister actions and criminalised anyone who speaks out about them.

Australia let Britain explode nuclear bombs in the Australian outback during the 1950s and '60s, exposing 35,000 uninformed soldiers, and the wider public, to nuclear fallout. Indigenous locals were not even told the tests were happening on their land, nor that

---

1. Commonwealth of Australia 2018.

they lived near the blast sites. In those same decades, Australia allowed the US to build bases capable of spying on most of the world and starting a nuclear war. Since the 1980s, politicians have handed unchecked power and funding to ASIO and the Australian Federal Police. Agents of the Australian Secret Intelligence Service (ASIS – Australian spies abroad) conduct espionage against our poorest regional neighbours for commercial gain.

Several chapters of *Secret* are devoted to the years of the Whitlam Labor government of 1972 to 1975. Toohey sketches a history which contradicts the usual liberal fawning over Whitlam, although Toohey himself can't help but fawn on occasion. Left-wing agitation within Labor and in broader society led Gough Whitlam, who had been to the right of most party members on issues like the Vietnam War, to include a series of popular promises in his electoral program. One of these was to "tell the public, in general terms, what Pine Gap and Nurrungar [US military bases in Australia] did" (p. 85). But Whitlam and his cabinet "immediately after the election... accepted without protest the advice of...[Secretary of the Department of Defence] Tange, that the need for extreme secrecy" meant Labor should abandon its commitment on the bases (p. 85). Whitlam also turned his back on popular opposition to the base at North West Cape, which the US could use to start a nuclear war.

Despite praise for Whitlam, *Secret* may be read as a searing critique of Labor, which has been just as likely as the Liberals to gift new powers to the federal police and ASIO, arrest whistle blowers and send Australia to war. Toohey's history underlines the extreme hawkishness of recent Labor leaders like Kim Beazley and Julia Gillard. He quotes Gillard's adulation for Australia's brutal colonial wars, and her promise in 2005 that Australian troops would stay in Afghanistan for "at least another decade" (p. 288). Beazley's name surfaces again and again. He has spent three decades arguing for a close military relationship with the US and has furiously defended America's right to launch nuclear missiles from its Australian bases.

Toohey smashes much of the mythology about a kind, rational Australian foreign policy based on respect for treaties, democracy and human rights. It is almost comical how little Australia's actions conform to the image of a "rules-based order". In the mid-1970s an

American company sold a telecommunications system to Indonesia, but "built a near-identical ground station at Shoal Bay [NSW]" (p. 30) to allow the American and Australian signals organisations (NSA and DSD) to intercept everything the Indonesians sent via satellite. The company "did not tell its Indonesian customer about this side deal". This hostility towards Indonesia did not stop Whitlam from making what Toohey calls his "worst foreign-policy mistake" (p. 158) in 1975, when the Australian government condoned and supported Indonesia's plans to invade Timor.

A central point in *Secret* is that "Australia has surrendered much of its sovereignty to the US" (p. 189), viewing Australia as hapless victim of its "bellicose ally" (p. 146). Toohey believes that a faithful adherence to the ANZUS treaty would prevent Australia being dragged into another American war. However, his own evidence shows that Australia was never dragged. Toohey notes that Australia "has not been invaded since 1788" (p. 328) but has enthusiastically thrown itself into and campaigned for wars, even when Britain or America have been reluctant either to receive Australian troops or to go to war at all. Australia has always sought to expand its power in the Asia-Pacific region, attaching itself to a super-power – first Britain and then the US – which can help it achieve this.

Tom O'Lincoln's short book *The Neighbour From Hell* provides a more powerful explanation for such behaviour than can be found in *Secret*. O'Lincoln paints a picture of Australia as an imperialist state, whose core objectives of "stability and security for profits and trade routes" make a strong alliance with America essential.[2] Journalist Paul Kelly describes Australia's contribution to the American alliance as "clever, cynical, calculated" and Australia itself as "a junior partner skilled in utilising the great and powerful in its own interest while imposing firm limits upon its own sacrifices".[3]

At times *Secret* provides a fascinating insight into the interdependent, though often fraught, relationship between the American and Australian states. A vehemently anti-Labor CIA official, James Angleton, worked with ASIO staff to try to topple Whitlam in the early 1970s, although this says less about any genuine danger Whitlam

2. O'Lincoln 2014, page xi.
3. Cited in O'Lincoln, p. 34.

posed to American interests and more about the inherent paranoia of secretive institutions like the CIA. As chief of counter-intelligence, Angleton accused several foreign leaders of being KGB agents and was sacked in December 1974 for his "wild accusations of treachery" (p. 162). While not the ultimate kingmakers of Australia, American officials have shown intense interest in the country's internal politics. The CIA even used undeclared "labor attachés" (p. 180) to infiltrate the leadership of Australian unions and parties for decades during the Cold War. This obvious breach did not disturb most Australian officials and politicians, who preferred the CIA to communists.

The format and style of *Secret* renders it a less compelling book than the fascinating subject matter deserves. Consisting of sixty article-length chapters, *Secret* lacks any chronological order and its thematic structure feels disorganised and unsystematic.

Toohey's focus on certain episodes has more to do with his personal involvement as a journalist than their historical importance. Half a dozen chapters are devoted to a feud between Toohey and his old foil Arthur Tange, head of the Defence Department during the Whitlam era. Meanwhile, Toohey has surprisingly little to say about the massive expansion of the security state in recent years, devoting a mere six pages to the slate of 75 anti-terror laws introduced by the Liberals and Labor since 2001. The tendency of *Secret* to flit between archival research and the excavation of old grudges is of little benefit to the reader, and gives the impression that the personal predilections of figures like Tange are responsible for the outrageous powers of the modern security state.

Despite these criticisms, it is hard not to admire a liberal journalist who has been thoroughly committed to "the public's right to know" for over 50 years. Most of today's journalists and reporters have no such backbone. Toohey pours scorn on the supposedly liberal Australian media, pointing to *Four Corners'* role in uncritically promoting Howard's claims that Iraq had weapons of mass destruction. He mocks the recent cowardice of ABC journalists who refused to publish any papers stamped with "national security" (p. 235) from a potentially revelatory pile of leaked Cabinet documents.

The SAS stands accused of war crimes and ASIS was found

to have bugged East Timor's Cabinet room.[4] But in Australia, only speaking out about these acts is considered a crime. When the Australian security state has given itself the power to jail whistleblowers, kidnap Muslims and raid the homes of unionists and reporters, there has never been a more pressing time to blow the lid on government secrecy. Toohey's remarkable history is a worthy contribution to that goal.

References

Commonwealth of Australia 2018, *Telecommunications and Other Legislation Amendment (Assistance and Access) Act 2018*, Parliament of the Commonwealth of Australia, 14 August. https://www.legislation.gov.au/Details/C2018A00148

McGrath, Kim 2020, "Drawing the Line: Witness K and the ethics of spying", *Australian Foreign Affairs*, 9, July.

O'Lincoln, Tom 2014, *The Neighbour from Hell: Two centuries of Australian imperialism*, Interventions.

---

4. McGrath 2020, p. 53.

IAN BIRCHALL

Review: Victor Serge's final words

Ian Birchall is a writer and translator in London, UK. He has written books on Babeuf and Sartre, and a biography of Tony Cliff, and has translated Alfred and Marguerite Rosmer and Victor Serge. For many years a member of the British Socialist Workers Party, he is now not attached to any organisation, but still considers himself a revolutionary socialist.

Victor Serge, *Notebooks 1936-1947*, New York Review Books, 2019.

VICTOR SERGE WAS one of the great witnesses to the revolutionary history of the first half of the twentieth century. A participant witness, since those in the thick of the action see most. Imprisoned as an anarchist in pre-1914 France, he then took part in the failed syndicalist rising of 1917 in Barcelona, and went to Russia in 1919, where he became an active Bolshevik. He reported from Germany on the abortive revolution of 1923. Returning to Russia, he was confronted with the rise of Stalin, and became a member of the Left Opposition. Exiled to the remote town of Orenburg, he was allowed to return to the West after a vigorous campaign in his support in France, just before the purges became truly murderous.[1] When the Nazis occupied Western Europe, he managed to get to Mexico, where he died in 1947. Throughout his last years he wrote copiously; many will know his remarkable *Memoirs of a Revolutionary*[2] and novels such as *The Case of Comrade Tulayev*.

1. Greeman 1994.
2. For the first complete English translation see Serge 2012a.

From 1936 till his death Serge also wrote regularly in his private notebooks. A few extracts from these were published, but most remained unknown. Then in 2010 a researcher discovered a pile of notebooks, apparently abandoned for ever. They were published in French[3] and have now been translated into English by Richard Greeman and Mitchell Abidor. For all lovers of Serge's writing they are an unexpected and welcome bonus.

These 600 pages contain a wide range of material and are impossible to summarise. Right up to his death Serge shows his unflagging intellectual curiosity, and the remarkable eye for significant detail which characterises both his journalism and his fiction. There is for example a vivid description of an earthquake (pp. 229-30). He is clearly fascinated by both the natural environment and the culture of the new continent where he finds himself domiciled. There are perceptive if (to my mind) disappointingly conservative assessments of surrealism ("nothing but a revolt of literary cafés") (pp. 308-9) and abstract painting (pp. 477-9).

But not surprisingly Serge constantly returns to political themes, to the recollection and reassessment of the revolutionary achievements and defeats he had lived through and the prospects for a newly emerging world.

The book is haunted by death. The Russian purges, the Spanish war followed by world war, together with the inexorable passage of time, meant that Serge was constantly receiving news of deaths. As he noted grimly: "Dead men on top of dead men" (p. 37). His notebooks contain dozens of obituaries, assessments of former comrades or of those who had crossed his path in an eventful life. The 1917 Revolution in Russia had been a moment of hope, drawing together many from diverse backgrounds, united by the aspiration for a better world. Failure, defeat and the triumph of reaction in various forms had driven them in different directions. Two examples may sum up a generation cast to the winds.

In the 1920s Jacques Doriot had been one of the rising stars of the French Communist Party. By the 1940s he was an active and enthusiastic supporter of the Nazis. Serge, who had known Doriot in

---

3. Serge 2012b.

Moscow, does not resort to any lazy clichés about the equivalence of all extremisms. He does not question Doriot's sincerity, remembering him for "modesty and firmness. A young man on whom you could rely". (It is a comforting illusion to believe that all who go wrong were bad from the start; on the contrary, any of us can develop badly.) Serge tries to explain the historical circumstances which led to Doriot's bizarre but not unique evolution; it was the French Communist Party's refusal of a united front against fascism which led to the initial break (pp. 491-4).

There is a sharp contrast with the figure of David Riazanov, an old revolutionary and a scholar to whom we owe so much of our knowledge of the life and work of Karl Marx. Serge recalled him as a supporter of the Revolution, but already in 1921-22 debarred by the party from speaking in public because of his critical attitude. For years he was marginalised, but eventually the Stalinist machine had him put to death (pp. 186-9).

Death hangs over the book, including Serge's own impending death, as his health, undermined by years of hardship and poverty, breaks down. Yet it is not a pessimistic book – on the contrary. Serge is constantly looking to the future, trying to discern the form of the post-war world and the possibility of continuing to fight for the values that had inspired his struggles over the preceding years.

Serge died in November 1947, just as the post-war world was beginning to take shape. In March the so-called "Truman doctrine" was announced, promising American political, military and economic assistance to prevent the spread of Communism. This was followed by the exclusion of Communist ministers from the governments in France and Italy, and a sharp turn to the left by the Communist Parties. But it was too soon to see how the coming quarter of a century would turn out.

Serge's keen intellectual curiosity makes him an acute observer of the society and culture of the emerging new world. He even sees, without any great enthusiasm ("mixture of great imagination and unspeakable stupidity"), one of the very first *Superman* movies (p. 281). But Serge was a witness, not a prophet (in 1939 he had spent months arguing that there would be no world war).[4] His conclusions do not go beyond generalisations.

He insists that the aftermath of 1945 will be very different from the period at the end of the First World War – "the events of 1917-1918 can't be repeated at the end of this war" (p. 454) – and as early as 1943 he sees that "the seed of the Third World War is germinating in this one" (p. 349).

Moreover, all Serge's political experience was European – Spain, France, Germany, Russia. When a political discussion touches on colonial emancipation, his views tend to be rather cautious – "the emancipation of the peoples of the colonies can be the result only of close collaboration with the socially reorganized industrial countries" (p. 434). He cannot have realised that one of the most significant factors of the post-war world would be the rise of the so-called "Third World" and the collapse of the European colonial empires.

When his boat, bound across the Atlantic, briefly visits Algeria, he notes the "crushing poverty" of the indigenous population and comments that "the French live with these men almost without seeing them. Inhuman, this, and very dangerous" (pp. 52-53). But he can scarcely have foreseen that within just over twenty years the "Arabs" would have fought a bitter war and driven out their French rulers.

Yet he has a keen eye for ruling-class arrogance. Writing of the war on Japan, he notes that American hopes of an easy victory will be disappointed. They "[h]ave no idea of the energy of a very different race, terribly energetic, very poor, not at all bourgeoisified and backed into a desperate situation" (p. 110). For later readers the parallel with Vietnam is inescapable.

So it is difficult to imagine how Serge might have developed if he had lived another ten or twenty years. The fierce pressures of the Cold War were just beginning, and many fell victim to them. George Orwell's decline from *Homage to Catalonia* to government informer is a sad reminder of just what could happen. Only a tiny minority of the left hung on to a "neither Washington nor Moscow" line.

---

4. Serge 2010.

One of the translators of the *Notebooks*, Mitchell Abidor, has written an article in which he argues that Serge's Mexican years saw a "final political shift" in which "hatred of the Communists became one of his central tenets".[5] It is a thoughtful and balanced argument, based on months of immersion in the text of the *Notebooks*, and it deserves to be considered with respect. But my own view is that Serge's position in the *Notebooks* remains complex and contradictory.

Certainly Serge does come to see Stalinism as the main enemy. There was a good reason for this; as he describes repeatedly, there were Stalinists in Mexico who were systematically planning to kill him (p. 138). The people who had murdered Trotsky just a few years earlier wanted to eradicate what remained of the Left Opposition. Meetings addressed by Serge and other anti-Stalinists were physically attacked with vicious assaults (p. 102).

So it is scarcely surprising that when other leftists discuss the possibility of a united front with the Communist Party (CP), Serge is sceptical. As he argues, "the CP is a totalitarian party led by agents of a foreign power: it's not a party of the left" (p. 219).

Such an attitude is easy to explain in terms of Serge's experience. Nonetheless it was misguided. In countries like France and Italy, where the Communist Parties counted their members in hundreds of thousands and their voters in millions, those mass organisations could not be written off as not part of the left. The only possible strategy for revolutionaries was systematic anti-Stalinist propaganda, combined with a united front with Communist Party members. It was a hard road, with little to show for it, at least until the Stalinist monolith began to crumble after 1956, but there was no alternative. That Serge himself recognises this is shown by a letter written to the French socialist editor René Lefeuvre in 1946 in which he insists that it is necessary to relate to Stalinist workers: "We cannot adopt a purely negative attitude to the CP. We shall get nowhere if we seem more preoccupied with criticising Stalinism than with defending the working class. The reactionary danger is still there, and in practice we shall often have to act alongside the Communists".[6]

Thus Serge's position is not wholly consistent. But while it is

---

5. Abidor 2019.
6. Serge 2003.

impossible to say what his later development might have been, it is hard to imagine him becoming a reliable supporter for the Cold War anti-communists. The position, which increasingly became essential to their orthodoxy, that Lenin (and indeed Marx) led inexorably to the gulag, is quite alien to him. While accepting that Bolshevik Jacobinism "contained the seed of Stalinist totalitarianism", he insists that *"Bolshevism also contained other seeds, other possibilities of evolution"* (p. 512).

He continues to affirm that Bolshevism had been "an astounding historic success" (p. 109) and believes that "there is no one left who knows what the Russian Revolution was in reality" (p. 365).

Serge is not always a comfortable ally for the left; he recalls facts and questions which those in search of a more simplistic narrative would prefer to forget. But he would have been an even more awkward companion for the red-baiters, for he would have rejected their most basic assumptions.

Serge had no pretensions to be a political leader, and did not offer a strategy for the left. But with other political exiles in Mexico he takes part in vigorous discussions about the way forward.

About the murderous nature of Stalinism he is in no doubt. And he is quite clear that the regime in Russia has nothing in common with the socialist values to which he had devoted his life. The future of Stalinism is a more difficult question. Sometimes the friends and enemies of Stalinism seem to converge in overestimating its strength and stability. Serge sees prospects for change. Meeting Trotsky's grandson on a bus, he argues that "before much time has passed Russia will change greatly...we must remain faithful to her and sustain great hopes for her" (pp. 392-93).

Trotsky Serge sees as one of the great Marxists; he repeatedly expresses his admiration. During his years in Mexico he regularly visits Natalia Sedova, Trotsky's widow, with whom he jointly wrote a biography of Trotsky.[7] Trotskyism is a different matter. Serge had been involved in Trotsky's earliest efforts to regroup the Left Opposition into a "Fourth International", but he had soon broken with this.[8] He believes that "a new International can't be founded without first

---

7. Sedova and Serge 2016.
8. See Cotterill 1994.

having two or three real parties or groups in two or three important countries" (p. 170) and that Trotsky in his last years became a "sectarian" (p. 221). He proposed the alternative of an alliance of all left-wing currents, rejecting any idea of Leninist hegemony.

Certainly Serge's critique is a powerful one. The history of the Fourth International, once Trotsky's guiding intelligence was removed, became a series of splits, with each fragment claiming to be the true – and sole – heir. Whether Serge's alternative could have succeeded is a different question. Probably sectarianism on the left was too strong, and in any case the post-war triumph of Stalinism meant that the anti-Stalinist left was crushed and isolated. It would take the upheavals of 1956 and 1968 for it to revive.

Serge notes a degree of friction in his discussions with Natalia Sedova, since she remains a member of the Fourth International (p. 142). Yet perhaps he sowed some seeds of doubt, since a few years later, in 1951, she broke all connection with the Fourth International.[9]

In fact Serge seems to be pessimistic about the prospects of an independent revolutionary left. Thus he urges that socialism's "only salvation" will be found in "rallying along with the old (moderate) socialist movements and the democratic masses" (p. 464) – in other words in cooperation with the reformists. This is not a simple abandonment of revolutionary politics. For Trotsky on the eve of the World War, it had seemed that capitalism had exhausted the possibilities for reform – and hence for reformism. In the revived capitalism of the post-war period reformism was able to bring about real changes in the interest of the working class. But reformist parties were also guilty of some appalling abuses. The role of the French Socialist Party (SFIO) in opposing Algerian independence was just the most blatant example. How Serge might have responded to such developments we cannot be sure. But what is true is that the small and fragmented revolutionary current that survived existed mainly by working inside reformist parties.

Serge does not have a detailed strategy for the left and it would be foolish to expect him to. But in debate with other exiles, he is scornful of those who are satisfied to continue to promote relatively

---

9. Sedova 1951.

small organisations: as he argues "most would be charmed to have a tiny party of thirty thousand men in Spain or France that would believe itself pure and that would be powerless" (p. 348). The irony is that all too many fragments of the left have been satisfied with 300, let alone 30,000.

Ultimately Serge gives us no answers, but leaves us with some very relevant questions. With the benefit of hindsight we can see where Serge was perceptive and where he was misguided. But an encounter with the critical thought and experience of a revolutionary like Serge cannot fail to be rewarding.

References

Abidor, Mitchell 2019, "Victor Serge: Indispensable Critic of Leftist Illusion", *The New York Review*, 28 February. https://www.nybooks.com/daily/2019/02/28/victor-serge-indispensable-critic-of-leftist-illusion/

Cotterill, David (ed.) 1994, *The Serge-Trotsky Papers*, Pluto.

Greeman, Richard 1994, "The Victor Serge Affair and the French Literary Left", *Revolutionary History*, 5, 3. https://www.marxists.org/history/etol/revhist/backiss/vol5/no3/greeman.html

Sedova, Natalia 1951, Letter of Resignation, *The Militant*, 15, 23, 4 June. https://www.marxists.org/archive/sedova-natalia/1951/05/09.htm

Sedova, Natalia and Victor Serge 2016, *Life and Death of Leon Trotsky*, Haymarket.

Serge, Victor 2003, "To René Lefeuvre", *Revolutionary History*, 8, 3. https://www.marxists.org/archive/serge/194x/xx/lefeuvre.html

Serge Victor 2010, *Retour à l'Ouest: Chroniques (juin 1936-mai 1940)*, Agone.

Serge, Victor 2012a, *Memoirs of a Revolutionary*, New York Review Books.

Serge, Victor 2012b, *Carnets 1936-1947*, Agone.

www.ingramcontent.com/pod-product-compliance
Lightning Source LLC
Chambersburg PA
CBHW010244010526
44107CB00063B/2679